The Rise of Literary Journalism in the Eighteenth Century

The 1980s, 1990s and 2000s have witnessed a heightened interest in eighteenth-century literary journalism, an interest that reflects growing critical fascination with the development of the public sphere in the Enlightenment. While there are a number of individual studies on specific categories of publications, until now there has been little attempt to survey the broad field of the periodical itself as a literary phenomenon.

The Rise of Literary Journalism in the Eighteenth Century fills this gap in the existing scholarship. Examining the period from the launch of the first essay-periodical, Richard Steele's *Tatler* (1709), to the domination of the market by magazines in the 1760s, Italia surveys a range of monthly, weekly and sub-weekly publications, producing a study remarkable for its scope and admirable for its depth. The ten individual chapters focus on publications ranging from the *Spectator* to Frances Brooke's *Old Maid*.

Appealing to scholars studying media, history and literature, *The Rise of Literary Journalism* is a much-needed addition to the fruitful areas of literary journalism studies and the Enlightenment.

Iona Italia is a Lecturer in English Literature at the University of East Anglia.

Routledge studies in eighteenth-century literature

The Rise of Literary Journalism in the Eighteenth Century

Anxious employment

Iona Italia

Routledge
Taylor & Francis Group

LONDON AND NEW YORK

First published 2005
by Routledge
2 Park Square, Milton Park, Abingdon, Oxon OX14 4RN

Simultaneously published in the USA and Canada
by Routledge
270 Madison Ave, New York, NY 10016

Routledge is an imprint of the Taylor & Francis Group

© 2005 Iona Italia

Typeset in Garamond by Wearset Ltd, Boldon, Tyne and Wear
Printed and bound in Great Britain by MPG Books Ltd, Bodmin

British Library Cataloguing in Publication Data
A catalogue record for this book is available from the British Library

Library of Congress Cataloging in Publication Data
A catalog record for this book has been requested

ISBN 0–415–34392–5

For Oliver

Contents

Preface and acknowledgements

This book was inspired by the need for a basic, introductory critical study of the eighteenth-century periodical which would be more than simply a brief survey or annotated bibliography of publications, and which would range widely over the period 1690–1770, looking at the literary questions raised by a number of different publications. I hope to shed light on the traditions of eighteenth-century non-political journalism, in particular essay-periodicals and magazines, traditions which also raise more general questions about eighteenth-century authors and readers and provide a fresh perspective on the contemporary, but very different, development of the eighteenth-century novel. I make no claims to have written a definitive study of eighteenth-century journalism. It is a wide field, and some important publications and interesting aspects of journalism had to be left out of the book, for lack of space. I hope, however, that the book will form part of an ongoing debate about the literary characteristics of the periodical press in the Enlightenment and stimulate further studies of journalism, which was such a central part of the contemporary literary scene.

A version of Chapter 7 has appeared as 'Samuel Johnson as moralist in *The Rambler*' in *The Age of Johnson: a scholarly annual* (May 2003). I'd like to thank the editor for permission to use it here. Illustrations from the following texts were supplied courtesy of the British Library: the *Compleat Library* (C.189.a.1); *The Dunciad Variorum* (642.k.2.(1.)); the *Female Spectator* (94.c.12); the *Friendly Writer* (P.P.596.(1.)); the *General Magazine of Arts and Sciences* (205.k.8); the *Midwife* (1081.d.14); and the *Universal Magazine of Knowledge and Pleasure* (P.P.5439). Illustrations from the following texts were supplied courtesy of Cambridge University Library: the *Female Tatler* (item no. 1391 in Microfilm P247) and Charles Gildon's *History of the Athenian Society* (R.8.52).

A number of people have read and commented on various stages of the manuscript and shared ideas about the development of this book. I'd like to thank Peter Barry, John Brewer, Beatrice Clarke, Elizabeth Eger, Richard

Elgar, Melissa Goodman Elgar, Johannes Haubold, David Hornsby, Scott Kleinman, Jim McDonnell, Shawn Lisa Maurer, James Raven, Timothy Raylor, David Shuttleton, Stephan Schmuck, Jane Spencer, Constance Walker, Penny Wilson and Tim Woods. I'd also like to thank the staff at the Cambridge University Library, the Wren Library, the Bodleian Library and, especially, the staff at the British Library Rare Books and Music Room.

Very special thanks are due to six people. John Mullan supervised the PhD at Jesus College, Cambridge, which formed the original germ of this book. Isobel Grundy gave me extensive help and advice when I was contemplating the arduous task of turning the thesis into a book. My friends Father Paul Kennington and Jonathan Bailey provided hospitality at their vicarages in East Sheen and Battersea, where I spent several happy summers during the initial stages of the writing. Nadia Valman has offered unstinting academic and personal support during almost every stage of this project. My biggest debt is to Oliver Josephs, who has immeasurably enriched my intellectual and personal life. The book's many faults are, of course, entirely my own.

Iona Italia

Notes on the text

Quotations from the *Tatler* are taken from Richard Steele, *The Tatler*, ed. Donald F. Bond, Oxford: Clarendon Press, 1987.

Quotations from the *Spectator* are taken from Joseph Addison and Richard Steele, *et al., The Spectator*, ed. Donald F. Bond, Oxford: Clarendon Press, 1965.

Quotations from the *Nonsense of Common Sense* are taken from Lady Mary Wortley Montagu, *Essays and Poems and Simplicity, A Comedy*, ed. Robert Halsband and Isobel Grundy, Oxford: Clarendon Press, 1993.

Quotations from the *Female Spectator* are taken from *Selected Works of Eliza Haywood*, series II, vols. 2 and 3, *The Female Spectator*, eds Kathryn R. King and Alexander Pettit, London: Pickering and Chatto, 2001.

Quotations from the *Rambler* are taken from *The Yale Edition of the Works of Samuel Johnson*, ed. W. J. Bate and Albrecht B. Strauss, New Haven and London: Yale University Press, 1958–: III-V.

Quotations from Oliver Goldsmith's journalism are taken from *The Collected Works of Oliver Goldsmith*, ed. Arthur Friedman, Oxford: Clarendon, 1966.

I have used the modern system for dates before 1752.

References to shorter periodicals give issue number (where available) in Arabic numerals, followed by date (where available). References to longer periodicals, such as magazines, generally cite the annual volume number, in Roman numerals, followed by the date (where available) and page number (if appropriate). Some periodicals have their own, more unusual, systems of references. I have noted within the text where this is the case.

The place of publication of all periodicals is London, unless otherwise stated.

Introduction
The rise of the periodical

In her review of George Frisbie Whicher's 1915 biography of Eliza Haywood, Virginia Woolf roundly dismisses Haywood's periodical writing, arguing that she 'left behind her a mass of unreadable journalism which both by its form and by the inferiority of the writer's talent throws no light upon her age or upon herself' (1979: 93). Woolf's comment reveals not only her low opinion of Haywood's skill as a writer, but her attitudes towards eighteenth-century journalism. For Woolf, it is the *form* in which Haywood wrote, as well as her lack of talent, which renders her journalism unworthy of scholarly attention.

The rise of the periodical coincided with an increasingly commercial literary marketplace, and journalism was often regarded as typifying all the worst qualities of the mass market, as unscrupulous hacks produced disposable literature, the 'Journals, Medleys, Merc'ries, Magazines . . . and all the Grub-street race', which cannot "scape the martyrdom of jakes and fire' in Pope's *Dunciad* (1951: 5.273–4, 5.280). The frontispiece to the 1729 edition of Pope's mock-epic shows the crumpled sheets of periodicals dropping from the donkey's back, being blown away and littering the ground, conveying a vivid image of the transience of journalism (Figure I.1). Henry Fielding comments acidly in 1752 that most journalism serves only as toilet paper: the large number of periodicals proves 'there are . . . many B–ms in the World' (*Covent-Garden Journal* 1, 4 January 1752).

This book provides an account of the eighteenth-century periodical as a literary genre. The 1980s, 90s and 2000s have witnessed a heightened interest in eighteenth-century literary journalism, an interest that reflects growing critical fascination with the development of the public sphere in the Enlightenment. While there are a number of studies of individual papers or specific categories of publications – most notably, several books on periodicals by and for women (Ballaster *et al.* 1991; Maurer 1998; Shevelow 1989) – there has been little attempt to study the periodical itself as a literary phenomenon. Eighteenth-century genres are usually defined by their

THE

DUNCIAD,

VARIORVM.

WITH THE

PROLEGOMENA of *SCRIBLERUS.*

DEFEROR IN VICVM

VENDENTEM THVS ET ODORES

LONDON.

Printed for A. DOB . 1729.

Figure I.1 Frontispiece of *The Dunciad Variorum* (1729).

structure – as novels, drama or poetry – or in terms of the specific themes and approaches which characterize particular styles such as the sentimental or the Gothic. The periodical does not fit easily within this scheme of categorization. While we might see the essay as a particular genre, governed by specific conventions and influenced by a rich literary tradition, the essay-periodical, we might argue, is not a genre in itself, but simply a form in which to market, distribute and publish essays.

An essay published in a book is very different, however, from one which appears as a single issue of an essay-serial and also distinct from an essay 'buried', as Oliver Goldsmith puts it, 'among the essays upon liberty, eastern tales, and cures for the bite of a mad dog' in the pages of a bulky magazine (1966: 4.111). The format and context in which a work is to appear profoundly affects its writer's choice of literary strategies. In this book, I will describe and analyse the set of literary conventions which characterize the eighteenth-century periodical and suggest reasons why the periodical developed its distinctive literary traits.

The study encompasses the period between the launch of the first essay-periodical, Richard Steele's *Tatler*, in 1709 and the domination of the market by the magazines in the 1760s. It spans the height of the essay-periodical's popularity and describes the conception and early development of its powerful rival the magazine. By an essay-periodical, I mean a publication issued weekly or sub-weekly with a long leader essay, sometimes accompanied by a brief section of foreign and domestic news and a selection of advertisements. These publications were often written by a single writer, and were usually no more than two folio pages long. Magazines were bulky publications, usually issued monthly, with very diverse contents that often included abridged essays reprinted from weekly and sub-weekly publications, as well as articles on politics, scientific discoveries, mathematical questions, readers' letters, poetry, serialized fiction, shipping news and the prices of goods and stocks.

While the distinction between essay-periodicals and magazines is central to this study, eighteenth-century periodicals cannot always be easily classified. Some studies of the genre have suffered from dividing the publications into somewhat arbitrary and often misleading categories. This study does not attempt to impose a strict system of taxonomy: the terms *periodical*, *journal* and *paper* are treated as approximately synonymous, and the anachronistic word *journalism* is used to describe periodical writing in general, not simply political reporting. Journals in this period were not always clearly defined by special interest, audience and approach. Many periodicals borrow features from several types of publication. Haywood's lengthy and varied issues in the *Female Spectator* share features with both the essay-periodical and the magazine, for instance. It is often difficult to distinguish literary from political papers. Publications such as the *Craftsman* (1726–50), which was primarily devoted to news reporting, often diversified their material with essays on manners and morals.

In addition, it is almost impossible to identify a separate tradition of periodical writing by or for women. While the titles of many papers – *ladies' magazines, museums, companions* and others – suggest that they were aimed at a female readership, there is evidence to suggest that male readers constituted a sizeable proportion of the audience of these periodicals. The editor of the *Ladies Journal* (1727) promises that his paper will contain 'nothing . . . but the lighter Affairs of the Ladies', such as 'Love and Gallantry' (no. 1), but there is a clear assumption that such material will also appeal to men. His advertisement explains that '*several Gentlemen*' had subscribed to a songbook that could not be published, as the printer absconded with the copy. The periodical, he assures them, '*was chiefly writ on their Accounts, wherein they have the . . . Songs, but also variety of the most entertaining Subjects*' (no. 1). The poetry miscellany *Flowers of Parnassus* (1734–6) is explicitly aimed at 'THE LADIES *of* Great-Britain', but the editor adds that if women endorse the publication 'our own Sex must relish and approve' (1736, Preface). Helen Berry has calculated that 'seven out of ten "Ladies" issues of the *Athenian Mercury* (which were purportedly devoted to questions from women) where the sex of the correspondent was mentioned, there were in fact as many or more questions from men than from women' (2003: 61). She notes that these 'Ladies' issues were gradually phased out after vol. v of the *Mercury* and that the *Ladies Mercury* folded after only a few issues, 'suggesting that segregation by gender was not a profitable venture' (*ibid.*). Jean Hunter has shown that never less than a third and frequently more than half of all letters to the *Lady's Magazine* (1770–1832) bear a male signature (1977: 103–71). We cannot be certain of the actual sex of some of these writers, but their sheer numbers indicate that the magazine was regarded as eminently suitable for male readers. Publications which are addressed specifically to women often do not differ from those which claim a mixed readership. Jasper Goodwill's *Ladies Magazine* (1749–53) printed serialized histories of Britain, accounts of the 'Proceedings of the *British* Parliament' and the Court of Session, criminal biographies, reviews of novels, and a 'Chronological Diary of Foreign and Domestic Affairs' as regular features, beside occasional items of more traditionally feminine interest. In addition, the style of a female-edited paper is not always distinct from one written under a male pen-name. Oliver Goldsmith's pacifist essay 'Some Thoughts Preliminary to a General Peace' was first published in the *Weekly Magazine* for 29 December 1759, where he wrote as a male journalist addressing a male readership. Just over a year later, the article reappeared in an only slightly altered form in the *Lady's Magazine; or, Polite Companion* (1759–63) for October 1761 under the heading 'Thoughts Upon the Present State of Affairs', written in the guise of the woman editor, Mrs Caroline Stanhope, and addressed to an explicitly female audience. Goldsmith allows the fictional Mrs Stanhope to apologize gracefully for 'indulging herself in political speculations', telling readers that 'none, not even women, should sit unconcerned in the calamities ... of their country' (*Lady's Magazine*: II.150). However, the political sentiments expressed are considered as suitable to a female, as to a male pen. Papers like the *Orphan Reviv'd* (1718–20) combine a news section, '*Containing all Remarkable Occurrences Foreign and Domestick*', with material specifically intended to appeal to women such as '*The Tea Table Tatler; or, The Ladies Delight*'. Contemporaries did not necessarily think that a female pen-name indicated female authorship. The *Female Tatler* was often attributed to Thomas Baker (see Chapter 2). Roxana Termagant, editor of the *Drury-Lane Journal*, imagines male readers commenting sceptically on her sex: 'A woman pretend to write! – Pshaw, 'tis impossible. – No, no, – a mere humbug – a stale pretence – 'twon't do, 'twon't do' (2, 23 January 1752). Her female readers, however, 'all of them strenuously maintain, that I must be, and most certainly am what I pretend to be, – a woman', variously attributing the periodical's authorship to Eliza Haywood, Sarah Fielding and the transvestite soldier Hannah Snell (1723–92) (*ibid.*). Correspondents to the *Female Spectator*, ostensibly written by a club of four women, address the editors as '*Ladies*, or *Gentlemen*, / *Madam*, or *Sir*' (bk VII: 2.233) and express their doubts of the Female Spectator's sex: 'I very much Question whether you are of the *Feminine* Gender or not' (bk XXIV: 3.405).

Some papers modified their titles, perhaps to reflect the changing gender balance of their readership. The *Ladies Diary* (1704–1871) became first the *Lady's and Gentleman's Diary* and then the *Gentleman's Diary; or, the Mathematical Repository*, before finally reverting to the title of the *Lady's and Gentleman's Diary*. Tipper's companion publication the *Monthly Entertainments* (1713) begins as a collection of 'Delightful Arithmetical Questions ... sent me by the Fair Sex' (*Ladies Diary* 1713, Advertisement). By 1728 almost all the mathematical questions are both proposed and answered by male correspondents, but Tipper still describes his readership as '*British Ladies*' (*Ladies Diary* 1728, Advertisement). Tipper's *Delights for the Ingenious* (1711) is addressed 'to all Gentlemen, Ladies, and Others' (January 1711) and alternately singles out male readers – 'Which are the most prevailing Arguments to persuade a *Woman*, that we *really love her*?' (*ibid.*) – and female ones – 'Oh ye charming fair Female Readers' (*ibid.*). By the middle years of the century, most literary publications promise to contain articles of interest to men and women. This is reflected in their titles and subtitles: in the *Gentleman and Lady's Companion*, *Gentleman and Lady's Polite Magazine*, *Gentleman and Lady's Repository* and *Gentleman and Lady's Palladium* among many others.[1]

Addresses to the fair sex, together with letters from female correspondents and discussion of issues of relevance to women, are ubiquitous in eighteenth-century journalism, whether written by men or women. In the first issue of his *Tatler*, Steele promises to include material 'which may be of Entertainment to the Fair Sex', in whose honour, he claims wryly, he has chosen the name of his publication. The editor of the *Free-thinker* addresses his paper to 'the Fair Sex (whose Approbation most flatters the Heart of a Writer)' (1, 24 March 1718), and the editor of the *Visiter* proclaims that 'the Ladies I design as my peculiar Care' (1, 18 June 1723). Adam Fitz-Adam of the *World* claims proudly that 'during the course of these my labours, there is nothing that I have applied myself to with more diligence and attention ... than the reformation of the fair sex' (158, 8 January 1756). The editor of Haywood's *Parrot* declares, 'I thought it my Duty, as well as found it my Inclination, to pay a peculiar Homage to that Sex [women]' (no. 7). In the second issue of the *Gray's Inn Journal*, the editor, Charles Ranger, tells his readers, 'Having recommended myself, in my last *Saturday*'s Paper, to the Patronage of the male Part of my Readers, I shall dedicate the present Essay to the *British* Fair' (6 October 1753). Samuel Johnson complains in his *Rambler* that he has been 'censured for not imitating the politeness of his predecessors, having hitherto neglected to take the ladies under his protection' (*Rambler* 23), while the editor of the *Connoisseur* tells us in the periodical's fourth issue that his female readers already 'exclaim against me for not having as yet paid my particular addresses to the Fair' (21 February 1754). A correspondent of Fielding's *Champion* rebukes him for having 'most shamefully neglected the Ladies; as if we had foresworn reading', threatening that he ignores her 'at his Peril' (327, 15 December 1741).

The feminization of the periodical is linked to a gentrification of the genre. Studies of the eighteenth-century novel have often focused on the figure of the vulnerable and naïve female reader and have seen the novel's associations with women as a sign of its lack of literary respectability. In the periodical, by contrast, addressing a female audience and discussing topics of traditionally feminine interest came to be viewed as a mark of literary and social cachet. As women were increasingly portrayed as indifferent to party politics, an address to women was taken to signal a high-minded political disinterestedness and preference for literary subjects, which would guarantee that the publication would outlast the scurrilous work of mercenary hacks, paid to inflame and perpetuate party squabbles. Periodical editors tried to shake off journalism's associations with a male, urban, trading readership who anxiously monitored foreign policy and the prices of goods and stocks. While gentlemen were merely a sub-group of male readers, by polite convention all female readers were regarded as ladies.

The periodical's early literary history clearly demonstrates the ways in which the conditions of the literary marketplace can shape the development of a genre. The neglected periodical is, perhaps, a casualty of our abiding fascination with the novel. However, it shares a number of important historical features with the novel: most notably its historical youth, relatively low price, dubious respectability, widespread availability and particular association with female readers. Its popularity raises important questions about the transition from intensive to extensive reading, the growth of a non-aristocratic readership and the status of the professional writer in the eighteenth century. The majority of the writers, both male and female, who form the focus of this study were professionals who turned to journalism as an opportunity of making a living.

The periodical illustrates a central tension in eighteenth-century writing: a preoccupation with class coupled with a blurring of traditional class boundaries. While editors were increasingly seen as mercenary hacks writing for a semi-literate mass audience, within the periodicals they maintain a pretence of gentility. More than in any other form of eighteenth-century writing, class and genre are intricately connected in the periodical. All the major features of the genre were influenced by the desires of periodical writers to shake off journalism's disreputable image. The work of each of the individual writers in this study represents a different approach to the problem of securing a measure of literary respectability.

While some of the works examined by this study were to gain lasting literary fame, the periodical as a genre was never to attain significant literary prestige. The essay-periodical, which represents the genre's most literary, least commercial product, was moribund by the end of the period covered by this study. While essay-periodicals continued to be published after 1770, they were never to regain the popularity they enjoyed during the early decades of the century. In the course of this study, I will suggest some reasons for the failure of journalism to achieve the privileged literary status accorded to the novel. First, however, I will place the study's central texts in their wider context by describing the historical conditions which led to the development of journalism and charting the main features of the genre.

General historical background

Periodicals flourished and grew both in number and diversity throughout the period 1690–1770. They ranged from the learned to the lewd. The scholarly *Phoenix Britannicus* (1731), which contains rare pamphlets from the Civil War period, together with the equally erudite *Miscellaneous Observations* (1731–2), which offers textual criticism of the Classics, appealed to '*the* Curiosi *of these Realms*' (*Phoenix Britannicus* 1, January 1731). At the other end of the scale, comic miscellanies like *Heraclitus Ridens* (1703–4 and 1718) and Ned Ward's *Humours of a Coffee-House* (1707–8) published collections of bawdy jokes, riddles and anecdotes. Learned abstracts such as the *Philosophical Transactions of the Royal Society* (1665–present day) and De la Crose's *History of the Works of the Learned* (1699–1712) carried reviews of scholarly publications, together with accounts of scientific experiments and theological debates. These erudite publications were later to develop into book reviewing journals such as the *Monthly Review* (1749–1844) and the *Critical Review* (1756–1817), which began by reprinting lengthy extracts and summaries of mainly non-fictional texts and gradually diversified to provide critical comment on a wide range of publications.[2] The ambitious *Edinburgh Review* (1755–6) presents itself as a 'national benefit', which will encourage 'a more eager pursuit of learning' among Scots, enabling them 'to distinguish themselves, and to do honour to their country' (1, July 1755). The *Scots Magazine* (1739–1826) also wishes to 'revive that universal esteem which SCOTLAND so justly acquir'd among her neighbours by the valour and learning of our ancestors' (vol. I, Preface).

A number of historical circumstances concurred to make the early to mid-eighteenth century a particularly propitious time for the development and proliferation of journalism. The first English newsbooks and corantos, modelled on Dutch publications, appeared in the 1620s in London (Harris 1978: 83). The breakdown of governmental controls during the Civil War fostered the appearance of a multitude of periodical publications. With the Restoration, conditions of publication became far more restrictive. The Licensing Act of 1662 placed the press under the supervision of a series of licensers. In 1684, the Stationers' Company was granted a royal charter and a monopoly on printing. Printing was restricted to 20 master printers from the Company, each of whom was allocated a set number of presses. In 1695, the Licensing Act was allowed to lapse, and at the same time the Stationers' Company lost their monopoly. There was to be no further registry of printing presses until 1799 (Brewer 1997: 135–7).

The official government vehicle for news, the twice-weekly *London Gazette*, had been established in 1665, but in 1695 non-official newspapers appeared, beginning with the *Post Boy*. The first daily newspaper, the *Daily Courant*, was launched in 1702 and the first evening paper, the *Evening Post*, in 1709. Provincial presses were quickly established, and local newspapers rapidly emerged, beginning with the *Norwich Post* in 1708. A newspaper provided a steady source of income and required only a small investment. It was also a cheap advertising medium for the bookseller or printer's other wares. By the 1730s, every major provincial centre had its own newspaper (*ibid.* 132). Provincial bookshops spread rapidly, increasing from 400 outlets in 200 towns in 1749 to nearly 1,000 in 300 locations in the 1790s (*ibid.* 137). The number of journals rose steadily throughout the eighteenth century. R.P. Bond has estimated that in 1711 there were 66 periodicals available in the British Isles, 90 in 1750 and 140 in 1775 (1969: 4). Robert Mayo lists 120 essay-periodicals for the period 1740–1815, about half of which were non-political papers (1962: 72).

The size of the readership of eighteenth-century periodicals is difficult to gauge. We do not usually have access to printers' and booksellers' ledgers, and print historians have often been forced to rely on the claims of editors, who may well have exaggerated their own success. Since periodicals were frequently lent out, shared, read aloud or consulted in a public place, a single copy may have been read by many people. Addison claims that each copy of the *Spectator* had 20 readers (*Spectator* 10) whilst one contemporary describes the *Craftsman* as having 'no more than 40 Readers to a Paper' (Harris 1987: 48). Historians have estimated the sales figures of some of the most popular publications. The *Craftsman*, an enormously successful polemical paper, achieved a sale of around 13,000 per week (*ibid.* 86). At the height of their influence, the major Opposition papers were bringing in profits of around £1,000 p.a. (*ibid.* 92). Major weekly periodicals of mid-century, which combined news and non-political features, often enjoyed sales of up to 10,000 per issue (*ibid.*). Monthly magazines had a readership of between 5,000 and 15,000 from the 1760s onwards (Mayo 1962: 84). In 1710, the official news organ, the *London Gazette*, printed 1,000 copies per issue, some of which may have been remaindered (R.P. Bond 1971: 39).

Very few estimates have been made of the circulation of literary periodicals: that is, all publications whose content was not primarily political. Most publishing history studies focus on newspapers. The *Tatler* and the *Spectator* were the most successful essay-periodicals, with sales of the original issues estimated at 3,000 and 4,000 respectively (R.P. Bond 1971: 39 and D.F. Bond 1965: lxxiv). Richmond P. Bond estimates the *Tatler*'s original profits at around £37 per week (1971: 39). The mid-century literary essay-sheet the *World*, published by Robert Dodsley, edited by the dramatist Edward Moore and numbering among its star-studded band of contributors Lord Chesterfield, Horace Walpole, William Whitehead, Soame Jenyns, Richard Owen Cambridge and Joseph Warton, reputedly sold 25,000 copies per week (Mayo 1962: 118). Very few literary essay-periodicals achieved comparable readerships. Most probably had a circulation of no more than a few hundred in their original sheets. It was customary, however, to bind and print collected issues of a periodical at the end of the run, and many publications reached much larger audiences in volume form (*ibid.* 71). Those who owned incomplete sets of the original sheets were also encouraged to replace issues they had missed and bind them themselves. Back copies, indexes and title pages were often available from the printer (R.P. Bond 1971: 41). Literary essay-periodicals tended to have much shorter lifespans than most of today's publications: in the majority of cases, the papers appear to have ended within a year, and many are only extant in two or three issues.

Periodicals were very widely available, especially in the capital. They could be bought at the publisher's office or ordered by subscription from the printer or from metropolitan or provincial booksellers. They could be purchased or hired from hawkers on the London streets, read at taverns, barbers' shops, chandlers and India houses (Jeremy Black 1991: 99–108). J.H. Plumb has estimated that there were around 2,000 coffee-houses in London during the reign of Queen Anne (1983: 269). Most held periodicals, which could be read on site or sometimes borrowed, and some played host to private book clubs, whose members purchased periodicals as a group and read them aloud over drinks or a meal (*ibid.* 269–70). By the 1720s, collected editions of periodicals could also be obtained from the new circulating libraries (*ibid.* 270).

Relatively little is known about the readership of eighteenth-century journalism. The extent of literacy in the period is difficult to estimate, and the means of defining literacy are contested. Those able to sign their names on a legal document – the usual measure of literacy in this period – were probably not all capable of reading Johnson's polysyllabic prose in the *Rambler*, for instance. However, most historians agree that literacy levels were rising rapidly, particularly in London and among women and merchants. John Brewer estimates that 45% of men could read and write in 1714, rising to 60% by mid-century and that female literacy rose from 25% in 1714 to 40% in 1750 (Brewer 1997: 167–8). He argues that the percentage of literate women in London changed more dramatically than elsewhere in the country, increasing from 22 to 66% between the 1670s and 1720s (*ibid.*). Wages for skilled workers in the capital seldom fell below 10s. a week, making periodicals affordable to many (Harris 1987: 192). Of the lower classes, shopkeepers were the most likely to be literate: 95% of them could read and write by 1775 (Brewer 1997: 168). The audience for periodicals in the first few decades of the century, then, was probably predominantly urban and included some shopkeepers, domestic servants and apprentices and their masters. It is likely that a significant proportion of that readership was female.

The cost of purchasing periodicals rose faster than the rate of inflation throughout the century, putting them quickly out of the price range of most unskilled and semi-skilled workers (Jeremy Black 1991: 107–8). This price rise is reflected in the style and focus of the periodicals themselves. As the century progresses, periodical editors increasingly portray their publications as genteel entertainment. The maverick literary entrepreneur John Dunton edited a number of popular epistolary periodicals in the late seventeenth and early eighteenth centuries, which reached a large and socially diverse audience. Dunton's papers, in particular the *Athenian Mercury* (1691–7) and the *Post-Angel* (1701–2), together with their later imitators, the *British Apollo* (1708–11) and the *Athenian News* (1710), contained a number of readers' queries and editors' responses on questions ranging from the nature of the soul to the reasons why prostitutes have so few pregnancies (*Athenian Mercury* I.1, 17 March 1690; I.18, 23 May 1691). The editor promises to answer queries sent in by 'All Persons whatsoever', providing a source of information to 'those whose Pockets could not arrive to a better Education' (*Athenian Mercury* I.1). No original letters to the *Mercury* have survived. However, Helen Berry's research suggests that Dunton's readership encompassed a wide range of society, including servant maids, shop assistants and apprentices (2003: 36–43, 63–5). Referring to the *British Apollo*, a correspondent of the *Female Tatler* comments acidly that 'the chief Querists are Drapers, Haberdashers, Grocers, Ale-house-keepers and such sort of Trash' (30, 14 September 1709).

Early journals frequently describe their role as that of disseminating knowledge to those without the leisure, money or education to read books. The *Weekly Pacquet* (1678) promises to cater for 'meaner capacities', arguing that 'though there be good Books enow abroad, yet every Mans Purse will not allow him to buy . . . This Method is therefore chosen, as most likely to fall into Vulgar hands' (qtd. Jeremy Black 1991: 6). In a similar manner, the *Weekly Amusement* (1734–6) reassures its readers that 'nothing shall be inserted but what may be understood by persons of the meanest capacities' (no. 1). Few periodicals of the mid- to late eighteenth century acknowledge such a humble readership. Robert Mayo has noted the predominance of phrases such as 'elegant amusement', 'entertaining companions' and 'taste, fashion and politeness' in editors' descriptions of their publications after 1750 (1962: 220–1). The editor of the immensely popular *World* defines his readership as high society or 'the well-dressed, and . . . *everybody one knows*' (162, 5 February 1756). The titles of publications such as the *Royal Magazine* (1750–1), the *Court Miscellany*,[3] the *St. James's Magazine* (1762–4) and the *Court and City Magazine; or, a Fund of Entertainment for the Man of Quality* (1770–1), announce their aristocratic pretensions. This does not necessarily imply that their readers were drawn from the upper echelons of society. As the authors of *Women's Worlds* have pointed out, 'Publishers and editors recognise their readers as "aspirational", aspiring to . . . a higher class or social bracket' (Ballaster *et al.* 1991: 11). A correspondent tells the *Court Magazine* that, although it is bought by 'the nobility', its chief readers are 'the servant in waiting, or the journeyman hair-dresser' (January 1762).

Michael Harris has argued that 'the press in this period did not succeed in substantially broadening the basis of its readership' (1978: 97) and believes that the readership of newspapers was largely drawn from the aristocracy, gentry and clergy, although it also included a substantial number of self-employed craftsmen, tradesmen and shopkeepers (1987: 191–5). The readership of literary essay-periodicals was almost certainly smaller and less diverse than that of newspapers. While few editors and not many readers were actually drawn from the upper classes, by mid-century most editors maintained a pretence of mutual gentility when addressing their audiences.

Taxation and the cost of paper kept the price of periodicals high after the first quarter of the century. The Stamp Act of 1712 taxed single-sheet newspapers 1d. for every copy printed: printing, say, 8 copies would cost 8d. Publications of more than one sheet paid only 2s. per sheet irrespective of the number of copies: a 4-sheet publication, for example, would pay only 8s. duty, no matter how large its print run. Multi-sheet publications were also exempted from advertisement duty (Harris 1987: 19–20). It became more profitable to publish several sheets weekly, instead of one daily sheet. A number of newspapers converted to the miscellany format, combining news items with literary essays and miscellaneous items, including 'scraps of Poetry, Trials of Highwaymen, pickpockets and many other subjects, that tend to debauch the morals of the community', as one reader complained in the early 1720s (Harris 1978: 85–6). The Stamp Act of 1725 closed this loophole by requiring all newspapers to be stamped on every page, regardless of length. In the 1740s, tough legislation was introduced to suppress the illegal sales of cut-price, unstamped papers. The hawkers who sold them on the streets were liable to up to three months' hard labour, and rewards were offered for information leading to a conviction (Harris 1987: 29–30). The stamp duty was doubled in 1757.

The stamp tax and the cost of paper were the largest expenses involved in setting up a periodical. At least £200 was needed to launch a newspaper in the 1730s (*ibid.* 49). Essay-periodicals brought in smaller profits, but also had smaller initial costs and overheads and could often be financed by individuals. As the costs of periodical production increased, there was a shift in the ownership of London papers, especially daily newspapers, from individual printer entrepreneurs to large groups of shareholding booksellers (Harris 1978: 92). This in turn was to bring about a significant change, not just in the way in which periodicals were produced, but in their form and content. It was to lead to a conception of journals not as the literary work of specific individuals, but as business enterprises undertaken primarily for profit, without a distinctive single editorial voice or artistic vision.

Although there was no pre-publication censorship, periodical printers and publishers were liable to prosecution for obscenity, blasphemy or seditious libel. Between 1715 and 1759 over 70 warrants were issued against newspapers, not including prosecutions for breach of parliamentary privilege. The reporting of parliamentary debates was to remain illegal until 1771 (*ibid.* 96). Printers and publishers were more likely to be arrested than authors, since they printed their names and addresses on their title pages, for commercial correspondence. Printers could be sentenced to a maximum of two years' imprisonment and fined up to £200. Even when a prosecution was unsuccessful, they were often imprisoned pending trial for a number of months – in some cases several years – and were released only when substantial bail had been raised. Printing materials and presses were often confiscated or damaged in government raids (Harris 1987: 142–7). A conviction could, however, make a paper more popular, by advertising its radical, salacious or titillating content. As well as taking legal measures, government officials at the Post Office could prevent the distribution of issues or threaten a paper's finances by intercepting orders and advertisements (*ibid.* 136–9). Despite these difficulties and restrictions, periodicals continued to flourish throughout this period, although these historical developments led to changes in the relative popularity of different forms of journalism. In the early part of the century the essay-periodical enjoyed considerable popularity, but by mid-century the periodical market was dominated by the magazines. I will be tracing the effects of these changes within the individual chapters of this book. First, however, it is important to understand the main characteristics of these two forms of periodical writing.

The essay-periodical

The single-essay periodical was pioneered by Richard Steele in his *Tatler* (1709–11) and then developed further by Steele and Joseph Addison in the *Spectator* (1711–12 and 1714). These periodicals were written in the guise of fictional personae. Both the *Tatler*'s Isaac Bickerstaff and Mr Spectator were genial, mildly eccentric figures, who combined moral *gravitas* with loveable idiosyncrasy. The concise and manageable form of the single essay meant that the papers could be written by one individual. In most essay-periodicals, one writer had editorial responsibility for the publication, as well as composing most of the material him- or herself. I use the term *editor* in this context almost interchangeably with *writer*. Richmond Bond has attributed 47 *Tatler* papers to Addison, estimating that he wrote a further 22 in collaboration with Steele. Other possible contributors to the *Tatler* include John Hughes, Arthur Maynwaring, Anthony Henley, Temple Stanyan, William Congreve, William Asplin, Richard Parker, Charles Dartiquenave, Jonathan Swift and Lady Mary Wortley Montagu (R.P. Bond 1971: 14–20). I treat the *Tatler*, however, as the work of Steele throughout, since he not only wrote 181 of the paper's 271 issues, but exercised full editorial control over all the material that was published (*ibid.* 15).

The use of a fictional persona allowed Steele to censure the faults and follies of his society, without exposing himself to personal attacks or to the charge of hypocrisy. The device brilliantly combines wit with morality, ironic distance with direct appeal. As the editor of the *Medley* comments in 1711,

> *Isaac Bickerstaff* ... had the Skill to talk in a superior Air to his Opponents, and support himself in it, by giving himself a comical Figure at the same time. Without this Subtlety ... the *Tatler* had been the most insufferably arrogant of any Writer that ever appear'd in the World.
>
> (38, 18 June 1711)

In the *Spectator*, Addison also describes the liberating effect of writing in a mask. He tells his readers, 'That might pass for Humour, in the *Spectator*, which would look like Arrogance in a Writer who sets his Name to his Work. The Fictitious Person might ... assume a Mock-Authority, without being looked upon as vain and conceited' (no. 555). Henry Fielding's *Jacobite's Journal* is unusual in the level of irony with which the author handles his persona, John Trott-Plaid. Fielding chooses to pose as a Jacobite in order 'to be laughed at for the Good of my Country' and to 'reduce all Men to be *as great and as sincere* Jacobites as myself' (*Jacobite's Journal* 1, 5 December 1747). However, Fielding abandons his alter ego after only 16 issues, declaring himself 'weary of personating a Character for whom I have so solemn a Contempt' and fearing that there is 'no Species of Wit and Humour so little adapted to the Palat of the present Age' as irony, as well as 'no kind of Humour so liable to be mistaken' (*Jacobite's Journal* 17, 26 March 1748). Most editors employ their personae more or less as mouthpieces – they are eccentric, perhaps, but ultimately respectable and authoritative spokespeople. The idea of the editor as a figure of moral authority was to remain central to conceptions of the genre.

It is impossible to overestimate Addison and Steele's influence on later periodicalists. The *Spectator*, in particular, continued to be read, anthologized and praised as a model of English prose and moral thought until the early part of the twentieth century. Editors frequently complain that because of the *Spectator* 'it is a ... fashion to condemn all other writings of the same kind' (*World* 173, 22 April 1756). The editor of the *Gray's Inn Journal* sees the eminence of Addison and Steele's publications as a hindrance to other journalists: 'It has for a long Time been the Objection to the periodical Writer of Essays, that every Subject is pre-occupied; that the *Spectators*, *Tatlers* and *Guardians* have cultivated every Field of Reflection' (29 December 1753). Addison is lionized in Edward Young's *Conjectures on Original Composition* (1759) and in John Gilbert Cooper's *Letters Concerning Taste* (1755). In 1760, Hugh Blair held a series of lectures on rhetoric, many of them involving painstakingly close readings of individual numbers of the *Spectator*. Blair comments that 'the "Spectator" . . . is a book which is in the hands of every one, and which cannot be praised too highly' (Bloom and Bloom 1980: 368). The copyright to the collected edition of the *Spectator* was sold for £1,150 in 1712, while the copyright to a part-book of the periodical was valued at the very high figure of £1,300 in 1767. Shakespeare's entire works, by comparison, were worth £1,800 (Brewer 1997: 100). Jane Austen complains of the continued veneration of Addison in her celebrated defence of the novel in *Northanger Abbey*. Young girls, she writes, are generally ashamed to be caught reading a novel. The author comments dryly 'Now, had the same young lady been engaged with a volume of the Spectator . . . how proudly would she have produced the book, and told its name' (Austen 1988: 38).

As Robert D. Mayo has pointed out, the eighteenth-century periodical was a genre characterized by 'journalistic orthodoxy' (1962: 71). In an age in which skilful imitation and adaptation of Classical models was highly prized, the periodical lacked a venerable literary ancestry. Ironically, this very deficiency made the essay-periodical, in particular, a highly conservative genre, as editors attempted to establish clear traditions and guidelines for periodical writing. The genre's historical youth, coupled with editors' aspirations to literary gentility, led to the establishment of the *Tatler* and the *Spectator* as prescribed models for every journalist. Mayo has discovered over a hundred imitators of the *Tatler* and the *Spectator* in the period 1715–40 alone (*ibid.* 43). In the preface to the collected edition of the *Censor*, the editor describes the 1710s, following the publication of '*the inimitable* Spectator', as '*the Age of* Counsellors, *when every Blockhead who could write his own Name attempted to inform and amuse the Publick*' (1717).

This attempt to compensate for the paucity of illustrious journalists by canonizing Addison and Steele also led to the periodical's relative immunity to literary fashion. The early periodical was a highly self-absorbed literary genre and appears to have neither influenced, nor been influenced by, the novel to any significant extent.[4] Mayo has noted that Addison and Steele's writing formed the 'single most important influence upon magazine fiction in the eighteenth century – Richardson, Sterne, and other popular novelists not excepted' (1962: 84). Henry Fielding wrote or edited at least five periodicals: the *Grub-Street Journal* (1730–8), the *Champion* (1739–43), the *True Patriot* (1745–6), the *Jacobite's Journal* (1747–8) and the *Covent-Garden Journal* (1752). The journalism of the author of *Joseph Andrews* (1742), *Tom Jones* (1749) and *Amelia* (1751) conforms to the Addisonian tradition and shares very few features with his novels. Fielding frequently adopts a Spectatorial persona. His alter ego in the *Covent-Garden Journal*, 'Sir Alexander Drawcansir, Knt. Censor of Great Britain', is a knight-errant in the

Bickerstaffian tradition. Fielding also assumes the identity of the colourfully named cudgel player Captain Hercules Vinegar in the *Champion* and of the fanatical Jacobite John Trott-Plaid, whose cousin, the Tory fox-hunter Humphrey Gibbins, resembles the *Spectator*'s Sir Roger de Coverley. In addition, Fielding's use of fictional letters to the editor, verse, political allegory and a 'Court *of* Censorial Enquiry', which echoes the *Tatler*'s 'Court of Honour', all bear witness to the influence of Addison and Steele. The novelist Frances Brooke was almost unique in her efforts to combine the characteristics of the two popular genres; Chapter 8 will explore her reinterpretation of the Addisonian essay-paper.

A large number of essay-periodicalists followed Addison and Steele's example by writing in the guise of a quirky and eccentric editor figure, often referred to by historians of journalism as the editor's *eidolon*, taken from the Greek word meaning 'ghost'. Almost all eighteenth-century journalism, like much other contemporary literature, was published anonymously. Editors wrote under colourful, patently fictitious pseudonyms, which were usually ironically self-deprecatory. Aaron Hill tells his readers in the *Prompter* (1734–6) that 'Custom has made it necessary . . . to assume a *Character* . . . either heroic or ludicrous' and 'take up some *Soubriquet*, or mock Name' (1, 12 November 1734). The convention was so well established by 1723 that the editor of the *Visiter* felt the need to apologize to his readers for not adopting a 'Character . . . which I think can be of little Use . . . to them, or my self' (1, 18 June 1723). Many of the names and titles chosen refer to those traits that seem particularly appropriate to a journalist. The *Busy Body* (1759), the *Prattler* (1747) the *Prater* (1756) and the 'Babbler',[5] and fictional creations like Mrs Prattle of the *Parrot* (1728) and Mrs Penelope Pry of the *Lady's Weekly Magazine* (1747) allude to the proverbial loquacity and nosiness of editors, whereas the *Grumbler* (1715), the *Grouler* (1711) and Lewis Theobald's irascible Mr Censor (1715–17) exploit the stereotype of the disaffected and misanthropic critic of society. Editors adopted a host of bizarre and flamboyant identities. They wrote as hermits, Jesuits, lay-monks and pilgrims; high German doctors, hyp-doctors, conjurors and mountebanks; dreamers, rhapsodists and projectors; and lovers, devils, fairies and knights-errant.[6]

It is difficult to judge how frequently their original readers knew the real authors of such publications. Contemporaries were quick to attribute the *Tatler* to Richard Steele, whereas the authorship of the *Female Tatler* aroused some controversy and remains uncertain. Some writers hint playfully at their real personalities within their periodicals, allowing fleeting glimpses of the author behind the mask. Guessing the editor's identity may have sometimes been part of the pleasure of reading a periodical, but more frequently it probably served to disguise and protect the writer. Editors usually handled their assumed characters with comic distance. Sheltering their true identities behind personae, editors were able to treat their alter egos with self-deprecatory humour, while still retaining their own dignity and credibility as social commentators, educators or moralists.

Female personae range from Eliza Haywood's genteel Euphrosine in the *Young Lady* (1756)[7] to Mother Bawdycoat of the *Tatling Harlot* (1709). There were, however, far fewer female pseudonyms, probably because of the narrower range of female occupations. Women were also allowed less freedom than men to display eccentricity of character. Any extreme personality trait in a woman was liable to be interpreted as a vice, whereas in a man it could be seen as a charming eccentricity.

A bizarre pseudonym was sometimes employed simply as an eye-catching marketing device, and the character of the editor was not developed further. As a correspondent of the *Lady's Museum* puts it, 'It is common enough among periodical authors to forget their titles: they fill their heads with the theory of a plan which experience soon shews them to be too narrow to last long' (3: 1.163). The editor of the *Hermit* (1711–12), for example, is never described, nor is anything about the paper's presentation or political stance especially appropriate to a hermit. In many periodicals, however, the fiction is taken to far greater lengths. The *High-German Doctor* (1714–15) is edited by a series of quacks and circus performers: among them the mountebank 'Hermodactyl'; Harry Gambol, a tumbler and rope dancer; and 'Orlando Mezereon, *Professor of the* Occult Sciences, *Adept in* Palmistry *and* Physiognomy . . . *Licentiate in* Surgery *and* Midwifery, Second-Sighted, *and a* Seventh Son' (II.1, 26 October 1714). Each editor relates his own life story, which is distorted and discredited by his successor, who presents the readers with a different version of the same events. Much of the periodical is dedicated to these varied and involved histories. An equally unusual strategy is adopted in *News from the Dead* (1715–16). One Saturday night, the printer enters his printing house to find Mercury, 'a little dapper Fellow, about twice the size of an *Umble-Bee*', playing on a pipe, at which 'the *Letters came hopping out*' of their own accord and '*fill'd up . . . half a Sheet*' (no. 1). The diminutive messenger from hell promises to supply '*a* Weekly *Account of all the Remarkable Passages that happened in the Infernal Regions*' (*ibid.*).

Christopher Smart developed perhaps the most flamboyant editorial persona of all in his *Midwife* (1750–3). Its editor, Mary Midnight, represents a distillation of all the stereotypes surrounding the figure of the female editor in their most extreme form: her sexuality, her ambition and her vanity. The frontispiece to the periodical shows two plump old women, the editor and her confederate Succubus Canidia, in a shabby, bare room, dressed in mob-caps and spectacles. The editor is smoking a pipe, seated next to a privy labelled 'The Jakes of Genius'. A witch's pointed hat hangs on the door. The scene is Hogarthian in its detailed squalor, and Mother Midnight resembles the infamous bawd Mother Needham in Hogarth's *Harlot's Progress* (1732). The disreputable nature of women's writing could not be more clearly emphasized than in the figure of an editor who is also both a witch and a bawd (Figure I.2). However, despite this, Mother Midnight is a figure of extraordinary vitality and fertility of both body and brain – she is the mother of 26 children (*Midwife* II.3), has visited Turkey and Cairo (II.5) and has some impressive academic publications to her name (see II.2, II.6). From December 1751, Smart extended the periodical into a circus and drag show called 'The Old Woman's Concert', in which he himself appeared dressed as Mother Midnight (Sherbo 1967: 75–81). The show featured the Midwife playing on the Jew's harp and hurdy-gurdy and also included imitations of Italian opera, pseudo-sermons in the manner of Orator Henley, animal pantomime, a company of Lilliputians and a dancer with a wooden leg.[8] It ran intermittently at the Castle Tavern in Paternoster Row until at least 1760.

Although most editors did not surround their personae with such intricate narratives, some of them did create subtle, complex characters, whose personalities shed light on the literary strategies and aims of their authors. This study will begin with an exploration of the figure of Bickerstaff, the first vividly realized fictitious portrait of a periodical editor, and will go on to examine the varied identities assumed by Steele's successors. The personae chosen by almost all the other editors in this survey are, in varied ways, responses to Bickerstaff.

The magazine

The essay-periodical was usually the work of a single author or small group of writers, who combined editorial and authorial responsibilities. However, in 1731 the printer and entrepreneur Edward Cave launched a periodical that signalled a radical new departure. Adopting a metaphor drawn from the commercial world, he called his publication a *magazine* and was the first to use the word in its modern sense. The *Oxford English Dictionary* defines the original meaning of *magazine* as a 'storehouse or repository of goods or merchandise' and cites Cave's publication as the first example of its figurative meaning of a 'periodical publication . . . consisting of a miscellany of critical and descriptive articles, essays, works of fiction etc'. Eighteenth-century editors like Charlotte Lennox and Mark Akenside also adopted the term *museum* to refer to a collection of fugitive pieces, a journalistic 'repository for the preservation and exhibition of objects' ('Museum', *OED* 1989 ed.) – or, as one of Akenside's correspondents puts it, 'an Hospital for every thing that

Figure I.2 Mother Midnight and Succubus Canidia of Christopher Smart's *Midwife* (1750–3).

is *singular*' (*Museum* 2, 12 April 1746) – but the coinage was to be short-lived.[9]

The Copyright Act of 1710 only applied to publication in volume form and did not affect periodicals. Cave conceived of his *Gentleman's Magazine* as a monthly anthology of all the best essays from the daily and weekly papers, combined with book reviews, translations, short biographies, poetry and readers' correspondence, as well as items of practical interest to businessmen, such as the prices of grain and stocks, shipping reports and foreign affairs that might affect the course of trade. He aimed to offer his readers a wide variety of material at a modest price and expected them to browse and select articles of personal interest, rather than reading cover to cover. The *Magazine* took no political stance, printing articles from the Whig and Tory press side by side, and had no distinctive editorial persona or voice. It aspired to the widest possible readership. Cave, who was a highly conscientious worka-holic, superintended the publication himself, but employed journalists and sub-editors, most famously Johnson, who seems to have been paid £100 p.a. to edit the paper and provide copy (Bloom 1957: 7). As Edward Bloom has pointed out, Cave was one of the first editors to provide a team of staff writers with more or less permanent and reliable employment (*ibid*. 71).

Like Addison and Steele's periodicals, Cave's successful formula was copied by many other editors. Beginning with the appearance of the rival *London Magazine* (1732–97), a year after the launch of Cave's paper, there quickly followed such publications as the *Bee* (1733–5), the *Country Magazine* (1736–7), the *Scots Magazine* (1739–1826), the *Gentleman's and London Maga-zine* (1741), the *Museum* (1746–7) and the *Universal Magazine* (1747–1815).

By mid-century, magazines dominated the periodical market. Essay-periodicals became fewer in number, with a rapidly decreasing share of the available readership. With their extensive format, magazines could reprint essay-periodicals in their entirety within their pages. When Johnson's *Rambler* was published in 1750–2, it achieved a sale of less than 500 in its single sheets, but reached a very wide audience through reprintings in London and provincial magazines (see Chapter 7). The editors of the *British Magazine* proudly announce that they '*propose to enrich every number . . . with one paper from the* Idler' (January 1760: 25) and also print individual numbers of Goldsmith's 'Chinese Letters'. Magazines also carried their own essay-series within the periodical. Charlotte Lennox's *Lady's Museum* (1760–1), which I discuss in Chapter 9, is a magazine that incorporates an essay-serial in the Spectatorial mode within its pages.

Magazines and miscellanies were bulky and diverse publications which relied heavily on teams of staff writers and readers' contributions. Cave and his followers were magazine editors in an almost twenty-first century sense: overseeing and correcting, rather than providing copy. Cave oscillates between portraying himself as an author and as a businessman, blurring the boundaries between literature and the commercial venture. By mid-century, few periodicals centred on the personality and adventures of an individual fictitious creation. The cranks and spinsters were relegated to essay-series within the magazine. From editors, they had dwindled into columnists. These historical developments reflect changing attitudes towards the nature of authorship, the purposes of journalism and the relationship between the writer and his or her audience. The magazines' increasing reliance on second-hand copy both reflected and influenced a growing disparity between literary values and journalistic practice. While poets and novelists came to value originality ever more highly, journalism was increasingly associated with the derivative, hackneyed and commonplace.

This association of journalism with the second-rate and with unscrupulous plagiarism was strengthened by the editorial practices of many of the later magazines modelled on Cave's format. Not all magazines achieved the high standards of Cave's publication. Many, particularly in the provinces, were scissors-and-paste operations, offering little or no original material and lacking any kind of editorial agenda or rationale to guide them in the inclusion or rejection of copy. Many of the same tales, letters, poems and essays were reprinted on numerous occasions in many different publications, and it is often difficult to trace the origin of a popular piece of writing. Sometimes the editors acknowledge their sources and at other times present these repertory pieces as original work. Issues of the *Tatler* and the *Spectator* were still appearing in magazines, under the guise of new writing, almost a century after their original publication (Mayo 1962: 225–31). As Mayo has shown in his comprehensive survey, magazine editors increasingly relied on the anonymous unpaid contributions of their readers (1962). No matter how fraught with difficulties, it was cheaper to print copy sent in by readers or to plagiarize existing material, than to pay professional journalists. Mark Akenside, as a well known author, was paid £100 a year to edit Robert Dodsley's bi-weekly *Museum*, but his salary was atypically generous (Brewer 1997: 144). A mid-century reviewer for the magazines would receive 2 guineas as a standard fee for writing eighty pages of reviews (*ibid*. 148).

The *Lady's Magazine* (1770–1832), which printed a large volume of fiction submitted by its readers, provides a striking example of contemporary editorial incompetence. The editor mislays manuscripts, prints the same short story twice and reprints articles that have already appeared. He or she prints episodes of serial fiction in the wrong order. Narrative pieces contributed by readers are frequently abandoned in mid-flow, and the editor is forced to beg remiss correspondents to send in further chapters of their stories. In the absence of continuations, the stories are sometimes brought to a sudden, perfunctory end. Sometimes other readers come forward, offering to continue the story, only to abandon it in their turn. There are lapses of months and even years between instalments (Mayo 1962: 220–3).

The voluminous magazines of the later eighteenth century are filled with repertory pieces of dubious origin and sometimes of venerable antiquity, which have often been plagiarized many times over. They rely on readers' contributions, which can seldom be attributed to specific authors, and rarely display any consistency of editorial stance or purpose. A number of literary periodicals and essay-series in the Spectatorial mould appeared during the last quarter of the century, but they represent only a minority of the total number of publications and did not exert a significant influence over the development of the genre. The periodicals of the late eighteenth century form a vital link in the history of journalism, but they call for a very different approach from their predecessors up to 1770.

The periodical and the mock-heroic

In the *Museum*, Mark Akenside comments with wry irony that 'hereafter I expect, that ... *Sylvanus Urban*, and myself, shall be as good Classics as Mr. *Pope* and Mr. *Prior*' (2, 12 April 1757). Like Akenside, most eighteenth-century periodical writers treat the genre in which they work with gentle mockery. With genteel but disingenuous irony, they relinquish all claims to posterity. A writer for the *Examiner* laments the fate of '*Half-Sheet* Authors' in a typically elegiac tone: 'We are like those little Animals ... that are born, and live, and dye, within the Compass of a Day. If we please [or] amuse our Readers ... between Sun and Sun, 'tis sufficient; but our Fame seldom lasts till late in the Evening; and the very Remembrance of us is usually lost by the next Morning' (5, 31 August 1710). The image of the editor as an insect, with its humorous connotations of a short-lived and mildly irritating creature, was a popular one. The *Covent-Garden Journal* compares journalists to a swarm: 'Homer's Simile of the Bees gives us scarce too vast an Idea of them. ... Some of them fly abroad only every other Day; some send forth their Works once a Week; others once a Fortnight' (1, 4 January 1752). Fielding describes the individual issues of the *London Gazette* surviving 'little longer than the Life of that posting Insect, whose Flash of Being endures but six Hours' (*Champion* 328, 17 December 1741), while Frances Brooke compares contemporary journalists with 'summer insects', which 'just make their appearance, and are gone', and wishes to 'buzz amongst them a little' (*Old Maid* 1, 15 November 1755). In this context, the periodical could be seen as a mock genre, bearing the same relationship to history as mock-epic does to epic or town eclogues to pastoral. Journalistic work will survive because of its author's wit and eloquence, despite the triviality of his or her medium.

1 'Censor-General of *Great Britain*'
The *Tatler* and the editor as social monitor

With his *Tatler*, Richard Steele inaugurated a wholly new departure in periodical writing: an essay-paper centred on the character of its fictional editor, Isaac Bickerstaff. No journalist before Steele had explored the possibilities of writing a paper which would be both objective and amusing, appeal to a wide readership and yet present its views through the figure of an eccentric, elderly man. Steele's subtle and highly successful blend of literary characterization and social commentary was to influence periodical writers throughout the century.

Steele tells us in his final issue that he assumed the persona of Bickerstaff for didactic aims. If he wished to reform, as well as entertain his readers, he would lay himself open to the charge of hypocrisy if he did so *in propria persona*: 'I considered, that Severity of Manners was absolutely necessary to him who would censure others, and for that Reason, and that only, chose to talk in a Mask' (*Tatler* 271). The idiosyncrasies of Bickerstaff's character provide the humour that sugars the bitter pill of moral censure, making his periodical a model of the *utile dulci*. Steele tells us that he 'spoke in the Character of an old Man, a Philosopher, an Humorist, an Astrologer, and a Censor, to allure my Reader with the Variety of my Subjects, and insinuate, if I could, the Weight of Reason with the Agreeableness of Wit' (*ibid.*). These two aims might at first appear to be potentially at odds. Steele had a difficult balance to achieve: he needed to create a figure of loveable and comic eccentricity, who would not repel readers by his saintliness, without, however, forfeiting his moral *gravitas*. The portrait of Bickerstaff was not autobiographical: he is a frail old man in his sixties and a social outsider, while Steele was a well-known playwright and a career politician aged 37.[10] Some contemporaries quickly identified the periodical as Steele's (Bloom and Bloom 1980: 103–30), but Steele's alias served not merely to protect his anonymity. The use of a comic alter ego enabled Steele to make his moral points with humorous exaggeration: to entertain, rather than preach. Before we can consider Steele's depiction of Bickerstaff as an *eidolon*, we need first briefly to examine Bickerstaff's method of attack, his moral categories and the system of which he was the spokesman.

In a humorously hyperbolic image, Bickerstaff describes himself as the 'Censor-General of *Great Britain*' (*Tatler* 163), an image which he borrows from Classical history. In ancient Rome, the censor-general's task was to count the population and establish the numbers of citizens in each rank, in order to assess them for tax purposes. The image suggests an obsession with taxonomy which is evident throughout the *Tatler*. It also betrays the *Tatler*'s strongly urban bias: it is a paper primarily concerned with London society. While the Roman censor's categories were based on income and rank, Bickerstaff categorizes men (I use the gender-specific term intentionally) not by their social position, religious or political affiliations, but by their dress and behaviour. The implications of Bickerstaff's categories are clearly didactic: the *Tatler*'s readers can choose to be smarts, pretty fellows, coffee-house statesmen or dappers (all subspecies of coxcomb, for Bickerstaff) or they can, as Bickerstaff instructs, avoid the various fashionable foibles which characterize these kinds of men.

The image of the editor as Roman censor was to be taken up by Lewis Theobald in his periodical the *Censor*. Theobald's *eidolon*, Benjamin Johnson, takes as his model 'my great Predecessor in this *Office*, *Marcus Cato* the *Censor*' (*Censor* 30, 17 June 1715). Like Bickerstaff, he is concerned with modish follies, declaring himself the enemy of 'Nonsense, Bad Poets, illiterate Fops, affected Coxcombs, and all the Spawn of Follies and Impertinence, that make up and incumber the present Generation' (*Censor* 1, 11 April 1715). Concerned chiefly with the '*Beau Monde*, in all its Views and Varieties', he promises to 'make a strict Inquisition into the *licens'd* Vanities of both Sexes, and lay an Interdict upon any Importation of new ones' (*Censor* 1). The *Censor* shows little interest, however, in the individual 'Varieties' of folly or in enumerating the '*licens'd* Vanities' of the '*Beau Monde*'. Prone to fits of misanthropic rage, the editor has a tendency towards wholesale condemnations of the age in which he lives. In his 'testy Humours' he has 'discharg'd my Venom in a *Satyr* on the *Times*, wrote Declamations against the *Stage* and *Pulpit*, and begun an *Examen* on the Modern Poets' (*Censor* 2, 13 April 1715). He also demonstrates less interest in foolish, foppish behaviour than in bad writing, focusing his criticism on 'the heavy Pages of the Moderns' (*Censor* 1) and, in particular, the theatre. The image of the censor simply endows Theobald's figure with authority and also alludes to the volatile temper that leads him to express censure so frequently.

Mark Akenside's definition of a censor in the *Museum* is much closer to Steele's conception of the term. In an essay 'On the Office of a Censor', Akenside proposes the institution of a modern, civil censor, to enforce good manners and punish antisocial behaviour, a role which he regards as necessary in a liberal and prosperous country:

The quick Circulation of Property, and the Latitudinarian Temper of the national Liberty, inevitably produce many Irregularities, grievous Nuisances to Society, and such as well deserve to be punished, though they are not within the Letter of the Law, nor under the Jurisdiction of any Court of Justice.

(*Museum* 2, 12 April 1746)

The *Tatler* often exercises a similar function of passing judgement on offences which are too petty or too common for the reach of the law and too ludicrous for the pulpit. The contemporary *Records of Love* (1710) adapts this idea of the editorial court, instituting a 'High Court of Judicature at *Paphos*, against Criminals in Love', who are tried for such crimes as 'Feloniously Stealing' a woman's virginity, 'being Enamour'd of a very ugly Woman' and falling in love with a horse (9, 4 March 1710). Fielding adopts the same pseudo-legal device in his *Covent-Garden Journal*, where the editor presides as 'Mr. Censor' over a '*Court of* Censorial Enquiry', hearing such cases as that of an indictment against a recently published novel 'on the Statute of Dulness' (15, 22 February 1752), a disbanded officer accused of attempting to raise a false alarm of fire at the theatre (16, 25 February 1752) and the complaint of the word 'No-body' (41, 23 May 1752). One of Fielding's correspondents offers the same reason for the necessity of a censor as Akenside does in the *Museum*: 'The greatest Evils in Society are those which are out of the reach of the Law' (*Covent-Garden Journal* 64, 30 September 1752). Fielding equates the roles of periodical editor and censor. In the *Jacobite's Journal*, he accuses the contemporary newspapers of having 'vilified and degraded the Office of Censor ... which [has] formerly exercised the Pens of Men of true Learning and Genius' (1, 5 December 1747) and institutes a 'Court of Criticism' where he judges contemporary literature (6, 9 January 1747), assuming the title of '*Censor of* Great Britain'. Fielding's use of the word 'censor' as almost synonymous with periodical editor is repeated in the *Connoisseur*, where Mr Town describes himself 'the CENSOR-GENERAL of all *England*' (140, 30 September 1756).

By focusing this chapter on Steele's moral programme in the *Tatler*, I do not mean to suggest that this periodical is always entirely serious in its aims. Many of its essays seem to have been written for sheer amusement value (such as a wonderful issue on the baffling antics of a dance teacher in *Tatler* 88). Bickerstaff's grave prose often contrasts ludicrously with the triviality of the subjects he turns his attention to, as in the issues on Bickerstaff's 'Court of Honour', where Steele's earnest sexagenarian alter ego presides over trials involving the abuse of canes, failure to return a bow and removing the hassock from a neighbouring pew (see *Tatlers* 103, 265, 259). However, in the *Tatler*, as in Steele's plays, comedy and didacticism are by no means mutually exclusive. The *Tatler* is strongly concerned with the ways in which our choices of clothing, mannerisms and social behaviour reflect our conceptions of ourselves as individuals and therefore our ethical codes. The periodical's pedagogical programme is concerned with the ways in which these choices shape our identity.

This idea of self-fashioning, of choosing an identity, is central to the *Tatler*'s vision of society. When Richard Steele began the *Tatler*, he was already a successful playwright, author of *The Funeral* (1701), *The Lying Lover* (1704) and *The Tender Husband* (1705). In the *Tatler*, Steele borrows from contemporary theories of acting in order to comment on the posturing and role-playing of his society, as well as to suggest new models of behaviour. He views the periodical as the natural successor to the theatre as a school of morality and presents his views through the dramatic persona of Isaac Bickerstaff. In the first part of this chapter, I will discuss Bickerstaff's taxonomic activities and the importance of theatrical imagery to Steele's conception of his society.

While Bickerstaff does include some definitions of female types, on the whole women do not fit easily into the schemes of classification he adopts for men, yet the periodical demonstrates a keen interest in monitoring and reforming female behaviour. In the second part of this chapter, I will examine some of the ways in which Steele approaches this task. Bickerstaff himself is a feminized editor. As an old man, he is represented as both desexed, too old to feel sexual desire, while still vested with masculine authority. He bridges the male and female worlds. Bickerstaff provides a model for female editorship and female moral reformation in his half-sister, Jenny Distaff.

The *Tatler* and the theatre

For Bickerstaff, the *Tatler*'s moral decorum, and in particular its celebration of marriage and family life, form an antidote to a Restoration ethic in which 'Love and Wenching were the Business of Life' (*Tatler* 3). Contemporary writers, especially the 'Stage-Scribblers' of the day, exploited the corrupt taste of their audiences and helped further to promote sexual immorality: 'The Wits of this Island, for above Fifty Years past, instead of correcting the Vices of the Age, have done all they could to inflame them' (*Tatler* 159). Bickerstaff's publication, by contrast, aims 'to put an honest Father of a Family in Countenance' (*Tatler* 159) and focuses, not on the masculine world of court, but on domestic values. The periodical offers an alternative to the amorality of the Restoration stage.[11]

Bickerstaff's comments can also be seen as a reflection on some of Steele's journalistic predecessors, who took the theatre as their model. Publications like the weekly *Momus Ridens* (1690–1) contained alternating stanzas of 'Report' on the news and irreverent 'Remark'. The *Observator* (1705–6) is written in the form of a dialogue between the editor and a 'Countryman'. Ned Ward's *Weekly Comedy* (1699) has speech headings and a list of dramatis personae. As its name suggests, each issue resembles a scene from a play, with such stock characters as 'Snarl, *a Disbanded Captain*', 'Squabble, *a Lawyer*' and 'Prim, *a Beau*' (*Weekly Comedy* 2, 17 May 1699). Ward's paper combines political satire with tales of 'Love and Wenching' of the kind of which Bickerstaff disapproves. In the *Weekly Comedy* 8 (28 June 1699), for example, the poet 'Scan-all' and the journalist 'Scribble' exchange salacious gossip about a woman's obscene revenge on her seducer.

Peter Motteux's monthly *Gentleman's Journal* (1692–4) also combines the political and the mildly pornographic. Motteux juxtaposes summaries of the news, theological essays and scientific treatises on such topics as 'the *Saltness, and Flux ... of* the *Sea*' (3 April 1692) with erotic poetry like the '*Verses from a Lover to his Mistress*' describing the delights of sex (1 February 1692) and lewd ballads, such as '*Acteon; or, the Original of Horn-Fair*' (2 March 1692). The *Journal*, with its short prose narratives, poetry and news, has often been regarded as a precursor of the *Tatler* (see, for example, R.P. Bond 1969), but it has little in common with Steele's publication. The editor's personality remains undeveloped, and Motteux adopts no pen-name, referring to himself simply as 'the Author of this *Journal*' (1 February 1692). The *Journal*'s obscene verses and erotic short stories contrast vividly with Bickerstaff's genteel irony and moral decorum and recall a tradition of bawdy farce.

The stage, for Bickerstaff, is the ideal instrument of social and moral reformation. 'There is no Human Invention so aptly calculated for the forming a Free-born People as that of a Theatre', he writes (*Tatler* 167). The statement appropriately forms part of an elegiac passage on the death of the actor Thomas Betterton, for the stage itself is moribund, in Bickerstaff's eyes. Infected by the lascivious and amoral spirit of Restoration wit, playwrights attract audiences by scoffing at moral values. A country gentleman discusses the decay of social manners in London and asks why playwrights have not turned their pens to the eradication of contemporary folly, which would surely 'give an excellent Field to Writers for the Stage', only to be told that 'there might be some Hopes of Redress of these Grievances, if there were proper Care taken of the Theatre; but the History of that is yet more lamentable' (*Tatler* 12).

Just as Addison was later to claim that the *Spectator* had brought philosophy 'out of Closets and Libraries, Schools and Colleges, to dwell in Clubs and Assemblies, at Tea-Tables, and in Coffee-Houses' (*Spectator* 10), we are told that the *Tatler* will 'bring the Stage as it were into the Coffee-house' (*Tatler* 64). Both periodicals, in fact, frequently employ theatrical metaphors to describe their journalistic enterprises. The title of the *Spectator*, as its editors point out, recalls the stage: 'The Word SPECTATOR being most usually understood as one of the Audience at publick Representations in our Theatres' (*Spectator* 22). Bickerstaff's correspondent Josiah Couplet tells him, 'You will always have a large Scene before you, and can never be at a Loss for Characters to entertain a Town so plentifully stock'd with 'em' (*Tatler* 64).

Bickerstaff's pleasure in the theatre comes as much from observing the audience, however, as from the play itself. He is the discerning spectator and critic of London society, confessing that he loves

> to sit unobserved and unknown in the Gallery, and entertain my self
> either with what is personated on the Stage, or observe what Appear-
> ances present themselves in the Audience ... Our Thoughts are in our
> Features; and the Visage of those in whom Love, Rage, Jealousy or
> Envy, have their frequent Mansions, carries the Traces of those Passions.
> (*Tatler* 182)

The notion of the *theatrum mundi* is, of course, a commonplace. What is more striking is the ironic suggestion that the place where we can best observe mankind is when they themselves form the audience in a theatre. The response to a theatrical representation is itself one of the surest tests of character: 'I would undertake to find out all the Persons of Sense and Breed-ing by the Effect of a single Sentence [of a play], and to distinguish a Gen-tleman as much by his Laugh, as his Bow' (*Tatler* 122). This focus on the theatre audience is perhaps unsurprising in a period in which there was no method of dimming the house lights, and the auditorium was frequently better lit than the stage itself.

Bickerstaff reads the minds and characters of the members of the audience with ease. The editor tells us frequently, not that appearances can be decep-tive, but just how revealing our facial expressions can be: 'Our Thoughts are in our Features'. He cautions that 'you may trace the usual Thoughts of Men in their Countenances' (*Tatler* 198) and tells us that 'the Balls of Sight are so form'd, that one Man's Eyes are Spectacles to another to read his Heart with' (*Tatler* 145). Appearances are far more than merely superficial: they are the outward expression of the inner personality and, as such, must be closely scrutinized, analysed and controlled. The self is not private and invisible, but public and conspicuous. It is foolish to attempt to disguise our feelings and motivations; the bad actor is quickly exposed: 'This Town will not allow us to be the Things we seem to aim at, and are too discerning to be fob'd off with Pretences' (*Tatler* 14).

As a successful playwright himself, Steele's ideas may have been influ-enced by contemporary theories of acting. Charles Gildon's *Life of Mr.*

Thomas Betterton (1710), which was dedicated to Steele, emphasizes the links between a person's outward appearance and his or her emotional state. He likens the body to a musical instrument, passively responding to the impulses of the mind: *'The whole Body of Man, all his Looks, and every Sound of his Voice, like Strings on an Instrument, receive their Sounds from the various Impulse of the Passions'* (Gildon 1710: 43). Gildon argues that a person's facial expression is a reliable guide to their feelings: *'The Countenance . . . is commonly the most certain* Index *of the Passions of the Mind'* (*ibid.* 45). Each emotion leaves its mark on the countenance, and we can read the character from the traces left by habitual *'Passions and Habits of the Mind'*, such as a 'rolling Eye', which indicates 'a quick but light Wit', or a ruddy complexion, a sign of its owner's 'inconstant and impatient mind' (*ibid.* 41). Aaron Hill's *The Art of Acting* expresses this philosophy succinctly: 'The Idea prints the Look' (1746: v). Both Gildon's and Hill's works serve at least partly as instruction manuals for actors. Not only do we assume a certain facial expression when we feel an emotion, but if we mould our features into that expression and perform the appropriate bodily gestures, we will automatically experience the emotion itself. As Hill puts it, 'Rightly to *seem*, is transiently, to BE' (*ibid.* 9). Hill even cautions against the power of the emotions that can be unleashed through the mimicry of gesture and expression. He relates the cautionary tale of an actor playing Ajax who was so successful at capturing the antic postures of madness that he suffered from temporary insanity and narrowly avoided killing a fellow actor during the performance. Hill praises, by contrast, an actor who was wary of performing the madman's role too convincingly and, paradoxically, *'represented* Ajax *raving so gracefully and discreetly, that he gain'd a great Applause'* (*ibid.* 142).

Steele represents his readers as constantly on stage to an audience of their peers. When Bickerstaff tells his readers that the theatre is the perfect instrument for reforming a free-born people, he refers us not to the moral lessons that a play may inculcate, nor to the theatre as an exercise in judgement and empathy. Instead, he concentrates on the figure of the actor, who provides a model for our emulation. Bickerstaff has been describing Betterton's classical predecessor Roscius:

> *The Perfection of an Actor is only to become what he is doing.* Young Men, who are too unattentive to receive Lectures, are irresistibly taken with Performances . . . to speak justly, and move gracefully, is what every Man thinks he does perform, or wishes he did.
>
> (*Tatler* 167)

Bickerstaff places physical poise and elegance of speech and action at the heart of his programme of moral reformation. To be a gentleman, it seems, it is necessary first to learn to appear one, to be a fit representative of a class and culture. Unexpectedly, it is the actor who is the perfect gentleman, though not usually a member of the gentry himself. To act convincingly, the actor must '*become what he is doing*': that is, of course, he must suit the part, but it also means that by 'speaking justly and moving gracefully' he is transformed into an embodiment of the ideal. He is performing, but also behaving perfectly naturally. His charm is irresistible to young and impressionable men and, by modelling themselves on him, they too become gentlemen and are able to perform their social roles with equal poise.

The theatrical metaphor pervades many of the periodical's discussions of morality. Bickerstaff himself assumes the 'Office of Prompter', an image that was later adopted by Aaron Hill in the *Prompter* (1734–6), whose editor, 'Broomstick', recalls Bickerstaff. The prompter, Hill writes, 'stands in a Corner, unseen and unobserved by the Audience, but diligently attended to by every one, who plays a Part' (*Prompter* 1, 12 November 1734). The editor can notify those who are blind to their foibles of the impression which their behaviour makes upon the 'well-bred'. A careful attention to the minutiae of one's own behaviour is vital for the smooth functioning of social interaction. The *Tatler*'s world is highly codified, and people must be seen, in their actions, facial expressions and manner, to be treating others with due politeness to avoid giving offence. Bickerstaff's 'Court of Honour' provides a tribunal at which the affronted can complain of coldness or ungraciousness of manner in others: 'short Bows, cold Salutations, supercilious Looks, unreturned Smiles', as well as the 'ambiguous Expression, accidental Justle, or unkind Repartee' (*Tatler* 250). The *Tatler* paints a vivid picture of a world in which the subtlest nuances of behaviour are subjected to constant scrutiny by the proud and touchy. By asking his readers to correct and regulate their behaviour, the editor is not only redressing social grievances, but protecting the well-meaning, but thoughtless, from censure.

Eccentricities of dress and behaviour are, to Bickerstaff, a form of perverted ambition: a wish to distinguish oneself for mere superficialities. People attempt to force themselves on society's notice with an unusual waistcoat or an outlandish habit of speech: 'The Desire of Fame in Men . . . who have the Ambition without proper Faculties, runs wild, and discovers it self in a Thousand Extravagancies, by which they wou'd signalize themselves from others' (*Tatler* 77). This wild desire for personal conspicuousness leads to the affectation of fashionable disabilities: such as the use of a pierglass to scrutinize one's acquaintance because 'it was the Fashion to be short-sighted' (*Tatler* 77) or the adoption of a 'jaunty limp', rendering the owner 'genteely a Cripple' (*ibid.*). Others assume a modish lisp: 'Some never utter'd the Letter *H*; and others had as mortal an Aversion to *S*' (*ibid.*).

For Bickerstaff, such departures from social norms of self-presentation signal a dangerous disregard for society's sanctions:

> The giving into uncommon Habits of this Nature, is a Want of that humble Deference which is due to Mankind; and (what is worst of all) the certain Indication of some secret Flaw in the Mind of the Person that commits them. . . . I remember a Gentleman of great Integrity and Worth was very remarkable for wearing a broad Belt and an Hanger instead of a fashionable Sword, tho' in all other Points a very well-bred Man. I suspected him at first Sight to have something wrong in him, but was not able for a long while to discover any collateral Proofs of it. I watched him narrowly for Six and Thirty Years, when at last, to the Surprize of every body but my self, who had long expected to see the Folly break out, he married his own Cook-Maid.
>
> (*Tatler* 103)

Of course, Bickerstaff's close attention to details of dress, and his deep interest in eccentricities is itself an eccentricity, but the humorous exaggeration of this passage does not disguise the centrality of these ideas for the periodical as a whole. Bickerstaff is a censor in the modern, as well as the Roman, sense of the word, asking his readers to edit out those aspects of their behaviour which are undignified, uncivilized and odd. Dress, that supposedly most superficial of all concerns, is an important form of self-representation, and it is a politeness that we owe to society to defer to its opinion in such matters. An inordinate attachment to an article of clothing, whether it be broad belt and hanger, red heels, or a cane dangling from a buttonhole, demonstrates a preoccupation with life's trivia and an unbecoming personal vanity.

At the same time, however, whilst 'unjustifiable Singularity' is to be avoided, Bickerstaff warns against a slavish dependence on fashion. Virtue and piety are out of fashion: people 'have generally taken up a Kind of inverted Ambition, and affect even Faults and Imperfections of which they are innocent' (*Tatler* 77). These sheep in wolves' clothing have inherited the idea of the dashing, witty and gallant villain from Restoration comedy and imported it into a more moral and sober age. It is a mere piece of theatre and verbal bravado, a game played by men like the young gentleman 'who talks atheistically all Day in Coffee-houses, and in his Degrees of Understanding sets up for a *Free-Thinker;* tho' it can be prov'd upon him, he says his Prayers every Morning and Evening' (*ibid.*). It is also a short step, for Bickerstaff, from an idiosyncratic sartorial taste to a 'secret Flaw in the Mind'. Just as some disfigure their bodies with canes and monocles, others disable their own intellectual integrity.

The coffee-house atheists are playing a dangerous game, for Bickerstaff. Imitating the appearance of vice can lead to condoning real evil. Such play-acting attracts some of Bickerstaff's bitterest scorn in the unlikely context of a discussion of rakes. As professed 'Knight Errant' of the fair sex (*Tatler* 195), we might imagine that no character could be more despicable to Bickerstaff. The editor, however, shows surprising sympathy for the rake as a man in the grip of a powerful addiction. His strongest moral disgust is reserved for the rake's imitators, who are motivated merely by pride and affectation:

> Second-hand Vice sure of all is the most nauseous: there is hardly a Folly more absurd, or which seems less to be accounted for . . . But the Fatal-ity (under which most Men labour) of desiring to be what they are not, makes 'em go out of a Method, in which they might be receiv'd with Applause . . . into one, wherein they will all their Life have the Air of Strangers to what they aim at.
>
> (*Tatler* 27)

For Bickerstaff, it is not only dishonest, but also futile, to attempt to assume a role in which we have not been cast by nature. We can only 'be receiv'd with Applause' when we are playing ourselves.

Steele is an irrepressibly optimistic and cheerful moralist. He would never have subscribed to Samuel Johnson's pessimistic belief that '*the Majority are wicked*' (*Rambler* 175). Opaque hypocrisy and secret guilt are rarities in the *Tatler*'s moral vision. On the contrary, most people are incapable of effective deception, being poor actors. Far from being worse than they appear, many – or even most – are better. They may imitate the appearance of vice, but they usually stop short of its commission. The *Tatler*'s emphasis on avoiding eccentricities is not simply a doctrine of rigid conformism. It also testifies to Steele's deep respect for his society and to a basic faith in human nature and in 'the Deference due to the Sense of Mankind' (*Tatler* 138). Society ideally acts as a corrective to the follies and vanities of individuals. The society that Steele describes is a shame, not a guilt, culture and in such a society a popular and fashionable periodical publication could exert a powerful influence over the lives of its readers. Their concern for the ways in which others regard them may make many of those readers slaves to fashion and copiers of petty vices, but it also makes them keenly susceptible to criticism. They do not like to be laughed at, and Steele, the gifted humorist, is supremely qualified to laugh them out of their follies. Bickerstaff's friend Sophronius advises the editor to treat sharpers in this manner:

> The Acceptance of these Men being an Ill which hath crept into the Conversation-Part of our Lives . . . [it] is to be amended only by bring-

ing Raillery and Derision upon the Persons who are guilty, or those who
converse with 'em.

(*Tatler* 56)

Steele believes in the centrality of the 'Conversation-Part of our Lives', an
evocative phrase that suggests mixed company discussing matters of general
interest in a domestic setting. The *Tatler* takes as its ideal the domestic and
social setting rather than the professional or mercantile and recommends the
kind of behaviour that would be suitable at a gathering or a dinner party,
where ladies were present, rather than in a tavern or coffee-house.

Bickerstaff attempts to reform the 'Conversation Part of our Lives' by cat-
egorizing the members of London society, 'disposing them into proper
Classes' (*Tatler* 162). He defines the characteristics of 'a *Gentleman*, a *Pretty
Fellow*, a *Toast*, a *Coquet*, a *Critick*, a *Wit*, and other Appellations of those
now in the gayer World' (*Tatler* 21). The '*Smart Fellow*', for example, can be
identified both by his dress – a 'Cane on his Button' and 'red heel'd Shoes' –
and by his behaviour: he elbows his way into theatres without paying and
'sends his Children a begging before they can go' (*Tatler* 26), while a '*very
Pretty Fellow*' is one who is 'successfully loud among the Wits, familiar
among the Ladies, and dissolute among the Rakes' (*Tatler* 24). While ostensibly defining terms, Bickerstaff is clearly also pronouncing social and moral
judgements, in order to expose the true characters of those who shelter
under specious appellations.

Bickerstaff's preoccupation with ordering and sorting reveals a characteristically eighteenth-century conception of judgement as a discriminating
faculty, drawing fine distinctions between things which are outwardly
similar, in opposition to the combinative activities of wit and imagination, in
which dissimilar things are yoked together in new and fantastic combinations
or parallels are drawn between things superficially unlike. Addison was to
distinguish the 'knotty and subtile Disquisitions' that characterize the activity of the understanding from the imagination's power of 'retaining, altering
and compounding those Images, which we have once received, into all the
varieties of Picture and Vision' (*Spectator* 411). Johnson, in his *Dictionary*
entry under 'Wit', cites Locke's distinction between wit and judgement:

Wit lying most in the assemblage of ideas, and putting those together
with quickness and variety, wherein can be found any resemblance, or
congruity, thereby to make up pleasant pictures in the fancy. Judgment,
on the contrary, lies in separating carefully one from another, ideas
wherein can be found the least difference, thereby to avoid being misled
by similitude.

(Johnson 1755 and Locke 1975: 156)

Addison cites the same passage from Locke in his essay series on wit in the *Spectator*, in which he describes wit as consisting in 'such a Resemblance and Congruity of Ideas' as 'is capable of giving the Reader some Surprize' (*Spectator* 62).[12] Coleridge draws on the same distinction in Chapter 13 of his *Biographia Literaria* (1817) when he describes imagination as the force that 'dissolves, diffuses, dissipates, in order to re-create', in implied contrast with judgement, which separates and distinguishes (1983: 1.304).

Bickerstaff's many definitions and classifications make his periodical into a reference book of social folly. He tells his readers that he has made it his study 'to marshal and fix People under their proper Denominations, and to range them according to their respective Characters' (*Tatler* 96). By drawing pen-portraits of character-types, Steele is drawing on a long-established comic tradition, whose most recent proponent was Jean de la Bruyère. Bruyère's *Les Caractères de Théophraste*, published in 1688 and still very popular in Steele's day, also contains a number of comic thumbnail sketches. However, Bruyère's characters are eternal types, characters whose main features have not changed since the time of Theophrastus, their original source. Henry Fielding was to use stock characters of this kind in his novel *Joseph Andrews*, where he tells us, 'I describe not men, but manners; not an individual, but a species' (Fielding 2001: 242). He depicts a selfish lawyer as an unchanging example of human depravity: 'The lawyer is not only alive, but hath been so these 4000 years' (*ibid.*). By contrast, Bickerstaff, like a naturalist, constantly adds new species to his catalogue and acknowledges the field research of his correspondents, reporting, for instance: 'Letters from *Hampstead* say, there is a Coxcomb arriv'd there, of a Kind which is utterly new' (*Tatler* 57).

The *Tatler* demonstrates a keen interest in the latest London foibles. The critic J. Paul Hunter has described journalism as characterized by a 'commitment to contemporaneity' (1990: 167–94), a concern with news in the widest sense. While the *Tatler*'s news section is short-lived, Bickerstaff presents London society as a fertile source of 'utterly new' fools and fops who need to be catalogued, described, warned against and discouraged, as soon as they come to his notice. The editor's cataloguing tasks are unending, as new species of folly are constantly evolving:

> The World is so overgrown with Singularities in Behaviour and Method of Living, that I have no sooner laid before Mankind the Absurdity of one Species of Men, but there starts up to my View some new Sect of Impertinents that had before escaped Notice.
>
> (*Tatler* 166)

All those who indulge in any ostentation or peculiarity of dress are liable to be judged by their dress alone, the editor warns. Bickerstaff labels such people according to their appearance, as a naturalist would unusual specimens:

> I . . . shall take it as a Favour of all the Coxcombs in the Town, if they will set Marks upon themselves, and by some Particular in their Dress show to what Class they belong . . . A Cane upon the Fifth Button shall from henceforth be the Type of a Dapper; Red-heeled Shoes, and a Hat hung upon one Side of the Head, shall signify a Smart; a good Periwig made into a Twist, with a brisk Cock, shall speak a mettled Fellow; and an upper Lip covered with Snuff, denotes a Coffee-House Statesman. But as it is required that all Coxcombs hang out their Signs, it is on the other Hand expected, that Men of real Merit should avoid any thing particular in their Dress, Gait, or Behaviour.
>
> (*Tatler* 96)

A reader writes to tell the editor that he has called a gentleman with red-heeled shoes and a cane dangling from his button a 'smart Fellow' on the strength of Bickerstaff's definition. The other, clearly also a *Tatler* reader since he is duly offended by the epithet, has challenged him to a duel. Bickerstaff defends his correspondent: 'Indeed, it is a most lamentable Thing, that there should be a Dispute rais'd upon a Man's saying another is, what he plainly takes Pains to be thought' (*Tatler* 28). Like an actor in a *commedia dell'arte* production, the smart fellow has assumed a role with his red heels and suspended cane. He is 'what his Taylor, his Hosier, and his Milliner, have conspired to make him' (*ibid*.). He is the natural property of the satirist since his attention-seeking behaviour deserves a public chastisement. All those 'who labour to distinguish themselves, whether it be by Vice or Virtue' (*Tatler* 50) are subjected to Bickerstaff's scrutiny.

The most damning of Bickerstaff's 'proper Distinctions' (*Tatler* 67) is that of his so-called dead men. The editor pronounces the deaths of all those

> who bestow most of their Time in Eating and Drinking, to support that imaginary Existence of theirs, which they call Life; or in dressing and adorning those Shadows and Apparitions, which are looked upon by the Vulgar as real Men and Women.
>
> (*Tatler* 96)

Bickerstaff's dead lack the moral and intellectual qualifications to be considered as full human beings. They may think of themselves as unique, yet they 'differ from each other but as Flies [butterflies] do by a little Colouring or Fluttering of their Wings' (*Tatler* 174). Steele's comic exuberance as a satirist gives way here to a tone of cynical pessimism. Bickerstaff is weary of a society in which superficial differences in apparel and behaviour have come to be seen as a substitute for any real strength of personality, in which the dressing and adorning of shadows and apparitions has replaced character and individuality. He is forced to categorize people by superficial attributes such as their dress because they lack any other distinguishing features: their minds and personalities are unformed blanks. To use an anachronistic term, they are zombies. The naturalist who took delighted note of the new species of coxcomb has become a bored butterfly-collector, contemplating with apathy the gaudy markings of the short-lived insects.

Bickerstaff's own character and personal habits avoid the two extremes of a slavish adherence to fashion and an obstinate affectation of singularity. Steele's old bachelor has a developed sensibility and a tenderness and gallantry towards women, whilst remaining celibate. Bickerstaff's love affairs, both past and present, provide a touch of humour which does not detract from his moral *gravitas*. The champion and promoter of marriage and family life, Bickerstaff himself resembles a lay monk, a fatherly adviser whose readers form a substitute for the wife and children which he has never had. Some of his successors were to imitate Bickerstaff's age and celibacy. The editor of the *Censor* has never been married, and now 'my Years are turned of that Date, when *Love* and the *Small-Pox* are most wholesome and most natural' (16, 6 May 1715). The editor of the *Plain Dealer* (1724–5) is 'a talkative *Old Batchelor*, in my grand Climacterick' (1, 23 March 1724). Jeoffry Wagstaffe of the *Batchelor* tells us that he is 'now past my grand climacteric' and has been single all his life (1, 29 March 1769) and Nicholas Babble of the *Prater* (1756) is 'an oldish man, sixty odd' (1, 13 March 1756) and a bachelor.

Bickerstaff and his women readers

Bickerstaff divides women into far fewer distinct types and much less systematically than he does men.[13] When he separates people into their proper classes, the editor refers only to male categories, explaining that he has not yet reduced 'the soft Sex . . . into any tolerable Order' (*Tatler* 162). With their far more limited range of available occupations, women have fewer opportunities for adopting the idiosyncratic manners of any particular profession and, with their more private and domestic lives, they are not as likely to expose themselves in public. Their faults and foibles are not those of individuals, or of types, but of an entire sex. For Bickerstaff, as for Pope, 'Most Women have no Characters at all' (Pope 1951: 3.46). Woman may be satirized, but rarely individual women.[14] For women, even more than for men, personality is consistently equated with personal folly, idiosyncrasy with unattractive eccentricity, originality with dangerous and self-indulgent experimentation. Bickerstaff characterizes women in sweepingly Manichean language, as angels and devils: 'The Ill are employed in communicating Scandal, Infamy, and Disease, like Furies; the Good distribute Benevolence, Friendship, and Health, like Angels . . . Such is the destroying Fiend, such the guardian Angel, Woman' (*Tatler* 201).

Women occupy an unusual and contradictory position within Steele's publication. Bickerstaff stresses the importance of his women readers from the very first issue, in which he claims to have named his publication in their honour and promises to include material '*which may be of Entertainment to the Fair Sex*' (*Tatler* 1). During the course of the paper's run, Steele greatly increases the amount of material of interest to women and the numbers of female correspondents, as well as introducing Bickerstaff's half-sister, Jenny Distaff, as the author of a number of issues.

With their perceived leisure and insatiable appetite for light reading, Bickerstaff considers women the ideal audience for a publication which aims to reform its readers by stealth. This makes the natural subject matter of a periodicalist the correction of women's faults and follies: 'Business and Ambition take up Men's Thoughts too much to leave Room for Philosophy: But if you speak to Women in a Style and Manner proper to approach them, they never fail to improve by your Counsel' (*Tatler* 139). For Bickerstaff, men as a sex are engrossed by 'Business and Ambition', whilst women are receptive to the moral observations of 'Philosophy'. Rather than attempting to find topics for both sexes, Bickerstaff turns in mock-frustration from his unreceptive male readers to the more susceptible female audience, whom he must address 'in a Style and Manner proper to approach them'. The decision to focus on his female readers affects both his subject matter and the form and register of his writing.

Steele's pamphlet *The Ladies Library* (1714), whose title page announces that it was '*Written by a Lady*', is a lengthy and detailed reading list for women. The *Tatler* issue which announces this future project defines the kind of reading material that Steele considers suitable for women. Bickerstaff tells us that 'the Ideas which most frequently pass through our Imaginations, leave Traces of themselves in our Countenances. There shall be a strict Regard had to this in my Female Library' (*Tatler* 248).

As we have already noted, Bickerstaff proposes the graceful and skilful actor as a model for emulation by young men. He is far from suggesting, however, that actresses are models of decorum for women. Acting as a profession for women was frequently associated with prostitution, and some actresses were perceived to be – and were – the mistresses of wealthy theatre-goers.[15] Men are invited by Bickerstaff to consciously act the part of gentlemen. The personal appearance of women, on the other hand, is not formed by public emulation, but by their private reading activities. A secret enjoyment of imaginative fiction in the closet will be revealed in their faces, since 'the Ideas which most frequently pass through our Imaginations, leave Traces of themselves in our Countenances'. Women must subject themselves to far stricter forms of self-control than men, regulating not only their public behaviour, but their private thoughts and fantasies. By implication, women are far more dependent on their reading matter to form their characters. They are both more morally vulnerable and more impressionable, forming a malleable, receptive audience for Bickerstaff's writing. It is not surprising then that the *Tatler* is preoccupied with Bickerstaff's relationship with his female readers, a preoccupation which is evidenced by Bickerstaff's portrayal of himself as a chivalrous knight-errant, by the femininity of his own personality and by the portraits of his sister, Jenny Distaff, part-time journalist, bluestocking and eventually tamed shrew.

Bickerstaff warns his male readers, 'The great Source of our wrong Pursuits is the impertinent Manner with which we treat Women' (*Tatler* 201). For Bickerstaff, large numbers of single women constitute an indefinable threat to the peace and political stability of society: 'Some Provision [must] be made to take off the dead Stock of Women . . . Let there happen but the least Disorder in the Streets, and in an Instant you see in the Inequality of the Numbers of Males and Females' (*Tatler* 195). Idle and therefore mischievous, single women encourage rioting and civic disturbances. Whether influencing parents in favour of a love-match (*Tatler* 185), advising women on the choice of a husband (*Tatlers* 20 and 91), outwitting a coquette (*Tatler* 98) or encouraging his readers to be married by lottery (*Tatlers* 166, 168 and 195), Bickerstaff is a constant promoter of wedlock.

Bickerstaff's attitudes towards women are not, however, based entirely on considerations of social utility; he is 'of a Complexion truly amorous' (*Tatler* 10). For Bickerstaff, love and courtship, far from being merely the province of women, are essential to refine and polish the characters of men: 'Every Temper, except downright insipid, is to be animated and softned by the Influence of Beauty' (*ibid.*). For Bickerstaff, 'Love is the happy Composition of all the Accomplishments that make a fine Gentleman' (*Tatler* 49). Bickerstaff describes chivalrous behaviour towards women as 'the heroick Virtue of private Persons' (*Tatler* 94), a definition eminently suited to a periodical that champions domestic life and values. Bickerstaff himself could be viewed as a hero of private life. He uses language and imagery drawn from *Don Quixote* and the French romances to define his role as a knight-errant of the fair sex, a knight fighting for the cause of moral decorum in the distinctly unheroic setting of contemporary London. He assumes the role of 'a Champion of distressed Damsels', promising to 'employ my Right Hand for their Redress, and serve them to my last Drop of Ink' (*Tatler* 128). In a humorous reversal of the normal proceedings of knights who save virgins from rape and abduction, he is a 'studious Knight Errant' seeking 'the Relief of all *British* Females, who at Present seem to be devoted to involuntary Virginity' (*Tatler* 195), through his many injunctions to his male readers to marry.

The image of the editor as knight-errant was to be adopted by a number of Steele's successors. Lewis Theobald's 'Mr. Censor' promises to 'enter the Lists' on behalf of women as 'a *Knight-Errant* . . . in their Service' (*Censor* 72, 6 April 1717), while the anonymous editor of the *Visiter* describes himself as a 'Guardian of the Fair' and a 'sort of Knight-Errant' (2, 25 June 1723). The *Prompter* alludes to 'the generous Knights-Errant, my Progenitors' (1, 12 November 1734), and John Hawkesworth's *Adventurer* hopes that 'if the world has now no employment for the Knight Errant, the ADVENTURER may still do some good' (1, 7 November 1752). Henry Fielding adopts the persona of 'Sir Alexander Drawcansir, Knt.' in his *Covent-Garden Journal* (1752), in which the editor does battle against the forces of Grub Street, declaring proudly: 'How much more noble is it in a great Author to fall with his Pen in his Hand, than quietly to sit down, and see the Press in the Possession of an Army of Scribblers' (1, 4 January 1752). Fielding's persona alludes to a character in Buckingham's *The Rehearsal* (1671), a bombastic hero who claims to 'slay both friend and foe' (Buckingham 1976; V.i.332). Later in this scene, he kills everyone on stage. Buckingham uses Drawcansir to ridicule the theatrical convention of representing battles on stage using only a small number of actors – hence Drawcansir's ability to slay entire armies single-handedly. The editor of the Dublin *Ladies Journal* (1727) also declares himself a 'Champion' of women, defending them, like Bickerstaff, with 'a little Instrument, call'd a PEN, as sharp as the best point' (no. 1). In the *Knight-Errant*, the editor explicitly identifies himself with both Drawcansir and Don Quixote. He walks the London streets by moonlight in search of adventure, tilting at fashionable folly as Cervantes' knight did at windmills and, like him, in possession of an unlikely squire, Satyrano de Gorgona, 'lineally descended from *Orlando Furioso*' (*Knight-Errant* 2, 5 March 1729). The editor is haunted by the ghost of Isaac Bickerstaff, who blesses his publication by appearing at his bedside (*ibid.*). The image of the knight-errant would, for eighteenth-century readers, have been more likely to summon the ludicrous images of Don Quixote or Drawcansir than that of Camelot. Like Don Quixote, Bickerstaff is a comic figure doing battle against red-heeled shoes and hoop petticoats. It is comically paradoxical that such an archaic figure should edit a work in a self-consciously new and modern genre, and much of the *Tatler*'s humour stems from the contrast between the timeless heroic world of romance and the essay-periodical's concern with daily life in contemporary London.

Bickerstaff is not only a protector of women: his own personality has

many characteristics associated with femininity. He describes his temperament as '*Saturnine* and Melancholy' and claims to be working on a tragedy
(*Tatler* 22). He is prone to the spleen and 'Poetical Vapours' (*Tatler* 47) and
has a suggestible imagination: at midnight 'a Shower of Rain, or the
Whistling of Wind ... is apt to fill my Thoughts with something awful
and solemn' (*Tatler* 111). Bickerstaff's responsiveness to literature is so great
that even a newspaper can arouse his sorrow, and he has 'frequently been
caught with Tears in my Eyes over a melancholy Advertisement' (*Tatler*
224).

Bickerstaff's correspondents often hint that the editor must be 'well
acquainted with the Passion of Love' (*Tatler* 128). We are offered tantalizing
hints of the history of Bickerstaff's love affairs. We learn that one mistress
died suddenly just before their engagement could be completed (*Tatler* 181).
'Teraminta', who 'reigned in his heart' in Bickerstaff's youth (*Tatler* 95), has
become a kept mistress and now leads a miserable existence (*Tatler* 45).
Bickerstaff describes himself as an 'old *Beau*' who, in his youth, had 'a great
Pleasure in Dress' and wrote extravagant love-letters:

> When I was Five and Twenty, upon sight of one Syllable, even wrong
> spelt, by a Lady I never saw, I cou'd tell her ... All she cou'd say, tho'
> she had an infinite Deal of Wit, was but a Repetition of what was
> express'd by her Form; her Form! which struck her Beholders with Ideas
> more moving and forcible than ever were inspir'd by Musick, Painting,
> or Eloquence.
>
> (*Tatler* 83)

The editor as an ardent admirer of women is a frequent figure in the early
eighteenth-century periodical. A correspondent assures the editor of the
Plain Dealer that 'LOVE ... seems to have had a considerable Share in your
Composition' (91, 1 February 1725). The publication ends at the request of
the Plain Dealer's sweetheart, Patty Amble, who promises to marry the
editor on condition that he give up journalism. Patty's request seems to
imply that the editor's marriage would compromise his devotion to his
female readers. Literary gallantries are incompatible with domestic
monogamy. The editor of the *Ladies Journal* is another love-sick bachelor.
He is forced to leave one issue to the care of his printer after he is thrown
into a '*Delirium*' by 'a fatal Glance from the ... incomparable *Myra*' (12, 6
April 1727).

Bickerstaff possesses the 'Severity of Manners' (*Tatler* 271) of the celibate
devoted to nocturnal studies, yet he has a past as a gallant admirer of
women, enabling him to talk of love with the benefit of personal experience.
Bickerstaff's personality qualifies him as a satirist without malice, an editor

equally suited to social and political commentary and to narratives of love, to the humorous and the sentimental. He forms a link between the male worlds of politics and public life and the female preoccupations of love and courtship.

Bickerstaff's 'unmanly Gentleness of Mind' (*Tatler* 181), the 'certain Weakness in his Temper' (*Tatler* 224), his 'particular Cast' of mind (*Tatler* 111), his 'Vapours' (*Tatler* 47) and his ready tears (*Tatler* 224) all, according to his own account, stem from the death of his father when he was only 4 years old. The sight of his mother weeping, he tells us,

> struck me with an Instinct of Sorrow, which, before I was sensible of what it was to grieve, seized my very Soul, and has made Pity the Weakness of my Heart ever since. The Mind in Infancy, is, methinks, like the Body in Embrio, and receives Impressions so forcible, that they are as hard to be removed by Reason, as any Mark with which a Child is born to be taken away by any future Application.... I imbibed Commiseration, Remorse, and an unmanly Gentleness of Mind.
>
> (*Tatler* 181)

Bickerstaff's emphasis on the indelible nature of early childhood experiences anticipates Walter Shandy's well-intentioned but fatal accidents with his son Tristram in Laurence Sterne's *The Life and Opinions of Tristram Shandy* (1760–7) as well as the preoccupations of the Romantics in works like William Wordsworth's *The Prelude* (1799, 1805, 1850), Thomas De Quincey's *Confessions of an English Opium-Eater* (1822) and Mary Hays' *Memoirs of Emma Courtney* (1796). Steele's *eidolon* is a very unusual figure in early eighteenth-century literature: a man whose character is formed neither by education, choice, nor influence, but by accidental circumstances in infancy, which have profound and permanent consequences. Bickerstaff, a helpless child, with no real understanding of his situation, passively 'imbibes' 'Commiseration, Remorse, and an unmanly Gentleness of Mind' and receives 'Impressions so forcible' that they cannot be changed by reason. No other periodical editor describes a childhood event of such significance. We learn little about the past lives of Mr Spectator and his club and nothing about their early years. The *Tatler*'s oft-vaunted special appeal to women readers is associated with an 'unmanly', feminized, gentle editor, whose own past has a novelistic quality and whose sensibility is that of a poet.

Bickerstaff is able to be the confidant of his women readers because of his own celibacy. The editor repeatedly claims that at his advanced age all carnal desires have been extinguished. He feels no sexual interest even in the 'beauteous *Flavia*': 'Wrapped up in the Safety of my old Age, [I] could with much Pleasure, without Passion, behold her sleeping' (*Tatler* 139). When

Bickerstaff tells a female friend that 'those bright Eyes, which are the Bane of others, are my only Sun-shine' (*Tatler* 16), he clearly means that he is immune from the danger of falling in love with her.

Despite Bickerstaff's advanced age, his celebrity as the editor of the *Tatler* brings him a proposal of marriage. Other celibate editors, like the *Female Tatler*'s Mrs Crackenthorpe and Mary Singleton of the *Old Maid*, were also to receive bulging mail-bags of honourable propositions from readers attracted by the wit and intelligence of their writing: a phenomenon I shall discuss further in later chapters. Bickerstaff is flattered by Maria's attentions, but he is quick to discourage false expectations:

> If you have that kind Opinion of my Sense as you pretend, I question not, but you add to it, Complexion, Air, and Shape: But, dear *Molly*, a Man in his Grand Climacterick is of no Sex. Be a good Girl . . . love one younger than my self.
>
> (*Tatler* 83)

In a later issue, Maria requests Bickerstaff's advice on choosing a husband and follows his counsel of being a good girl and marrying someone younger (*Tatler* 91). The lover has been entirely subsumed in the fatherly adviser.

Despite these protestations, Bickerstaff is not entirely free from pretensions to marriage, but is cured by his encounter with a gold-digger. She woos him by embroidering a 'Wrought Nightcap' (*Tatler* 91), the same gift which he later requests from a female correspondent who wishes to send him a Valentine (*Tatler* 137). The night-cap appears to symbolize Bickerstaff's celibacy, old age and perhaps impotence. Nights spent snuggled up in bed with a night-cap against the cold are the antithesis of nights of steamy passion. In connection with Bickerstaff's would-be bride, Steele offers us one of the periodical's few descriptions of the frailty of the elderly editor, who has to be lifted on to his horse. Turning, he sees his mistress laughing at his physical debility and realizes that she is a hypocrite and that he himself cuts a ludicrous figure as a lover (*Tatler* 91).

Bickerstaff's sexual abstinence is an essential recommendation for his role as a physician for 'the Distempers which proceed from Affections of the Mind' (*Tatler* 34). Like a doctor, he is able to view women closely and in a state of moral and, on occasion, physical undress (*Tatlers* 139 and 215), without the suspicion of dishonourable motives, while, as a man, he can discuss topics that a woman could not broach. The periodical provides women with a forum in which to express their feelings in the security of anonymity. Through the male editor's mediation, they can speak of emotions and wishes without being thought immodest. Bickerstaff makes this explicit:

A Woman that is ill-treated, has no Refuge in her Griefs but in Silence and Secrecy. The World is so unjust, that a Female Heart which has been once touched, is thought for ever blemished. The very Grief in this Case is looked upon as a Reproach, and a Complaint almost a Breach of Chastity.

(*Tatler* 128)

Jenny Distaff

Early in the periodical's run, in *Tatler* 10, Steele introduces the figure of Jenny Distaff, Bickerstaff's much younger half-sister. The first portrayal of a female periodical editor, Steele's creation provides the paper with the claim to speak for and to women more directly. She writes six of the periodical's 152 issues, at her brother's invitation, using the 'Papers in his Closet', the political reports of Kidney, a waiter at St. James's coffee-house, and other materials which Bickerstaff has left her 'with liberty to speak it my own way' (*Tatler* 10). Four of the Jenny Distaff issues are featured in June and July of 1709 (*Tatlers* 35, 36, 37 and 38), after which she does not contribute another issue until November of the following year (*Tatler* 247). Jenny's fifth paper (7 July 1709) immediately precedes the launch of the rival *Female Tatler* on 8 July 1709. Not only can the *Female Tatler* be seen as a response to Steele's successful publication, therefore, but Steele may have decided to reduce the presence of Jenny Distaff in the periodical as a reaction to having been what he describes as 'scolded at by a *Female Tatler*' (*Tatler* 229). Six issues, spread over a period from October 1709 to June 1710, narrated by Bickerstaff, describe Jenny's marriage to Tranquillus and her behaviour as a young bride (*Tatlers* 75, 79, 85, 104, 143 and 184). The duties and quarrels of the early months of Jenny's marriage seem to preclude her journalistic contributions, and she only writes another issue after her power struggles with her husband have ceased and she has become 'a notable and deserving Wife' (*Tatler* 184).

From Jenny's first issue, it is assumed that a female journalist would address a primarily female audience on topics of exclusively feminine interest. In comic mock-apology, she begins:

It is so natural for Women to talk of themselves, that it is to be hop'd, all my own Sex at least will pardon me, that I could fall into no other Discourse. If we have their Favour, we give our selves very little Anxiety for the rest of our Readers.

(*Tatler* 10)

The natural instincts of a woman, newly offered access to publication, are the defence of her own sex against male aspersions. With 'Pen and Ink in my

Hand', Jenny is eager to 'give a right Idea of Things which, I thought, [Bickerstaff] put in a very odd Light, and some of them to the Disadvantage of my own Sex' (*Tatler* 33). Jenny espouses the 'Cause of my Sex' (*Tatler* 247) both by combating misogyny and by advising individual female readers. She proclaims her intention '*to propose Remedies against the greatest Vexations attending Female Life*' (*Tatler* 37).

In a bid for revenge against male satire, Jenny contributes a number of thumbnail sketches of ridiculous men of her acquaintance: the utterly passive 'Quid nunc' (*Tatler* 10), a coffee-house newspaper addict; 'Will Shoestring', her 'dear Outside', whose main activities are 'combing your Wig, Playing with your Box, or Picking your Teeth'; '*Umbra*'; an amateur physician who understands 'the Cure of a Pimple or a Rash'; and the scandalmonger '*Fly-blow*' (*Tatler* 38). All have one thing in common: their failings — passivity, vanity, laziness and addiction to gossip — are those of which women are most commonly accused. Jenny promises her female readers the enjoyment of further attacks on the common enemy: '*I have Ten Millions of Things more against Men, if I ever get the Pen again*' (*Tatler* 33). Without independent access to print, Jenny has to make the most of every opportunity. Her claim that men and women have the same faults should be regarded in this light less as a proto-feminist agenda than as a blow struck in the age-old battle of the sexes. Jenny does not call for social and political reform of any kind; neither does she incite her female readers to rebellion against the rules of an inherently sexist society or urge them to resist the accepted definitions of femininity as, for example, Mary Wollstonecraft was to do at the end of the century in her *A Vindication of the Rights of Woman* (1798). She simply aims to redress the balance of criticism a little and satirize men as effectively as Bickerstaff does women.

As a woman, Jenny regards men as potential lovers, and it is in this light that she evaluates them. She promises her readers marital advice in a comically grave tone and with an unshakeable confidence in her own judgement: 'No Vow shall deceive me, but that of Marriage: For I am turn'd of Twenty, and ... have heard all that can be said towards my Undoing' (*Tatler* 33). The irony of a 20-year-old solemnly avowing her insusceptibility to the temptations of illicit love fits perfectly the portrait of Jenny as the headstrong, impulsive, spirited bluestocking. She promises that her contributions to the periodical will be dominated by the most appropriately feminine of concerns, that of 'Love in all its Forms' (*Tatler* 36).

The association of women writers and readers with what the editors of the *Ladies Journal* call 'the lighter Affairs of the Ladies ... Love and Gallantry' (no. 1) was a frequent one in the first half of the eighteenth century. The *Athenian Mercury* regards 'Questions of *Courtship*, *Love* and *Marriage*' as particularly appropriate to women (III.13, 5 May 1691), and the editors of the *Ladies Mercury* ironically resign 'Learning, Nature, Arts, Sciences' to their male counterparts, restricting themselves to '*a little homely Cookery . . . a small Treat of* Love, &c' (1, 27 February 1693). The *Female Tatler*'s editors regard 'the Errors of Love' as one of the main themes of the woman journalist (87, 25 January 1710), and the annual *Ladies Complete Pocket-Book* 'By a LADY' promises its readers 'Moral Reflexions on the Passion of Love' (1769). Some periodicals offer romantic short fiction and verse to a female audience. *Records of Love* (1710) leads each issue with a 'Novel', a brief tale of love. The frontispiece to *Flowers of Parnassus* (1734–6), an annual poetry collection, is appropriately decorated with cupids, one of whom is taking aim at a couple walking arm in arm. John Tipper's monthly *Delights for the Ingenious*, with its mathematical questions, riddles and enigmas, also offers romantic tales. A story of two star-crossed lovers is specifically addressed to 'ye charming fair Female Readers, whose Souls have e'er been touched with tender Love!' (*Delights for the Ingenious* 1, 1 January 1711). Eliza Haywood, herself a writer of enormously successful amatory fictions, dedicates the first issue of her periodical the *Female Spectator* (1744–6) to love:

> Of all the Passions giv'n us from Above,
> The noblest, softest, and the best is Love.

(bk I: 2.20)

Jenny's most detailed description of her experiences in love bears all the stylistic hallmarks of an amatory novel: florid prose, a seduction scene, a young innocent girl and a man overwhelmed by physical passion. Her false friend the wicked Lady Sempronia has decoyed her young protégée to her country mansion, in order to leave her prey to the designs of an aristocratic rake:

> There was at the further End of her Garden a Kind of Wilderness, in the Middle of which ran a soft Rivulet by an Arbor of Jessamin. In this Place I usually pass'd my retir'd Hours, and read some Romantick or Poetical Tale till the Close of the Evening. It was near that Time in the Heat of Summer, when gentle Winds, soft Murmurs of Water, and Notes of Nightingals had giv'n my Mind an Indolence, which added to that Repose of Soul, which Twilight and the End of a Warm Day naturally throws upon the Spirits. It was at such an Hour, and in such a State of Tranquility I sat, when, to my unexpressible Amazement, I saw my Lord walking towards me . . .

(*Tatler* 33)

The sensuous setting, with its nightingales and jessamines, the lulling effects of the wind and water and the novel-reading heroine, whose mind is rendered susceptible to love by the excitements of her 'Romantick or Poetical Tale', could have been taken from a best-selling amatory novel by Steele's contemporary Delarivier Manley (compare Manley 1992: 20–1 and 39). Jenny, however, escapes rape or seduction and, less predictably, refuses to accept the lord when he repents, reforms and makes honourable proposals of marriage. She tells her readers, with spirit and a little self-dramatization: 'I glory in contemning a Man who had Thoughts to my Dishonour' (*Tatler* 33).

Jenny claims that her prudent attitude towards lovers allows her to be a disinterested judge of male behaviour. With playful lightheartedness, she anticipates Bickerstaff's image of men as butterflies (*Tatler* 174), promising her readers to 'stand among Beaux and Pretty Fellows, with as much Safety as in a Summer's Day among Grass-hoppers and Butterflies' (*Tatler* 33). The innocence of the metaphor reflects Jenny's chastity. Unlike many other female writers, Jenny is not suspected of sexual laxity. From this vantage point of personal immunity, Jenny deplores the sexual double standard: 'If we have Merit, as some allow, Why is it not as base in Men to injure us as one another?' (*Tatler* 247). At the same time, however, she believes that 'we have contributed to our own Deceit' (*ibid.*) because of female inability to judge male character: a skill 'which is the most important of all others in Female Life' (*ibid.*). Jenny advises women to evaluate their lovers in the light of their 'Reputation among the Men' and their behaviour in male-dominated settings 'in the Camp, at the Bar, on the 'Change, in the Country, or at Court' (*ibid.*). Ironically, Jenny, writing on a subject of traditionally feminine expertise, refers her women readers to the more objective and reliable knowledge that men have of the members of their own sex. Bickerstaff, the male editor, is the natural marital advisor and women's moral guide, since he can provide a disinterested male perspective on the male character.

'Love in all its Forms' (*Tatler* 36) appears a very inadequate topic for a journalist addressing women readers. In the same issue in which she claims that love is the only fitting topic for a female writer, Jenny writes of Sir Scipio Hill's speculation in life annuities. She paints the portraits of various habitués of St. James's and provides thumb-nail sketches of a variety of coffee-house denizens (*Tatler* 38). Jenny has her information from male gossips: 'Tho' I never visit these publick Haunts, I converse with those who do . . . they are as talkative as our Sex' (*Tatler* 37). The content of Jenny's papers does not differ significantly from that of Bickerstaff's: they both share the satirical pen-portraits of men and women, the news section, which Steele was later to cut, the correspondence, the short fiction and the concern with love, marriage and domesticity. These similarities bear testimony to Steele's belief that there are few, if any, topics of exclusively male or female concern.

Steele does not envisage a gender-specific audience for either the Bickerstaff or the Distaff issues of his paper.

A wit who loves to sit 'with her Nose full of Snuff, and a Man's Nightcap on her Head, reading Plays and Romances', Jenny bears most of the characteristic attributes of the much-satirized figure of the literary lady. Her brother hopes to find a husband to tame the spirited Jenny and 'let her see, that to be well dress'd, in good Humour, and chearful in the Command of her Family, are the Arts and Sciences of Female Life' (*Tatler* 75). Jenny is symbolically purified for her wedding by her brother who makes her renounce the masculine appendage of a snuff-box and 'half drown her self with washing away the Stench of the Musty' (*Tatler* 79).

The snuff-taking, play-reading, journal-writing Jenny's metamorphosis into 'a notable and deserving Wife' (*Tatler* 184) is a gradual and far from a complete one, and the choice of her husband's name, Tranquillus, allows us from the outset to suspect that he will be henpecked. Within a couple of weeks of her wedding, Jenny has quarrelled with her placid spouse. Her brother's intervention reconciles the couple, but it is clear that Jenny is in control of the relationship. She boasts to Bickerstaff that 'I find I can do any Thing with him' (*Tatler* 85). A couple of months later, Jenny visits her brother, who finds her very altered. Her sprightly wit has been replaced by a 'a decent and Matron-like Behaviour', and she has adopted 'a great deal of her Husband's Way and Manner in her Remarks, her Phrases, the Tone of her Voice, and the very Air of her Countenance'. Her identity appears to have been subsumed in her duties as a wife, and Bickerstaff notes with pleasure that 'she expected to be treated hereafter not as *Jenny Distaff*, but Mrs. *Tranquillus*' (*Tatler* 104).

Several months later, however, Jenny has a further 'Change in her Humour' (*ibid.*). Visiting her brother after a lengthy absence, she boasts to him that she has been living in London without Tranquillus and has bought a coach in her husband's absence. Once again, Bickerstaff has to intervene to restore domestic harmony by writing to Tranquillus and urging him to forbid his wife the luxury of an equipage. The taming of Jenny – by Bickerstaff, rather than by her husband – appears complete two months later, when, visiting the play with her husband, she is both 'sprightly and airy', but also a model wife and 'the true Figure of Conjugal Affection' (*Tatler* 184).

The fact that Jenny contributes another issue to the *Tatler* towards the close of the paper's run (*Tatler* 247) may be taken as an indication that only once she has accepted her position as a dutiful wife to Tranquillus can she be permitted by her brother to write for the periodical again. On the other hand, it also suggests that marriage is not incompatible with female editorship. Had Steele continued his periodical, he might have developed both her character and her journalistic style further. Instead, the figure of the female editor was to be explored by others in the *Female Tatler*, which I will turn to in the following chapter.

In the *Tatler*, Steele describes and catalogues a society governed by a multitude of social and sartorial codes: obsessed with status, reputation and public behaviour. Steele envisages his audience as primarily metropolitan, highly influenced by fashion and hence amenable to censure by the editor of a fashionable periodical. Through the figure of Bickerstaff, Steele is able to suggest ways to regulate that society, to order and categorize, without appearing censorious or dictatorial. By focusing on what Steele describes as the 'Conversation-Part of our Lives' (*Tatler* 56), he blurs the boundaries between public and private, to provide impish commentary on both male and female behaviour alike. The *Tatler* does not have a clearly gendered audience. There is an assumption, however, that genteel women, with their lack of occupation and their voracious appetite for print, will form a significant, if not the major, part of the readership of the essay-periodical. Steele named his paper in the fair sex's honour, and Bickerstaff, with his sensitivity, tenderness, gallantry towards women, his propensity to tears, his melancholy, his poetry and tragedy-writing and his chastity, is in many respects a feminized figure. Both these aspects of Steele's publication were to have almost prescriptive force for later journalists. Steele's moral aims and his successful ironic wit were to be cited as models by generations of journalists, who were to view literary journalism as necessarily characterized by a concern to record and catalogue the minutiae of contemporary life, coupled with a special focus on women readers.

2 'The Conversation of my Drawing-Room'

The female editor and the public sphere in the *Female Tatler*

Before we can turn to the *Female Tatler* in more detail, it is necessary to provide a few words of explanation on the subject of its publishing history and the vexed question of attribution. The *Female Tatler* ran for 115 issues, which were numbered 1–112 (there were three issues of *Female Tatler* 88, and one issue was unnumbered) and was issued three times a week, on non-post days: Mondays, Wednesdays and Fridays from 8 July 1709 to 31 March 1710. Issues 1–18 were printed by Benjamin Bragge. On 19 August 1709, two rival *Female Tatlers* appeared, one printed by Ann Baldwin, the other by Bragge, and the two publications continued to be issued concurrently, each strenuously denouncing the other as spurious, until *Female Tatler* 44 of 14 October, when the Bragge issue ceased publication, and the periodical appeared with Ann Baldwin's imprint until the end of its run. The first 51 issues of the *Female Tatler* were written under the sobriquet of 'Mrs. Crackenthorpe, a Lady that knows every thing', but in *Female Tatler* 51 the editor announces that she has 'resign'd her Pretensions of writing the *Female Tatler* to a Society of Modest Ladies', and the final 65 issues of the periodical are alternately ascribed to Lucinda (17), Emilia (16), Artesia (15), Rosella (10), Arabella (3) and Sophronia (3).[16]

It is beyond all reasonable doubt that the original author of the *Female Tatler* changed publishers with *Female Tatler* 19 and that Bragge continued to print the periodical under a different editorship (R.B. White 1974: 51–60), a practice which illustrates editors' lack of control over the use of their names or their literary property. Bragge's attempt to continue the publication suggests that it was a profitable venture. Its popularity was probably the result of its scandalous content, since Bragge's continuation appears to be a jumble of thinly veiled personal allegations, unskilfully presented in a bitter, humourless tone. All references in this chapter to *Female Tatler* 19ff. are to the Baldwin publication, unless otherwise stated.

The identity of Mrs Crackenthorpe remains uncertain but the two most likely contenders are Delarivier Manley and the lawyer and playwright

Thomas Baker. The *British Apollo*, which feuded with the *Female Tatler* between August and October of 1709, identifies Baker as the author of the *Female Tatler*:

> But others will swear that this wise *Undertaker*,
> By Trade's an *At---ney*, by Name is a *B---r*,
> Who rambles about with a Female Disguise on
> And lives upon Scandal, as Toads do on Poyson.
>
> (49, 12 September 1709)

It is unclear, however, whether the paper is referring to the Baldwin issue of the *Female Tatler* or to Bragge's rival publication. Fidelis Morgan has suggested that Baker may have authored the Bragge production, rather than the original paper (1992: viii). The *Dictionary of National Biography* (1997) includes the *Female Tatler* in a list of works credited to Baker and does not mention the periodical in its entry on Manley. John Harrington Smith has traced verbal echoes of Baker's plays in the *Female Tatler* (1952). In addition, he directs our attention to Baker's feud with rival playwright Thomas D'Urfey, who is attacked in *Female Tatler* 4 (15 July 1709), 8 (25 July 1709) and 26 (5 September 1709) (1952: 286–300). Baker lampoons D'Urfey in his prologue to Susannah Centlivre's play *The Busie Body* (Centlivre 1709a), which receives a favourable mention in *Female Tatler* 41 (10 October 1709). Baker's association with Centlivre strengthens his claim, since she may also have been involved in the editorship of the periodical. On 19 October 1709, the *Female Tatler* was indicted before the Grand Jury of Middlesex as a public nuisance due to the activities of a person posing as the editor of the *Female Tatler* and threatening to expose public figures in print if not paid for his silence. In the previous two issues of the publication, *Female Tatlers* 44 (17 October) and 45 (19 October), Mrs Crackenthorpe dissociates herself from '*those his* Rascally *and* Knavish Impositions' (*Female Tatler* 45). The court case may have prompted Mrs Crackenthorpe's resignation from her paper less than a month later, and Baker's increasing disillusionment with a literary career may have played a part in the decision, since he was to retire from Grub Street to the country in 1711 (Smith 1952: 286–300).

Paul Bunyan Anderson, on the other hand, has more convincingly ascribed the periodical to Delarivier Manley (1931: 354–60). His case for her authorship rests on the timing of Mrs Crackenthorpe's retirement from the paper on 4 November 1709, immediately following Manley's arrest for libel as the author of the *New Atalantis*, published that same year. Manley was held in custody from 29 October 1709 to 14 February 1710 (Luttrel 1857: 4:505–8). *Female Tatler* 51 might have been written immediately before Manley's arrest and a final Mrs Crackenthorpe paper issued subsequently to explain that editor's disappearance from the paper. Anderson also believes that a sarcastic reference to 'my Sister *Mickelthwait*' (*Female Tatler* 1, 8 July 1709) may allude to Manley's estranged elder sister, Mary Braithwaite, and that the ancient landed family of the Crackenthorpes, with their adherence to the royalist cause and their antiquity, resemble Manley's claims concerning her own family (*Female Tatler* 43, 14 October 1709). Fidelis Morgan, who also identifies Manley as the periodical's editor (1992), cites the *General Postscript*'s claim that the *Female Tatler* was written by '*Scandalosissima Scoundrelia* and her two Natural Brothers' (27 September 1709), a wonderfully appropriate sobriquet for the notorious novelist. Manley's long-running feud with Steele may have inspired her to edit a spoof of his periodical.[17] The periodical editor is playfully compared with the author of the *New Atalantis* (*Female Tatler* 45, 19 October 1709), whilst a lover of Mrs Crackenthorpe's hopes to impress his mistress by sending her a versification of a scene from the novel (*Female Tatlers* 8, 25 July 1709; 15, 10 August 1709). Steele may also be associating the editor of the periodical with the novelist when he complains that he was 'scolded at by a *Female Tatler*, and slandered by another of the same Character, under the Title of *Atlantis*' (*Tatler* 229). Manley's resourceful literary professionalism may well have led her to turn to journalism as an additional source of income, but there is little specific external evidence to link her with the publication.

The editorship of the periodical under the Society of Ladies has been ascribed by Anderson to the partnership of Bernard Mandeville as Lucinda/Artesia and Susannah Centlivre writing the remainder of the papers, on the grounds of strong internal, but no external, evidence (1936: 286–300). We can detect a characteristically Mandevillian brand of political theory in *Female Tatler* 64, which argues that 'to wish for a flourishing Trade, and the decrease of Pride and Luxury is as great an Absurdity, as to pray for Rain and Dry Weather', and similar ideas appear in future issues, including an attack on contentment as an economically unviable virtue (*Female Tatler* 109, 24 March 1710).

The case for Centlivre's involvement rests mainly on *Female Tatler* 69 (14 December 1709), in which Emilia reviews the dramatist's second comedy, *The Man's Bewitch'd* (Centlivre 1709b), which had been given its first performance at the Haymarket only two days previously. The issue details a visit which the playwright pays to the Society of Ladies, in which she complains bitterly at the affronts offered her by actors and managers. Rumours of Centlivre's authorship were clearly rife, since in her introduction to the printed play, the dramatist felt the need to deny any involvement with the periodical: '*I . . . declare I never was concern'd, either in Writing, or Publishing any of the* Tattlers' (*ibid.* Preface). In addition, *Female Tatler* 87 may have formed the basis for Centlivre's play *The Artifice* (1722), although its tale of a woman pretending to poison her lover seems to have been a common one and recurs in a slightly adapted form in Eliza Haywood's *Female Spectator* nearly 40 years later as 'The Lady's Revenge' (bk XIV: 3.58–70).

Contemporary readers clearly took a lively interest in the authorship of the *Female Tatler*, and it appears to have been both popular and controversial. Centlivre's wish to distance herself from the publication suggests that its scandalous content was considered less than respectable for a woman writer. Given the paucity of contemporary testimony, it is difficult to judge whether most original readers believed the periodical to have been written by a man or a woman or both. The paper's tone and level of irony is ambiguous at many points. The inappropriateness of a woman's writing an essay-paper may have provided some of the paper's humour. Some contemporaries may have regarded the *Female Tatler* as evidence of female journalistic skill, others as a thinly disguised and misogynistic drag act.

With ironic self-deprecation, the *Female Tatler*'s editor claims the non-political essay-sheet as a quintessentially feminine venture. Mrs Crackenthorpe envisages that the imminent end of the War of the Spanish Succession will lead to peacetime effeminacy and laziness and with it the demise of the newspaper and the rise of '*Tatlers*, both *Male* and *Female*' (*Female Tatler* 81, 11 January 1710):

> When our News Papers are laid aside; and when ... Peace ... shall, instead of promoting Religion, Virtue, and Sobriety, so far intoxicate Men's Minds, as to draw 'em into Pride, Luxury, and all Manner of ridiculous Excursions, an ingenious *Tatler* will conduce more to the Reformation of Mankind than an Hypocritical Society.[18]
>
> (*Female Tatler* 1, 8 July 1709)

Mrs Crackenthorpe claims that her publication will complement, rather than replace Steele's, since the market could support 'ten such Papers'. In such a venture, her gender is a qualification, rather than a handicap, since '*Tatling* was ever adjudg'd peculiar to our Sex' (*ibid.*). Eliding the differences between speech and writing, Mrs Crackenthorpe defines her periodical as a printed form of gossip, a more public version of the elegant chit-chat of drawing rooms and the scandal spread on visits to female friends. She asks Bickerstaff's leave 'to prate a little to the Town' (*ibid.*).

Dated from her own apartment, Mrs Crackenthorpe's periodical is, at least in part, a record of the conversation at her visiting days, almost like the minutes of a meeting. As Sarah Prescott and Jane Spencer have pointed out (2000), Mrs Crackenthorpe's drawing room is a public as well as a private space. The company is mixed and extensive: 'I have twice a Week a very great Assembly of both Sexes ... Grave Statesmen, Airy Beaus, Lawyers,

Citts, Poets, and Parsons, and Ladies of all Degrees assemble there' (*ibid.*). Business of both male and female import is transacted at Mrs Crackenthorpe's – 'Books are canvass'd, Removals at Court suggested, Law Cases disputed, the Price of Stocks told, the Beaus and Ladies inform us of new Fashions' – and the drawing room provides a social meeting place 'which comprehends, *White's*, *Will's*, *The Grecian*, *Garraway's* in *Exchange-Alley*, and all the *India Houses* within the Bills of Mortality' (*ibid.*). Mrs Crackenthorpe already presides over a forum for public discussion in her drawing room and, in this context, the periodical appears to be a natural extension of this. Her status as a society hostess qualifies her for editorship.

The authors of the rival *Female Tatler* are portrayed as men, and a correspondent of Mrs Crackenthorpe's is taken to meet the editor in a *locus classicus* of brutish masculinity, a 'common Ale-house', in St. Paul's Churchyard, an area full of booksellers' and printers' shops, 'where in a dark Rook [*sic*] . . . behind a slabber'd Table, sat a surly . . . old Dotard, snarling . . . and cursing . . . I expected to have seen a glittering Coquet, and wonder'd such a Monster shou'd Personate a Young Lady' (*Female Tatler* 35, 26 September 1709). This denizen of Grub Street could not be further from a society lady: educated by Puritans, his mother was a military prostitute. According to Mrs Crackenthorpe, it is grotesque that he '*talks of Ladies Drawing-Rooms, who was never yet admitted into tolerable Company*' (*Female Tatler* 20, 22 August 1709). The editors of the Bragge *Female Tatler* also claim that their rival is written by a man: Mrs Crackenthorpe's footman Francis Powder-Monkey, dismissed from her service for fornication and 'forc'd to pump for Bread' (*Female Tatler* ed. Bragge 23, 29 August 1709).

The sex of the *Female Tatler*'s editor is represented as a topic of intense interest among the periodical's readership. The '*Ridiculous Report of the Authors being a Man*' allegedly circulating around town (*Female Tatler* 47, 24 October 1709) can be seen as a flattering testimony to Mrs Crackenthorpe's competence, equal to that of any male writer, or as an ironic allusion to the gender of the periodical's actual author. Mrs Crackenthorpe dismisses the speculations as '*a splenetick and irrational Aspersion upon our whole Sex*' (*Female Tatler* 11, 1 August 1709) and as the belief that a woman would be incapable of authorship, protesting that '*those Ladies who have . . . div'd into Arts and Sciences, have ever discover'd a quicker Genius, and more sublime Notions*' (*ibid.*). Mrs Crackenthorpe claims the periodical as a feminist exercise, a proof to convince the sceptical of female literary skill. Such a claim must be seen in the context of a contemporary audience uncertain, and perhaps doubtful, that Mrs Crackenthorpe's creator was a woman.

The female editor is keen to distance herself from the inhabitants of Grub Street, insistent that she does not publish 'meerly for the Profit that may accrue to me by it', that she possesses 'an Estate of 300 *l. per An.*', together with a retinue of 'two Maids and a Footman' (*Female Tatler* 1, 8 July 1709). Mrs Crackenthorpe's claim to gentility echoes Charles Gildon's declaration in his *History of the Athenian Society* that the *Athenian Mercury* was not written for profit. Gildon asserts mendaciously that the founder member (John Dunton) thinks 'it so much below him to mingle Interest with so *noble a Design*, that I am confident it would be the only certain way to make him forsake it, to press any Reward' (c.1693: 14). The *British Apollo* claims to have been 'Perform'd by a Society of Gentlemen' (subtitle). Ruth Collins of the *Friendly Writer* claims to write '*without the Reward of filthy Lucre*' (vol. for 1732, Preface). Jean de la Crose tells a correspondent that 'it's my Bookseller's care to get Customers, and not mine, who am altogether unconcerned in the Sale' (*Memoirs for the Ingenious* March 1693). The editor of the *Patrician* (1719) loftily declares 'that he never intended or hop'd for, by such his Publication, any thing peculiar to himself, but the Pleasure of promoting his Country's Service' (no. 4), while the editor of the *Plain-Dealer*, though not rich, possesses 'an Estate, rather moderate than plentiful' (1, 23 March 1724). The *Old Whig* (1719) accuses the *Plebeian* (1719) of being, unlike himself, 'a Son of *Grubstreet*' (no. 2). Some contemporary editors argue that there is no profit to be made from journalism in any case. Defoe tells us that in editing the *Review* '*Profit, the* Press *would not allow; and therein I am not deceiv'd, for I expected none*' (vol. I, Preface). The editors of the *Athenian Mercury* refute the accusation that "tis a Mercenary Design to get a Peny' with the sarcastic riposte, '*A wondrous* Estate ... *he* [the paper's editor-bookseller, John Dunton] *is likely to raise by a* Peny-Paper' (vol I, Preface). De la Crose also argues that 'if I design'd any thing like getting an Estate by the writing of Books, I would make choice of a Matter more suitable to my ends' (*Memoirs for the Ingenious* March 1693). The editor of the *Visiter* is almost unique in his frank admission that 'I am not in a Capacity to make the Town a Present of my Paper' (4, 9 July 1723).

As a woman, Mrs Crackenthorpe is particularly eager to avoid the taint of being 'forc'd to pump for Bread' (*Female Tatler* ed. Bragge 23) and, in particular, the associations of the professional woman writer with prostitution. Bickerstaff writes for a living and retains his moral integrity; Mrs Crackenthorpe could scarcely do so – she must be seen to be a genteel amateur. The *Female Tatler*'s tone is characterized by an unrelenting snobbery. It bears many of the hallmarks of a coterie publication: written for a small and privileged audience who know each other and recognize the editor's satirical pen-portraits:

> the gay part of Mankind, who frequent Park, Plays, Chocolate-Houses, and every little fashionable Assembly, that rid away many a tedious hour in reading *Tatlers*, eating Jellies, disputing on twenty different

sorts of Snuff, and making pretty satirical Observations upon one another.

(*Female Tatler* 34, 23 September 1709)

We do not know to what extent the paper is a *periodical à clef*, nor the editor's real social standing or the social class of the majority of readers: whether they really consisted of 'those of Birth and Education' (*Female Tatler* 24, 31 August 1709), or whether a readership of lower social standing and less disposable income may have read the paper partly out of an aspiration to belong to such a select group or gain further knowledge of them. Mrs Crackenthorpe alludes consistently to a readership of 'Men and Women of Eminence and Figure' (*Female Tatler* 38, 3 October 1709). She offers her readers 'the Darling Quality Pleasure of Railing at Citizens' (*Female Tatler* 48, 26 October 1709), satirizing the social aspirations of such characters as 'Deputy *Bustle*, Cheesmonger, and Reformer of Manners' (*Female Tatler* 24, 31 August 1709), who is libelled in six issues of the *Female Tatler* (24, 26, 30, 39, 47 and 50). Like Bickerstaff, she prescribes norms of dress and behaviour to each particular branch of society and deplores the confusion resulting from those who do not conform: 'This town does so swarm with People in Masquerade that one hardly knows a Gentleman from his Taylor' (*Female Tatler* 26, 5 September 1709).

The editor's own life is a constant round of visiting and receiving visits from such aptly named friends as Lady Coupler, Lady Scandal, Mrs All-Talk and Colonel Tatalindus (*Female Tatlers* 2, 5, 11 and 28). Her claims that 'we ought to touch upon great Peoples *Characters*, with ... awful Respect' (*Female Tatler* 17, 15 August 1709) ring very hollow as she constantly requests new gossip from her friends and acquaintance. Not only does Mrs Crackenthorpe claim to be writing for 'those of Birth and Education' (*Female Tatler* 24), but she also invites only such readers to send in correspondence:

> Young People and Fools, think the TATLERS give 'em a mighty Opportunity to expose their Superiors ... Should such People be encourag'd, a Paper of this kind would be not only Useless, but Pernicious ... But if Gentlemen or Ladies please to write any thing ... it will be kindly receiv'd.
>
> (*Female Tatler* 7, 22 July 1709)

Mrs Crackenthorpe invites potential correspondents to introduce themselves at her visiting day. The periodical's correspondence is an extension of her social intercourse. Those who would not be admitted to Mrs Crackenthorpe's drawing room do not have the liberty of writing to the paper either. Despite Christine Blouch's claim that the *Female Tatler* is 'the first periodical written by a woman directed at a female audience' (2000a: lxxi), there are many more appeals to a class-based readership, than to one defined by gender. When Mrs Crackenthorpe first proposes launching a paper to a friend, she is told that 'the Ladies, more particularly would encourage it' (*Female Tatler* 2, 11 July 1709) and she herself maintains that '*the Ladies gave the first Reputation to this Paper*' (*Female Tatler* 20, 22 August 1709), yet such references to a predominantly female audience are rare. The editor more commonly describes her readers as 'Gentlemen and Ladies' and describes the aim of her paper as 'impartially to laugh at the Foibles of both Sexes' (*Female Tatler* 5, 18 July 1709).

The paper's audience's hunger for society gossip is attested by the revealingly self-contradictory nature of her readers' most common complaint, '*that . . . Characters are too plain when they are continually inquiring, 'Who's meant by this Lady, and T'other Gentleman*' (*Female Tatler* 47, 24 October 1709). Like Bickerstaff, the *Female Tatler*'s editors appeal to pride, rather than conscience. It is public behaviour, rather than private morals, which such a paper can correct: 'A *Tatler* alarms the World into a *Circumspection* . . . The *Giddy* Sort *Gossip* less for fear of being *laugh'd at*, and the *Libertines* of this Age, *Sin* more in private for fear of being *abhorr'd*' (*Female Tatler* 41, 10 October 1709). Her paper, Mrs Crackenthorpe claims, will continue popular until the objects of her satire outnumber her other readers: 'A Paper of this kind will flourish, till the whole Town at their own Instigation have been Ridicul'd, and then it will be generally exploded' (*Female Tatler* 44, 17 October 1709).

Mrs Crackenthorpe, by her own account, is herself of an ancient landed family, unsullied by trade (*Female Tatler* 43, 14 October 1709). Unlike the Bickerstaffs, whose family have inherited long chins, bad posture and other physical failings (*Tatler* 76), this hearty old English family have 'neither the Men nor the Women, had ever the least Deformity in Mind or Body' (*Female Tatler* 43). The editor roundly asserts of her ancestors, 'The *Crackenthorpes* were what ev'ry true *English* Family ought to be' (*Female Tatler* 43). Like her family, Mrs Crackenthorpe has no obvious failings or peculiarities. She defines herself as close to the norm: 'a middle ag'd, middle siz'd Brown Woman, that's neither Awkward nor Coquettish, Foppish nor Fantastical, but Dresses her self like a Gentlewoman, moderately in the Mode, with an Easy, Affable Disposition' (*Female Tatler* 43) (Figure 2.1). Steele distinguishes his creation with a number of loveable eccentricities, while, for Mrs Crackenthorpe, it appears to be enough to be a woman periodical editor to differentiate and characterize her, as journalists are necessarily a rare species among women, and women themselves are defined by their sexual characteristics and by their alleged differences from men, such as their loquacity and fondness for gossip.

Figure 2.1 Mrs Crackenthorpe of the *Female Tatler* (1710–11).

Mrs Crackenthorpe tells her readers that, with her few faults, she 'can never want Admirers' (*Female Tatler* 43). The single female editor's sexual availability is stressed from the opening of the periodical. The two periodicals, male and female, sharing a name, resemble a married couple, as the editor's friend Lady Coupler is quick to point out in the *Female Tatler*'s second issue, where she suggests a union of the pair: '*For our Progeny, the Sons would be all Bishops, Judges and Recorders, and the Daughters* Behns, Philips's *and* Daciers' (*Female Tatler* 2, 11 July 1709). In Lady Coupler's fantasy, the women are the creative writers, presumably resembling their mother, whilst the men become '*Bishops, Judges and Recorders*', following in the footsteps of their father Bickerstaff the 'Censor of *Great Britain*' (*Tatler* 163), who presides over his own 'Court of Honour'. Female periodical writing is here envisaged as closer to poetry and novel writing, whilst male journalism more closely resembles law and judgement.

Even Bickerstaff, at his advanced age, is popular with his female readers and receives proposals of marriage, and Mrs Crackenthorpe finds that 'since I published an Account of my Person and my Family, Lovers croud in upon me' (*Female Tatler* 47, 24 October 1709). The woman editor is in a peculiarly privileged position, since men are attracted to her wit and intelligence, without being influenced by her appearance. Mrs Crackenthorpe hints at this when she warns a suitor that 'if he saw my Face, he'd think no more of Adoration' (*Female Tatler* 8). Female editors have the rare luxury of wooing with their eloquence and can 'take more Pains to place their Words, than their Patches' (*Female Tatler* 8). However, since the periodical's male readership takes a keen sexual interest in Mrs Crackenthorpe, she cannot avoid being associated, like other women writers, with pornography and prostitution. She becomes an obscene toast among men '*in Taverns and dirty Eating-houses*': '*One wou'd give a Shilling, and t'other half a Crown to –––– –––* *Nasty Wretches! A third* Jack a-Dandy, *cries*, Hang her, she must be Three-score, or she cou'dn't know so much of the World' (*Female Tatler* 18, 17 August 1709). An Oxford undergraduate sends the editor a versification of a notorious incest-like seduction scene from Manley's *New Atalantis* (*Female Tatler* 8, 25 July 1709; see Manley 1992: 35–7). When he too promises to toast Mrs Crackenthorpe, it is unclear whether it is her authorship – he clearly ascribes the periodical to Manley – or her sexual attractions which he would like to celebrate.

The sexual innuendoes continue when Mrs Crackenthorpe has resigned her editorship to the Society of Ladies. Artesia is 'teiz'd out of my Senses' by her associates for her alleged fondness for her 'Brother, Practitioner in *Garrulity*' (*Female Tatler* 29, 12 September 1709). Alluding to Bickerstaff's own account of his impotence and decrepitude, her friends regret that a sexual union between the editors is no longer possible: 'If the *Male* had not been so Old, we might have encreased and multiply'd before now' (*Female Tatler* 97, 24 February 1710). Like Mrs Crackenthorpe, the Society of Ladies receive sexual propositions from their male readers. The correspondent Jack Rakish advises them to marry rich old fools and deceive them with dashing young lovers, offering his services in the latter capacity (*Female Tatler* 59, 21 November 1709). The ladies also receive a general proposal of marriage from a fortune-hunting colonel who advertises himself as a gigolo:

> I'm not quite Six Foot, well shap'd, clean limb'd, a good Rakish Air . . . a Woman of Twenty, with a tollerable Forehand – – – For as many Guineas, shall enjoy all, and every single part of me for the Space of Twenty Four Hours.
>
> (*Female Tatler* 82, 13 January 1710)

Jack Rakish assumes that the Society of Ladies are a group of young, desirable, unmarried women seeking husbands, implying that a woman with a husband would not be able to write a periodical and would have no motivation to do so. The army colonel seems to envisage a female readership hungry for titillation and eager to find lovers through the periodical. Gillian Teiman has argued that the *Female Tatler* as edited by the Society of Ladies is a more prudish version of Mrs Crackenthorpe's paper, that the ladies 'were virtually silent on issues of sexuality' (1993: 233), a tactic which Fidelis

Morgan regards as 'a cover for a more prurient attitude' (1992: x). Even though the change of editorship does reflect a decrease in the amount of sexual scandal and lewd innuendo, the paper is still considered an appropriate venue for a prospective male prostitute like the colonel to solicit custom, despite Mrs Crackenthorpe's claim that the new editors are *'a Society of Modest Ladies'* (*Female Tatler* 51, 2 November 1709).

Under the ladies' editorship, the focus of the periodical does shift, however, from the prominence of personal satire to topics ranging from Donne's poetry, through suicide, duelling, pacifism, Sacheverell's sermon and mothers-in-law to macroeconomics. Complaints from fictional readers that 'of late the Authors of the *Female Tatler* set up for Morality' (*Female Tatler* 98, 27 February 1709) serve to underline the periodical's increased variety. The editors are keen to point out that they have adopted the moral high ground at the expense of popularity. Most readers, we are reminded, 'love to find an Acquaintance exposed or a neighbour ridiculed' (*ibid.*). The correspondent Thomas Love-Truth warns the ladies that 'as Scandal was the rise of your Paper, so whenever that fails 'twill sink' (*Female Tatler* 59, 24 November 1709).

It is impossible to know how seriously to take such pseudo-complaints, which read like disclaimers on the part of the editors. Personal satire does continue in the periodical: both in the *divertissements*, in which individuals like 'Sarah Stroakings, at the Cow-House at Islington' are alluded to under fictional names (*Female Tatler* 67, 9 December 1709), and in the short narrative anecdotes. Often sensationalist, lurid and sexually titillating, tales of women like Chloë, whose garter was discovered in a lodger's bed (*Female Tatler* 56, 14 November 1709) and the voyeur Ephelia, who has had numerous abortions (*Female Tatler* 102, 10 March 1710), would not be out of place in the periodical's more suggestive early issues. It is impossible for the modern reader to judge whether such narratives are pure fiction or allude to contemporary scandals.

Since scandal can no longer be considered the paper's raison d'être, the Society of Ladies attempt to define a new agenda. The editors form an open collective, and the term 'Society' suggests a professional organization. The image of the periodical as a society recalls John Dunton's publications, particularly the *Athenian Mercury* (1691–7). Charles Gildon's *History of the Athenian Society* describes Dunton's editorial collective as a *'Learned Society'* with 'a Master in every Science' including a philosopher, physician, mathematician, poet and theologian (c.1693: 12–13). In grandiose and unconvincing terms, Gildon compares Dunton's venture with the Royal Society as a contribution to learning and science of national importance (*ibid.* 3). Daniel Defoe's *Little Review*, which imitates Dunton's epistolary format, also adopts the term, 'being *allegorically* rather than *significantly* call'd a

Society' (A Supplementary Journal September 1704). The *Weekly Oracle*, a publication also modelled on the *Athenian Mercury*, claims to be the work of 'a
SOCIETY of GENTLEMEN', comprising 'a SAGE AND VENERABLE DIVINE', 'a most
LEARNED PHYSICIAN', a 'GENTLEMAN OF THE LONG ROBE', 'a *Profound Adept in
the* MATHEMATICKS and NATURAL PHILOSOPHY' and a 'MORAL PHILOSOPHER',
along with 'AN EMINENT VIRTUOSO' and 'A MAN OF MODE'. The latter two
members are described as 'two Characters of lighter Freightage', included
'that our Vessel may not be in Danger of sinking by being overladen with
too great a Quantity of weighty and substantial Learning' (vol. I, Introduction). The *Oracle's* claims are grandiose – the details of the society members'
qualifications take up two closely printed half-sheets – and probably ironic:
the Introduction alludes to 'the Art and Mystery of *Puffing*' and describes the
members of the editorial committee as 'worthy and never-enough-to-be-
admir'd' (vol. I, Introduction). The editors of the *British Apollo*, a publication
which adheres closely to Dunton's model, also claim to be 'a Society of GEN-
TLEMEN' (1, February 13, 1708). The *Apollo's* social and academic pretensions
are mocked in the *Female Tatler* (30, 14 September 1709).[19] The convention
of the learned society is also satirized in the *Grub-Street Journal*, whose editor
playfully compares the members of his club – Mr Quidnunc, 'a wealthy old
Citizen'; the somnolent poet 'Mr. Poppy'; and the historian 'Giles Blunder-
buss' – with the Royal Society (1, 8 January 1730). The *Grub-Street Journal's*
collected issues were published in 1737 under the ostentatious title of
Memoirs of the Society of Grub Street, recalling the *Memoirs of the Royal Society*
(1665–1735), an abridgement of the Society's *Transactions*. The Society of
Ladies playfully mock the pseudo-erudition of male editors, whilst at the
same time their name leads the reader to expect a wider range of material
than Mrs Crackenthorpe provided.

In her first issue, Sophronia outlines the Society's editorial policy in
detail. The 'Conversation of my *Drawing-Room*' is to 'exclude all Politicks
... as a Topick most unfit for a Female Assembly' and focus instead
on 'Snuff, *Billet-Doux*, Joynts, Canes, Weather or Opera's &c'. (*Female Tatler*
87, 25 January 1710). The *Female Tatler* continues to be organized as a
series of ladies' visiting days, and Sophronia, like Mrs Crackenthorpe,
emphasizes the periodical's verbal origins: it is based on conversation,
which she as the society hostess directs and facilitates. She includes a wider
range of topics than Mrs Crackenthorpe: 'History, Philosophy, Poetry or
Prophecy'.

The unrestrained gossiping of Mrs Crackenthorpe's drawing room is to be
replaced by a kind of debating society, of which the periodical is to be the
minutes: 'We shou'd reduce our Conversation to general Heads, and alot a
Convenient Subject for each Day ... one of the Society shou'd relate a Story
by way of Example, and the rest approve or condemn' (*Female Tatler* 87). The

fiction of multiple authorship allows for a number of different viewpoints to be aired within the publication and for dissensions between individual members of the society, in particular between the two most frequent contributors, Lucinda and Artesia, who, though sisters, disagree fiercely on the ethics of duelling and on the merits of the War of the Spanish Succession (*Female Tatlers* 52, 53 and 59). Despite Sophronia's disclaimer, political topics are introduced by male guests. The most controversial views in the periodical are expressed by an '*Oxford* Gentleman', a regular visitor to all the ladies, who has usually been identified as Bernard Mandeville. The male guest can present theories which would be both too abstract and too provocative for a woman writer, such as his idea that content is no virtue (*Female Tatler* 109, 24 March 1710). He outlines his theories at greatest length on Lucinda's visiting day, telling the company that 'to wish for a flourishing Trade, and the decrease of Pride and Luxury is as great an Absurdity, as to pray for Rain and Dry Weather at the same time' (*Female Tatler* 64, 2 December 1709). Lucinda disclaims responsibility for such opinions, barring him from her house: 'I . . . told him . . . that I thought it not worth my Time to refute his abominable Principles . . . and desired him never to visit me any more' (*ibid.*). Nevertheless, she prints the episode, thereby disseminating his views, and offers no convincing counter-arguments. The '*Oxford* Gentleman' continues to expound his ideas in the periodical, condemning scholars as useless social parasites only two issues later (*Female Tatler* 66, 7 December 1709).

The female editors continually defend their right and ability to edit a periodical. A friend of Artesia's father tells the ladies that 'Young Women shou'd only study how to get Husbands', referring them to the example of Jenny Distaff: '*Mr. Bickerstaff*'s Sister *Jenny* . . . writ *Tatlers* almost as well as her Brother, but unless he was out of the way she never meddled with it' (*Female Tatler* 95, 20 February 1710). This prompts Artesia to ask 'why may not Women write *Tatlers* as well as Men?' and to deny that there is anything to be ashamed of in writing for money: 'Suppose *Tatlers* were writ for Money, were not Sermons the same?' (*ibid.*). Emilia also offers a spirited defence of female literary professionalism. Without attempting to curry favour by suggesting that the writing of such a periodical might be a moral or educational exercise of some kind, she simply asserts her right to act as she thinks fit:

> Why shou'd a Book or a Pen be more appropriate to a Man than a Woman, if we know how to use them? . . . 'Twas the Tyranny of Mankind that condemn'd us to the Glass and Needle, or we had sat in Parliament long before this time.
>
> (*Female Tatler* 101, 8 March 1710)

The publication of the *Female Tatler* itself is, in both cases, used to testify not only to female literary skill, but also to general female competence and potential. It might itself be viewed as a radical act, and where there are female journalists, female politicians seem more conceivable. Contemporary readers may, however, have found Emilia's vision of women MPs laughable and preposterous.

The periodical contains several impassioned appeals to its female readers, which might be regarded in modern terms as consciousness-raising exercises. Artesia's indignant indictment of women's collusion in their own oppression is the most striking example:

> What enrages me most is to see our Sex so stupid . . . How can People in their Senses think, that the fine Cloaths and all the Trinkets that are given us, are bestow'd upon the Sex any other ways than Play Things are given to Children, to amuse, keep their Thoughts employ'd, and their Hands from doing of Mischief?
>
> (*Female Tatler* 88, 27 January 1710)

Women are kept in deliberate ignorance, without any 'Knowledge of Arts and Sciences', to make them more tractable, Artesia claims (*ibid.*). She attempts to inspire her female readership with a disdain of luxury, of the 'fine Cloaths and . . . Trinkets' that distract them from more important issues. Her serious and moralistic attempts to turn women from dress to learning are counteracted, however, by her sister Lucinda's more light-hearted suggestions. Lucinda unashamedly celebrates fashion: 'Dress, be Vain and Gay, it being the best expedient yet found to defeat the Cunning, and defend you from the Treacherous Arts of Mankind' (*Female Tatler* 111, 31 March 1710).

Both the strengths and limitations of the ladies' feminism are most evident in the discussions surrounding their Tables of Fame. Bickerstaff describes a dinner table in an imaginary hall of fame and asks his readers for suggestions of suitable guests (see *Tatlers* 74, 78 and 182). When two female relatives challenge him as to his exclusion of women from this company, suggesting Lucretia as an eminent female figure, the editor agrees to have a 'small Tea-Table set apart in my Palace of Fame for . . . all of her Character' (*Tatler* 84). The Society of Ladies inaugurate their own 'Female Table of Fame' in response (*Female Tatler* 95, 20 February 1710), including rulers like Deborah, Zenobia and Queen Elizabeth I, as well as connubial heroines such as Panthea, Camma and Artemisia (*Female Tatler* 68, 12 December 1709; 88, 1 February 1710).

Tables of female fame were to become a convention of women's periodicals. Each issue of John Tipper's *Ladies Diary* displays the portrait of a celebrated woman on its cover. The *Nonsense of Common Sense* proposes instituting a picture gallery of women celebrated for their actions, rather than their appearance (no. 6). Short biographies of famous women were a common feature of mid-century magazines. The *Court Miscellany* relates the lives of Elizabeth Rowe (July 1765), Mme de Pompadour (September 1765), Susannah Centlivre (August 1765), Catherine the Great (February 1766) and Christina, Queen of Sweden (March 1766). A correspondent of the *Ladies Journal* argues that women are intellectually superior to men, citing the achievements of Sappho, Anne Dacier, Queen Elizabeth I, Katherine Phillips, Aphra Behn, Delarivier Manley, Centlivre and Eliza Haywood (no. 3). Attitudes towards prominent women are frequently highly ambivalent, however. A male writer for the *Court Miscellany* asserts that 'Genius has no sex', but stresses that women 'cannot appear on the stage [of life], but when they are called forth by particular circumstances' (October 1765). Those who have taken an active part in public life, he writes, 'shine . . . with as much dignity as men of the greatest renown', and he cites an impressive list of examples ranging from Boadicea and Joan of Arc to Mme de Scudéry and Elizabeth Carter. He ends, however, by recommending domestic virtue as 'a kind of heroism in private life' (*ibid.*).

The *Female Tatler*'s heroic historical women, drawn primarily from exotic, eastern locations and from the distant past, bear little resemblance to the modern British women who compose the periodical's readership. This leads Sophronia to lament the degeneration of her sex. The thought of 'so many dazling Heroigns' gives her 'extream Delight' and leads her to reflect that the Greeks personified wisdom as a goddess, from whom she takes her own name. Her pleasure is 'short-liv'd' however. When she turns to 'a Consideration of Womankind . . . as they deserve Applause or Reproof at the present Hour . . . the Motives of Vanity grew weak', and she is forced to abandon 'all Fond Idea's of Perfection' (*Female Tatler* 89, 3 February 1710). The historical women are further distanced from contemporary readers by being compared with Greek goddesses: they are the stuff of legend, the inhabitants of an idealized past. The famous women are, moreover, 'not given as Examples for *English* Women to Copy after' (*Female Tatler* 95, 20 February 1710), any more than Boadicea is held up as a role model for the readers of the *Court Miscellany*. The tables of fame are simply intended, Artesia claims, to show that women possess as much 'Intrepidity and Fortitude of the Soul' as men (*Female Tatler* 90, 5 February 1710). It is a question of women's moral worth and potential: 'We had a Mind for the Encouragement of our Sex, by those Examples to demonstrate, that Women were as capable as Men of that Sublimity of the Soul' (*Female Tatler* 95). The ladies do not advocate any form of social change. Emilia tells us that women are intelligent and sensible enough to be capable of sitting in Parliament (*Female Tatler*

101, 8 March 1710), but she does not suggest that they should actually run as candidates.

However limited the *Female Tatler*'s feminist programme, its editors always describe the essay-periodical itself as a feminine genre. An essay-periodical, Mrs Crackenthorpe writes, will gain popularity in a peacetime society, in which men have turned from the manly pursuits of politics and war (*Female Tatler* 1, 8 July 1709). Steele and the editors of the *Female Tatler* both emphasize the links between the essay-periodical and the 'Conversation Part of our Lives' (*Tatler* 56). In the *Female Tatler*, journalism is described as a particularly feminine activity because of women's association with verbal loquacity – with tattle, gossip and chit-chat. Writing a periodical is portrayed as a kind of written form of conversation, an activity half-way between authorship and normal sociability, an extension of a woman's social intercourse at her visiting days, albeit embracing a wider circle. The paper's tone is colloquial and intimate: the reported conversation of the guests at the visiting days of Mrs Crackenthorpe and the Society of Ladies often forms the basis of the periodical. This emphasis on conversation and sociability may be a response to contemporary anxieties about women's writing and, in particular, to the public aspects of publication. The *Female Tatler* demonstrates that the division between public and private arenas was not always clear-cut in eighteenth-century women's lives or writings. Both hosting a visiting day and writing a periodical – portrayed here as parallel activities – straddle the divide between the public and private.

The *Female Tatler*'s editors adopt a more modest stance than Bickerstaff in the *Tatler*. While Bickerstaff is an elderly male authority figure, Mrs Crackenthorpe is a loveable chatterbox, and the Society of Ladies are a group of young women addressing their contemporaries and social peers. Bickerstaff is an outsider, a commentator on society, while the *Female Tatler*'s editors are participators in the social scene. The periodical is rarely a vehicle for their own ideas. The Society of Ladies report a number of different and sometimes contradictory opinions within the publication, allowing readers to feel part of an ongoing conversation and to make up their own minds as to the validity or falsehood of individual viewpoints.

This idea of the periodical as the vehicle for conversation includes a sense that the *Female Tatler* is in constant dialogue with Steele's *Tatler*. Prophetically, the editors of the *Female Tatler* regard the *Tatler* as the first example of a new genre, a genre in which they stake a claim. As the title reminds us, the periodical is a female answer to Steele's publication and continually defines itself in reference to the *Tatler*. When Sophronia joins the Society of Ladies, she offers her readers a detailed description of her editorial policy. Every part of her plan, from Tables of Fame to dream allegories, is modelled 'according to the Practice of this polite Age', that is to say on Steele's successful formula (*Female Tatler* 87, 25 January 1710). The Society of Ladies sometimes view the *Tatler*'s content ironically, as frivolous and superficial, but they always identify it with their own strategy. Artesia sometimes satirizes Steele's aims, but she always writes in the first person plural: 'Some People care but little how others divert themselves, what Cloaths or Wigs they wear ... but we that watch and labour for the general Benefit of Mankind, take nothing more to Heart' (*Female Tatler* 74, 26 December 1709). The Ladies are constantly concerned to define the *Tatler* and *Female Tatler* as part of a new mode of periodical writing. Steele's publication is seen, not as an individual work, but as the prototype of a genre. Steele and Addison were to be invoked as talismanic figures by other periodical editors throughout the eighteenth century and, whether or not their work actually resembled the *Tatler* and *Spectator* in form or content, the sacred names of Addison and Steele were cited as precedents in defence of many later writers' own journalistic projects. This process of canonization, which makes the essay-periodical such a conservative genre, begins early, with the *Female Tatler*. Called upon to defend her writing to a sceptical friend, Lucinda vindicates herself as a follower of Bickerstaff's noble example:

> What they [the ancient philosophers and moralists] cut out roughly *Tatlers* endeavour to polish. Their Business was to reduce great Numbers into a Society, and ours is to make them a Civilis'd and Polite Society ... That Mr. *Bickerstaff* has a more happy Genius this way than anybody else yet discovered, we don't dispute, but his being the greatest Mastiff, proves not that all the rest are Curs.[20]
>
> (*Female Tatler* 95)

The term '*Tatlers*' here describes a burgeoning new genre with a number of clearly defined features, which was to be reinterpreted throughout the century, by male and female writers alike. It is a genre which emphasizes the 'Civilis'd and Polite' and which is centrally concerned with societies, both civic society and editorial societies, a genre in which the conversation of the drawing room appears in print. The *Female Tatler* ensured that the figure of the female editor was to be an important part of that tradition.

3 'In Clubs and Assemblies, at Tea-Tables, and in Coffee-Houses'

The *Spectator* and the shift from the editorial club to the club of correspondents

Less than two months after the demise of the *Tatler*, the first issue of Addison and Steele's new periodical the *Spectator* appeared. The paper was an immediate success, and contemporaries quickly attributed it to Steele (D.F. Bond 1965: lix, xcviii; Bloom and Bloom 1980: 231–65). Addison's association with the paper was not widely known until after the *Spectator*'s original run. The first series of the *Spectator* was published daily, except Sundays, from March 1711 until December 1712, a total of 555 issues, of which Addison and Steele each contributed 251 papers, Eustace Budgell 29, John Hughes 6 and other contributors 18 (D.F. Bond 1965: lxv). The second series, numbered 556–635, was published three times a week from June to December 1714 and written by Addison, with the collaboration of Budgell and Hughes. I will be concentrating in this chapter on the much livelier and more varied first series.

John Gay comments on the paper's initial reception in *The Present State of Wit* in May 1711:

> We were Surpriz'd all at once by a Paper called the *Spectator*, which was promised to be continued every day, and was writ in so excellent a Stile, with so nice a Judgment, and such a noble profusion of Wit and Humour, that it was not difficult to determine it could come from no other hands but those which had penn'd the *Lucubrations*.
>
> (1711: 11)

Gay's confidence in his estimation of the paper's worth, and his attribution of its authorship, just two months after the periodical's inaugural issue, are typical of the reactions of many contemporaries to the new paper. Its editor, Mr Spectator, was portrayed as the opposite of Isaac Bickerstaff: not a tattler, but a man whose most striking characteristic is his silence. Steele's biographer Calhoun Winton has suggested that Steele was allowed to retain his position as Commissioner of Stamps under the new Tory government of 1712 in return for ending the *Tatler* and ensuring Bickerstaff's silence (1964: 126–7). Mr Spectator's taciturnity may be a sly comic allusion to this demand.

The focus in the periodical's early issues is on creating a new kind of persona, an editorial figure who differs in important ways from Isaac Bickerstaff. One of the most striking differences is that Bickerstaff writes as a lone eccentric, while Mr Spectator is part of a club, whose members are described in detail in the periodical's second issue.[21] The Spectator Club is foregrounded at the opening of the periodical's run and is equally prominent towards the end of the first series of the *Spectator*. As the paper draws to a close, the club breaks up, as each of its members in turn die, leave London to live in the countryside full-time or decide to dedicate themselves exclusively to their professions. Budgell later suggested that the club members were retired and killed off in order to prevent other journalists from issuing spurious continuations of the paper. Of Sir Roger de Coverley, whose death is reported in *Spectator* 517, he writes:

> Mr. *Addison* was so fond of this Character, that a little before he laid down the *Spectator* (foreseeing that some nimble Gentleman would catch up his Pen the Moment he had quitted it) he said to an intimate Friend, *I'll kill Sir Roger, that no body else may murder him.*
>
> (Smithers 1968: 251)

This would seem to suggest that the club was an integral part of the periodical. In the final issue of the first series, Mr Spectator explains, 'All the Members of the imaginary Society, which were described in my First Papers, having disappeared one after another, it is high time for the *Spectator* himself to go off the Stage' (*Spectator* 555).

While the club fiction, then, would appear to be central to the *Spectator*, Addison and Steele make surprisingly sparing use of most of the club members within the main body of the periodical. Of the 555 issues of the *Spectator*'s first series, only 45 are either contributed by or concerned with the doings of members of the club, compared with 250, almost half the total number, which are largely or completely filled with readers' letters (D.F. Bond 1965: xxxviii). As Donald F. Bond has noted, with the exception of Will Honeycomb and Sir Roger de Coverley, the club members 'fail to play any very lively role as contributors or stimulants to discussion' (1965: xxii). The second series of the *Spectator* does not feature an editorial club at all. In the first half of this chapter, I'll be examining the club motif. I'll discuss some of the possible reasons for Addison and Steele's employment of this device within the paper and suggest some reasons why they do not make more extensive use of what appears such a promising journalistic strategy. One reason for the editors' relative neglect of the club fiction is their increasing use of correspondents. In the second part of this chapter, I'll examine the role of readers' letters in the *Spectator*, showing how the paper's correspondents come to replace the editorial club and to fulfil most of its roles and functions.

The club fiction

The second issue of the *Spectator* is dedicated to detailed descriptions of the individual members of the editor's club. The club members – the Tory landowner Sir Roger de Coverley; an unnamed lawyer who prefers the theatre to the bar; Sir Andrew Freeport, an eminent merchant; Captain Sentry, a former soldier; Will Honeycomb, an ageing man-about-town; and an unnamed clergyman – represent a wide variety of professions, as well as both Whig and Tory political allegiances. As Mr Spectator puts it, 'The Club of which I am a Member, is very luckily compos'd of such Persons as are engag'd in different Ways of Life, and deputed as it were out of the most conspicuous Classes of Mankind' (*Spectator* 34). The editor claims that each member of the club represents a constituency of readers:

> My Readers too have the Satisfaction to find, that there is no Rank or Degree among them who have not their Representative in this Club, and that there is always some Body present who will take Care of their respective Interests.
>
> (*Spectator* 34)

Ronald Paulson has described the Spectator club as 'a social microcosm, an England in little, of which the reader is meant to think he is a part' (1967: 210). The club's representativeness is limited, however. As Paulson himself notes, all the members of the club are actually 'on closer inspection, withdrawals or dropouts from society' (1967: 220). The Templar does not practise law, preferring to frequent the theatres instead; the Clergyman is too ill to take up a living; Captain Sentry has retired from the army, tired of his failure to advance in the military ranks; and both Will Honeycomb, the superannuated rake, and Sir Roger de Coverley, the Tory squire, subscribe to an outmoded Restoration code of political and ethical values. This code teaches passive obedience to the monarch, male sexual promiscuity and the values of land over trade. It is consistently opposed in the *Spectator*. Only Sir Andrew Freeport appears to be a productive member of his society. More importantly, the club does not contain any female members: a striking omission in a paper which so frequently addresses a female readership. Will Honeycomb could be seen as the women's representative, as 'all his Conversation and Knowledge has been in the female World' (*Spectator* 2), but his attitudes towards women are at best patronizing and often predatory. Towards the end of the paper, Mr Spectator reports that his female readers have felt aggrieved by their underrepresentation in the club. After Will's marriage and withdrawal from London the editor reports:

> the Ladies are in great Pain to know whom I intend to elect in the Room of WILL. HONEYCOMB. Some of them indeed are of Opinion that Mr. HONEYCOMB did not take sufficient Care of their Interests in the Club, and are therefore desirous of having in it hereafter a Representative of their own Sex.
>
> (*Spectator* 550)

The club is equally unrepresentative in its political leanings. While the inclusion of both the Whig Sir Andrew and the Tory Sir Roger appears to suggest that the paper will maintain a political neutrality, the *Spectator* contains a number of essays defending the trading interest and the Hanoverian succession, as contemporaries were quick to notice, and a number of modern critics have pointed out.[22] Sir Andrew's personality remains undefined in the *Spectator*, but his political allegiance to the interests of trade over land is defended in a number of the *Spectator* papers. Sir Roger, by contrast, is a fully-fleshed portrait of a loveable eccentric, but his political stance is never voiced convincingly within the paper. As one reader puts it, he is a model of virtue, but not of political prudence, he 'cannot . . . (*I mean as to his domestick Character*) be too often recommended to the Imitation of others' (*Spectator* 424; my italic). At least one paper contains an argument between Sir Roger and Sir Andrew in which each puts forward his political opinions (*Spectator* 174), but, on the whole, Sir Roger is far more often described than allowed to speak for himself.

Calhoun Winton has argued that the club fiction enables Addison and Steele to distance themselves from their political opinions: 'Like the dialogue and the play, the club kept the authors safely removed from their materials' (1964: 141). However, Addison avoids the club device altogether in his political periodicals. In Steele's partisan publications, he rarely allows his dramatis personae to voice his political views. Instead, Steele employs the rather tortuous device of writing letters on political subjects, signed with his own name, to his periodicals. Sir John Edgar of the *Theatre*, Nestor Ironside of the *Guardian* and the editor of the *Englishman* all receive and print letters on political topics signed by 'Richard Steele'. This allows Steele to maintain a fiction of editorial political impartiality, while including political commentary within the papers. Steele frequently suggests that although the use of a persona is necessary for a moral and social commentator, it is unethical to express political opinions without owning them. He comments in the *Theatre*:

> If a Man is disguis'd ... from a just and modest Reflection, that his Personal Infirmities would tarnish his Argument, and therefore assumes, for the sake of Virtue, an imaginary Character ... it is laudable to wear a Mask; but he who assumes one for any other Purpose, does a very ill Thing.
>
> (no. 11)

In Steele's paper wars with the *Examiner*, he repeatedly challenges the editor of that paper to reveal his or her identity and makes it a point of honour to sign his name to his own pieces. He asks angrily in the *Englishman*:

> What can a Man say who owns his Name, and is abused by one who does not own himself? Who is the more unjust, he who with his Name defends an Argument, or he who without any Name calumniates that Person without any Possibility of Recrimination?[23]
>
> (*Englishman* 4)

Steele clearly separates his moral commentary, voiced by an editorial *eidolon*, and his political opinions, which are stated *in propria persona*. In his *Review*, Defoe also puts his name to his political papers: Mr Review is always clearly identified with Daniel Defoe. Much of the *Review* is taken up with refutations of personal attacks on the author, forcing the editor to apologize for 'the Interruptions frequently given the Reader and my self, by the Apologies and Defences I have been Oblig'd to make' (31 May 1705). Taking personal responsibility for the views expressed in the paper is presented as a point of honour and a courageous stance: Defoe tells us that he has received '20 to 30' death threats (*Review* 7 July 1705).

The members of the Spectator Club are rarely employed as mouthpieces. Mr Spectator imagines some readers attempting to decipher the initial letters at the end of each paper and ascribing different issues to different members of the club:

> Some tell us, that C is the Mark of those Papers that are written by the Clergyman, though others ascribe them to the Club in general. That the Papers marked with R were written by my Friend Sir ROGER. That L signifies the Lawyer, whom I have described in my Second Speculation; and that T stands for the Trader or Merchant: But the Letter X, which is placed at the End of some few of my Papers is that which has puzled

the whole Town, as they cannot think of any Name which begins with that Letter, except *Xenophon* and *Xerxes*, who can neither of them be supposed to have had any Hand in these Speculations.

(*Spectator* 221)

This playful suggestion is clearly proposed in order to demonstrate its impossibility. The array of signature letters at the feet of the individual papers does suggest a number of different contributors to the paper, but very few of the numbers seem appropriate to specific members of the club. Addison may here be attempting to encourage speculation as to the paper's authorship – a good way of maintaining interest in the paper – but part of the paper's effectiveness lies in the uniformity of its tone, the impossibility of knowing whether authorship was single or multiple. On the whole, the members of the club are not distinctive voices within the paper. They are more often alluded to than discussed, more often discussed than ventriloquized.

Exceptions to this rule are relatively few: Will Honeycomb contributes long letters to the *Spectator*, which take up most of three issues (*Spectators* 499, 511 and 530); the Clergyman provides letters for *Spectator* 27 and materials for two more issues (*Spectators* 103 and 186); Sir Andrew Freeport's reported conversation provides the substance of one (*Spectator* 232); and the opinions of Captain Sentry and the Templar occupy one paper each (*Spectators* 152 and 541). Despite his prominence in the club, Sir Roger de Coverley does not write a paper, and it is striking how late in the periodical's run Captain Sentry's and Will Honeycomb's contributions appear. Addison introduces Will's first issue in a rather self-conscious manner, as if aware of the oddness of this omission:

My Friend WILL HONEYCOMB has told me, for above this half Year, that he had a great Mind to try his Hand at a *Spectator*, and that he would fain have one of his Writing in my Works. This Morning I received from him the following Letter, which, after having rectified some little Orthographical Mistakes, I shall make a Present of to the Publick.

(*Spectator* 499)

As D.F. Bond has pointed out, the *Spectator* frequently handles topics which seem particularly appropriate to one or other of the club members. He points out that the templar 'who might have been an obvious choice for the expression of opinions about the drama and other literary matters' features seldom, as does Captain Sentry, an obvious candidate for the expression of opinions about army life, a frequent topic in the paper (1965: xxxiii). Will Honeycomb's expertise in fashion – he 'knows the History of every

Mode' and 'remembers Habits as others do Men' (*Spectator* 2) – eminently qualifies him to comment on dress. Mr Spectator remarks that he has 'Thoughts of creating an Officer under me, to be entituled the *Censor of small Wares*' to critique the excesses of contemporary fashion (*Spectator* 16), but he does not suggest Will for this task. The Clergyman would also seem an appropriate persona to adopt for Addison's more serious Saturday papers on morality and religion.

The *Spectator* is not the only paper to begin with the introduction of an elaborate club fiction which turns out to be far less prominent in the body of the paper than the opening issues would lead us to expect. This is also true of Steele's other periodicals the *Lover* and the *Theatre* and Addison and Steele's *Guardian*. The first issue of the *Lover* (1714) introduces us to the members of its editor's club: each of them a man at a different stage of life and in a different romantic situation. The editor emphasizes the distinctive contribution which each of them makes to the conversation of the club, with the strong suggestion that this conversation will be minuted in the periodical. Mr Oswald is a recent widower with children, who 'is indulged by this Company to speak of [his wife] in the Terms she deserved of him, with allowance to mingle Family-Tales concerning the Merit of his Children'.[24] Mr Mullet is a wealthy older widower, sought in marriage by many mercenary young ladies. Mr Johnson is happily married with many children, leading the editor to comment that 'the manner of subjecting his Desires to his Circumstances, which are not too plentiful, may give Occasion in my future Discourses to draw many Incidents of Domestick Life'. Mr Wildgoose is a confirmed bachelor, inclined to be bitter and misogynistic, having been disappointed in love in his youth. Mr Oswald is reintroduced in *Lover* 29, with a telling preamble which must have reminded readers of the differences between the promises of the first issue and subsequent editorial practice: 'The Reader may remember that in my first Paper I described the Circumstances of the Persons, whose Lives and Conversations my future Discourses should principally describe'. Mr Oswald is the only member of the club to be mentioned again in the course of the paper.

Steele's *Theatre* (1720) describes a similar club in its first issue, this time a club of women who meet at the apartment of a Lady Sophronia: '*Flavia*, a very docile and ingenious Maiden; *Lysetta*, a Widow . . . and *Sophonisba*, a dependent Relation' (*Theatre* 1). We are told that '*Sophronia* and her three Friends are great Patronesses, and Advocates for the Theatre, and I shall from time to time give an Account of their Sentiments relating to it' (*ibid.*). The *Theatre*, however, quickly becomes embroiled in political and theatrical controversy, and the four female theatre critics are never heard of again.

The *Guardian* provides a particularly striking example of a similar elaborate framing device, although here the club is replaced by the family, a move

which enables Steele to incorporate both male and female figures and
perhaps reflects a wish to celebrate family life. The early issues of the
Guardian describe the Lizard family, to whom the editor, Nestor Ironside,
has been an unofficial guardian for decades. The Lizards, with their interests
(on the male side) in trade and economics and (on the female side) in love
and marriage, seem to provide a plethora of opportunities for use as mouthpieces or for reported conversation. The editor strengthens this supposition
by telling the reader 'that his chief Entertainment will arise from what
passes at the Tea Table of my Lady *Lizard*' (*Guardian* 2). The Lizard family,
we are told, can provide a perspective on every subject:

> There is no Circumstance in human Life, which may not directly or
> indirectly concern a Woman thus related [as Aspasia, the Lizard matri-
> arch], there will be abundant Matter offer it self from Passages in this
> Family, to supply my Readers with diverting, and perhaps useful
> Notices for their Conduct in all the Incidents of human Life.
>
> (*ibid.*)

Lady Lizard's daughters encompass a suggestive range of female types:
Jane, the good housewife; Annabella, a malicious wit; Cornelia, a bookworm
and would-be scholar; Betty, worldly wise and mercenary; and the spirited
and witty Mary, whom the editor always refers to as the Sparkler. We also
learn about their suitors: Sir William Oger (a suitor of Lady Lizard's) and his
son Oliver; a Mr Rigburt, who wishes two of his sons to marry two of the
daughters; and Sir Harry Pandolf (in *Guardian* 5). Lady Lizard's ambitious
marital plans for her daughters, coupled with the sheer number of unmarried young women and their suitors, suggest tantalizing narrative possibilities. Jane's story, in particular, seems ripe for plot developments. She is
in love with a worthy, but penniless suitor, while her mother is trying to
marry her off to a wealthy boor. The editor implies that he will unfold the
details of the lives of the Lizard family members when he tells us, 'As I write
Lives, I dwell upon small Matters, being of Opinion, with *Plutarch*, that
little Circumstances show the real Men better than things of greater
Moment' (*Guardian* 6). There are suggestions that the periodical will be,
among other things, a group memoir.

Despite their prominence in the early issues of the *Guardian*, the Lizard
family increasingly fade from view as the periodical progresses. Of the
Guardian's 175 issues, only 13 deal directly with the Lizards, and they are
alluded to briefly in only half a dozen more. Most of these issues are to be
found in the first third of the paper's run. In particular, none of the narrative
possibilities suggested by the Lizards are developed further. We hear
nothing more of Jane's marital prospects, for example. In *Guardian* 26 we

are told, tantalizingly, that Nestor is 'in Love by Proxy for Sir *Harry Lizard*', but the periodical contains no further mention of this interesting development. In some of the early issues, the Lizard daughters are used to illustrate the spectrum of contrasting female views and behaviour, for example, in a discussion of happiness (*Guardian* 31) and a visit to see *Othello* (*Guardian* 37), but as the periodical continues they are increasingly replaced as exempla by readers' letters and by frequent paraphrases of Classical literature, Eastern tales and allegorical dream visions. Some of the later issues betray a vagueness as to the exact details of the Lizard family situation that suggests that Addison and Steele had tired of this framing device. In *Guardian* 65, Nestor is interrupted at divine service by a gang of giggling women, amongst whom he spots one of Lady Lizard's daughters. Despite his careful delineation of their contrasting personalities in the early issues, he does not even specify which Lizard daughter this is.

Defoe's *Review* also introduces a club, appetizingly called 'the Scandalous Club', which the editor describes as 'a Corporation long since established in *Paris*' (19 February 1704). The 'Advice from the Scandalous Club' ran from February 1704 to November 1705: as a section in the *Review* itself until April 1705 and in the form of a monthly *Supplementary Journal* (1704–5). The project was resuscitated in June 1705 as a separate publication, the *Little Review*, which lasted for 23 issues. The Club begin by critiquing the daily newspapers and responding to readers' complaints of injustice and antisocial behaviour, but by August 1704 the 'Advice from the Scandalous Club' has become a forum for answering readers' queries on subjects ranging from marital problems to natural history, closely following the model of the *Athenian Mercury*. Despite the growing size and importance of this section of the *Review*, Defoe's use of the club fiction is rather perfunctory. When Defoe defends the Club against an accusation of libel, he refers to the 'author' of the Scandalous Club, and uses the third person singular throughout (*Review* 29 April 1704). Introducing the first number of the *Supplementary Journal*, he tells his readers that 'the Hand that operates in this Work' is '*allegorically* rather than *significantly* call'd a *Society*' (September 1704). A reader of the *Little Review*, who explicitly addresses his letter to 'Mr. de Foe', rather than to a fictional persona, asks '*what Appellation the Society assumes; and whether it consists of a Number, or a single Person*' (2, 15 August 1705). He receives the teasing answer that 'we are one Person, sometimes Mr. *Review*, sometimes the *Scandal Club*, sometimes one single Body, sometimes a Body Corporate' (*Little Review* 2). Charles Ranger of the *Gray's Inn Journal* is also a member of a rather shadowy club, which is only mentioned two or three times in the course of the paper's run; he himself points out that 'I must consider myself an unworthy Member, as I have not of late attended [meetings] with proper Punctuality' (37, 8 June 1754).

In view of this disproportion between the detail with which clubs are described in early issues of periodicals and the relative paucity of their role within the body of the periodicals, it seems necessary to ask why clubs were so popular with early editors. Part of the answer may lie in the particular demands of the periodical as a genre: periodicals could not conform to a plan set in stone from the opening issues. Editors needed to be able to respond to public interest in a particular current event or fad, to answer correspondence or to pursue areas which seemed to attract particular readerly approbation (as gauged by the volume of correspondence a particular subject generated or the sales figures for an individual issue). Perhaps readers simply did not respond with interest to the club fiction or address their correspondence to individual members of the club. In Lillie's collection of original correspondence to the *Tatler* and the *Spectator*, only one letter is addressed to Jenny Distaff, and none are addressed to members of the *Spectator* club (Lillie 1725: 1.125–9). The club fiction may have served as an editorial insurance policy, with characters and storylines which could be taken up if other copy was scarce. However, in addition to these pragmatic considerations, the club fiction probably served at least two important structural purposes. It provided an important middle ground between the editor as private individual and the public world of print, and it also offered a model of sociable reading and writing practices.

In the *Tatler*, Isaac Bickerstaff begins by dividing his paper into sections, each dated from a different coffee-house, but in the course of the *Tatler*'s run an increasing number of papers are headed 'Sheer-Lane' (where Bickerstaff lives) or 'From my own Apartment', and the paper's division into headings is gradually phased out. Writing is presented as an essentially solitary, private activity: the collected edition of the *Tatler* is subtitled the *Lucubrations of Isaac Bickerstaff Esq.*, suggesting that the issues were written late at night, alone, by flickering lamplight. In the *Spectator*, by contrast, writing is more sociable. Mr Spectator produces a series of papers during a visit to Sir Roger de Coverley, for example (*Spectators* 106–31), and papers are sometimes inspired by discussions in a club setting. In *Spectator* 99, for example, the editor tells us:

> The Club, of which I have often declared my self a Member, were last Night engaged in a Discourse upon that which passes for the chief Point of Honour among Men and Women, and started a great many Hints upon the Subject which I thought were entirely new. I shall therefore methodize the several Reflections that arose upon this Occasion, and present my Reader with them.
>
> (*Spectator* 99)

The *Spectator*'s presentation of public and private realms is a very unusual one. Mr Spectator combines some of the traditional characteristics of the retired scholarly writer with those of the clubbable man. Outside his club, he maintains a profound silence, communicating with his landlady by sign language, for example (see *Spectator* 12). In this, he is the opposite of the traditional periodical editor, usually portrayed as a blabbermouth, a *Babler*, *Tatler*, *Parrot*, *Tatling Harlot* or *Female Tatler*. Addison and Steele's later persona Nestor Ironside is more typical, his name alluding playfully to Steele's authorship but also to Homer's 'everlasting Story-teller' (*Guardian* 121), the original literary model of the garrulous old man. As Michael Ketcham has noted, there are two Mr Spectators (1985: 14–15): the confident, authoritative editor who reaches a wide audience and the shy, silent man, who rarely opens his lips outside his own club and is so inconspicuous that even Will Honeycomb fails to recognize him while staring him straight in the face. 'My Appearance before him just put him in mind of me, without making him reflect that I was actually present', the editor explains (*Spectator* 77). His silence in company leads many to suspect that he is a Jesuit, a disaffected courtier, a misanthropist or a white witch (see *Spectators* 4 and 131).

Ketcham argues that the *Spectator* breaks down the traditional oppositions between the retired and the active life. Mr Spectator has the shy reclusive qualities of the retired man but he is uncomfortable in the country and prefers to seek his solitude in a crowd. He tells us that 'he who comes into Assemblies only to gratifie his Curiosity, and not to make a Figure, enjoys the Pleasures of Retirement in a more exquisite Degree, than he possibly could in his Closet' (*Spectator* 4). Mr Spectator is 'frequently seen in most publick Places' and, indeed, tells us that 'there is no Place of general Resort, wherein I do not often make my Appearance' (*Spectator* 1). He mingles freely with every company – 'where-ever I see a Cluster of People I always mix with them' (*ibid.*) – and manages to be sociable without opening his lips: 'I always make one of the Company I am in; for though I say little my self, my Attention to others, and those Nods of Approbation which I never bestow unmerited, sufficiently shew that I am among them' (*Spectator* 77).

Ketcham's argument centres on the *Spectator*'s depiction of the family, which he claims 'exists as a mediator between the self-display of the public world, and the retired isolation of the private' (1985: 105). In a similar manner, the club provides a liminal space, one which is neither purely public nor purely private, not a place of business dealings and political intrigue, yet not a solitary space either. The coffee-house forms a parallel with the family hearth or the small village community: 'The Coffee-house is the Place of Rendezvous to all that live near it, who are thus turned to relish calm and ordinary Life' (*Spectator* 49). The editor comments further:

You see in their Countenances they are *at home* [my italic], and in quiet Possession of the present Instant, as it passes, without desiring to Quicken it by gratifying any Passion, or prosecuting any new Design. These are the Men formed for Society, and those little Communities which we express by the Word *Neighbourhoods*.

(*ibid.*)

Addison and Steele equate coffee-houses and clubs with tea-tables and assemblies, their domestic equivalents, throughout the paper. The coffee-house may be a place only frequented by men, but, in Addison and Steele's vision of it as a 'Place of Rendezvous', they imagine the ideal coffee-house club as one which acts as a substitute home and family for the bachelor editor and which has an equivalent in the domestic tea table. Mr Spectator expresses the hope:

> that I have brought Philosophy out of Closets and Libraries, Schools and Colleges, to dwell in Clubs and Assemblies, at Tea-Tables, and in Coffee-Houses.
>
> I would therefore in a very particular Manner recommend these my Speculations to all well regulated Families, that set apart an Hour in every Morning for Tea and Bread and Butter; and would earnestly advise them for their Good to order this Paper to be punctually served up, and to be looked upon as a Part of the Tea Equipage.
>
> (*Spectator* 10)

The parallel constructions here make clubs and assemblies, tea tables and coffee-houses seem almost interchangeable terms. The passage moves easily from the idea of the paper in the coffee-house to the particular recommendation that it should be read by families at home.

The common denominator which links the editor in his club and the reader at the tea table is sociability, a sociability which is part of the periodical's means of production, its consumption and its subject matter. 'My Paper', Mr Spectator claims, 'is in a Kind a Letter of News, but it regards rather what passes in the World of Conversation than that of Business' (*Spectator* 468). The paper will 'daily instil into [readers] such sound and wholesome Sentiments, as shall have a good Effect on their Conversation for the ensuing twelve Hours' (*Spectator* 10). The editor will take it 'for the greatest Glory of my Work, if among reasonable Women this Paper may furnish *Tea-Table Talk*' (*Spectator* 4). He tells us that in an essay-periodical, 'Knowledge, instead of being bound up in Books, and kept in Libraries and Retirements . . . is canvassed in every Assembly, and exposed upon every Table' (*Spectator* 124). Even the letters which the *Spectator* receives are a written version of conversation. The editor observes that 'it is wonderful that a Man cannot observe upon himself when he sits down to write, but that he will gravely commit to Paper the same Man that he is in the Freedom of Conversation' (*Spectator* 284).

While contemporary novels increasingly refer to their readers as silent and solitary (see J. Paul Hunter 1977; Sitter 1982: 9), the *Spectator* encourages group reading and reading aloud. Many of Mr Spectator's correspondents allude to these practices in their letters. The female correspondent who reports that she is part of 'a Company of young Females, who peruse your Speculations every Morning' (*Spectator* 319) is typical. Many readers bear witness to the popularity of the *Spectator* as a topic of female conversation. One reports that 'the Triumph of *Daphne* over her Sister *Letitia* [in *Spectator* 33] has been the Subject of Conversation at several Tea-Tables where I have been present' (*Spectator* 53), while another relates that he belongs to 'a private Assembly of Wits of both Sexes, where we generally descant upon your Speculations' (*Spectator* 547). A male correspondent relates that at a gathering of women he was asked to read the *Spectator* aloud to the assembled company (*Spectator* 271), and groups of men also seem to be fond of reading the paper aloud: references to reading the *Spectator* are frequently in the first person plural. Many letters begin like Philo-Spec's, who writes, 'I was this Morning in a Company of your Well-wishers, when we read over, with great Satisfaction, *Tully*'s Observations on Action adapted to the *British* theatre [in *Spectator* 541]' (*Spectator* 542). A group of Oxford men even gather together to read the collected *Spectator* aloud (*Spectator* 553). While all of these letters may be fictional, the correspondents in Lillie's collection of *Original and Genuine Letters* bear witness to equally sociable reading practices. The collection is peppered with references to tea table and coffee-house readings and discussions, and many letters claim to be the result of club resolutions. One correspondent tells Mr Spectator that, at a regular 'meeting of several wealthy and learned citizens', reading the *Spectator* aloud is always a fixed item on their agenda and that he has been 'ordered to send you the minutes of the board' (Lillie 1725: 2.15). The Spectator club mirrors and encourages the readers' own clubs, clubs for the enjoyment of the *Spectator*.

The club device provides a model of sociability, not only between editors or between readers, but also between writer and audience. As David Shields (1997) has argued, it is the means 'by which an anonymous readership was recruited into a sense of print fellowship' (qtd. Scott Black 1999: 29). The editor in the club is a far more accessible figure than the lone writer in the garret, particularly as clubs generally meet in public places, such as coffeehouses. The editor is a man-about-town, spending time in the same places as his readers. In the opening issue of the *Spectator*, the editor names the places where he is most likely to be found: at the coffee-houses Will's, Child's, Jonathan's, the Grecian and the Cocoa Tree; at the Exchange; and at the theatres in Covent Garden and Drury Lane (*Spectator* 1). Similarly, during the *Guardian*'s run, Steele set up a lion's head at Button's coffee-house that male readers could use as a kind of post box to communicate with the editor. Steele's *eidolon* Marmaduke Myrtle of the *Lover* explains the main difference between himself, a journalistic knight-errant in the Bickerstaffian mould, and the knights-errant of old: 'I am more accessible than any other Knights were before me, and in plain Terms … there is a Coffee-house under my Apartment' (*Lover* 2). He tells his readers, 'The two Theatres, and all the Polite Coffee-houses, I shall constantly frequent, but principally the Coffee-house under my Lodge, *Button*'s, and the Play house in *Covent-Garden*' (*Lover* 5).

Knowing the editor's haunts invited readers to guess at his real identity, and it also held out the promise that they might be able to read about events which they had witnessed first hand or recognize the pen-portraits of friends and acquaintance. Frequenting the same coffee-houses as the editor made them part of the extended club formed by the periodical's readers. The *Spectator*'s correspondents are used in many of the ways in which the fictional club members are not. They frequently serve to provide different perspectives and different voices. Within the periodical itself, this extended club was gradually to replace the fictional one.

The extended club of correspondents

The most immediate difference between correspondents and members of the *Spectator* club is that the club members are patently fictional, while the *Spectator*'s letter-writers may be real. There are, of course, different degrees of authenticity: some letters may have been printed unchanged, others may have been heavily edited, and even where the letters are genuine, the situations they describe and the identities which the correspondents claim could be fictions. Nearly half of all the *Spectator* issues are made up wholly or in part of letters, most of them in numbers attributed to Steele. The publication of daily issues of the *Spectator* for a period of 22 months must have been an onerous task, particularly for Steele, who as general editor was probably responsible for all aspects of the paper's publication. It seems likely that he would have lightened this task by having frequent recourse to readers' letters to provide copy. D.F. Bond has calculated that nearly two-thirds of Steele's issues contain correspondence, and many of these are exclusively collections of letters.[25] Steele usually presents the letters as a miscellany, rather than grouping letters on specific themes, suggesting that he printed whatever correspondence he had to hand on any particular occasion. The letters are often prefaced with little more than an introductory sentence, with the editor pleading business or laziness in his defence: claiming to publish letters 'for Want of Time to substitute something else in the Room of them' (*Spectator* 461); because of other duties – 'This being a Day of Business with me' (*Spectator* 518); or merely because, as he writes in the *Englishman*, he is 'at this present Writing a little touched with the Disease the Writer of the following Letter complains of [laziness]' (*Englishman* 33). It seems overwhelmingly likely that many of these letters were genuine.

As we have seen, a number of original letters to the *Spectator* have survived, most of which were never published in the periodical (see R.P. Bond 1959; Lillie 1725). During the paper's run, Addison and Steele suggest the value which these unpublished letters might have. They print a letter from Anthony Title-Page, a stationer who requests the use of the *Spectator*'s 'Refuse Letters', which, the correspondent claims, could at worst be sold 'by the Pound Weight to his good Customers the Pastry-Cooks' (*Spectator* 304). Writing in the second series of the *Spectator*, Thomas Tickell suggests

> that if the several Letters, which are Written to me under the Character of SPECTATOR, and which I have not made use of, were published in a Volume, they would not be an unentertaining Collection. The Variety of the Subjects, Stiles, Sentiments, and Informations, which are transmitted to me, would lead a very curious, or very idle Reader, insensibly along, through a great many Pages.
>
> (*Spectator* 619)

The rejected letters were to be published by Charles Lillie in two volumes in 1725. They were published by subscription, which implies that there was considerable public interest in them. The *Spectator* is not the only periodical to suggest that its correspondence is of independent worth – even if only to 'a very curious, or very idle Reader'. John Tipper's *Delights for the Ingenious* was a repository for letters which could not be printed in his *Ladies Diary*. He tells his readers that the 'Entertainment . . . is, for the most part, of their own providing' (*Delights for the Ingenious* 1, January 1711). Edward Cave launched the separate periodical *Miscellaneous Correspondence* (1742–8) to house 'Essays, Dissertations, etc. on various Subjects, sent to the Author of the *Gentleman's Magazine*, which could not be inserted' (subtitle).

In addition to the *Spectator*'s 'Refuse Letters', the originals of a few letters which appeared in the periodical have since been published. Comparing these with the printed versions reveals that Steele usually edited the correspondence, often extensively, and frequently completely rewrote the letters. As R.P. Bond points out, when Steele claims to include a letter in its original form, he states this explicitly – 'I am of Opinion that I ought some times to lay before the World the plain Letters of my Correspondents in the artless Dress in which they hastily send them' (*Spectator* 268) – implying that this is the exception, not the rule (1959: xlii–xliii).

In fact, Mr Spectator only occasionally singles out a letter as deserving of publication unaltered. A description of a female paragon is prefixed by the assertion that 'I . . . publish it just as it came to my Hands' (*Spectator* 302): it is important that the reader should believe that the woman described is a real person and therefore a suitable model for imitation, not a figment of the editor's imagination. Mr Spectator sometimes implies – though rarely explicitly states – that emotive letters expressing readers' grief have been little changed; they are meant to convey pathos, to be spontaneous and heartfelt, rather than products of careful and self-conscious artistry. In a paper on affliction, he publishes a letter from a woman whose lover has died, telling readers that 'the following Letter . . . though Subscribed by a ficti-tious Name, I have reason to believe is not Imaginary' (*Spectator* 163). He introduces a heartrending letter from a woman who has married against her father's will with the declaration that 'I am more pleased with a Letter that is filled with Touches of Nature than of Wit' (*Spectator* 181). Similarly, in *Spectator* 199, Steele tells us that 'the following Letters are written with such an Air of Sincerity, that I cannot deny the inserting of them'. Steele's choice of words is perhaps significant here. The letters have 'Touches of Nature' and 'an Air of Sincerity', but this does not mean that the editor has not improved them. The only letters of this kind that we know to have been published unchanged are the extracts from the correspondence between Steele and his second wife, Mary Scurlock, published as 'Genuine, and the Images of a Worthy Passion', as if submitted by a correspondent called Andromache (*Spectator* 142; see Steele 1968: 192–200, 273).

Mr Spectator makes no secret of the fact that correspondents could expect to see their letters appear with considerable alterations. He invites correspon-dence from those who have good ideas, but are not skilled at expressing them:

> If he [the reader] has started any Hint which he is not able to pursue, if he has met with any surprizing Story which he does not know how to tell, if he has discovered any epidemical Vice which has escaped my Observation, or has heard of any uncommon Vertue which he would desire to publish; in short, if he has any Materials that can furnish out an innocent Diversion, I shall promise him my best Assistance in the working of them up for a publick Entertainment.
>
> (*Spectator* 16)

Hints and information will suffice: the editor will know how to tell the story and work up the materials into something fit for public consumption. In an issue thanking his correspondents for their contributions, Addison explains:

> Sometimes indeed I do not make use of the Letter it self, but form the Hints of it into Plans of my own Invention, sometimes I take the Liberty to change the Language or Thought into my own way of speaking and thinking.
>
> (*Spectator* 271)

Correspondents frequently humbly offer to 'submit [their letters] to your better Judgment, to receive any other Model you think fit' (*Spectator* 302). In the preface to his collection, Lillie apologizes for what he describes as a deficiency in the 'correctness, stile, and beauty' of the *Spectator*'s original correspondents: 'As they were wrote with a view of being amended, it is hoped the reader will make allowances' (1725: n.p.).

The question of the status of the letters – whether genuine or fictional – is a complicated one and must have been as opaque to contemporaries as it is to us. As critics of the novel have noted, the blurring of the boundaries between fact and fiction is a conspicuous feature of early eighteenth-century writing. It takes a particularly involved form here. The letters may or may not describe real events, they may or may not have been sent in by real correspondents, and they may or may not have been slightly or radically altered by the paper's editors. Trying to discover which letters were real and to recognize the originals of the pen-portraits they contained must have been part of the fun of reading the paper for many contemporaries. While later papers were to make repeated claims for the authenticity of their letters, the *Spectator* contains several playful hints that many of the letters are inventions, a fact about which the editors are unapologetic. 'Some will have it', writes Addison,

> that I often write to my self, and am the only punctual Correspondent I have. This Objection would indeed be material, were the Letters I communicate to the Publick stuffed with my own Commendations, and if, instead of endeavouring to divert or instruct my Readers, I admired in them the Beauty of my own Performances.
>
> (*Spectator* 271)

From the point of view of the periodical's literary qualities or Addison and Steele's aims as writers, the question of the letters' provenance is irrelevant. However, Mr Spectator describes this question as arousing a keen interest among readers:

> When I have been present in Assemblies where my Paper has been talked of, I have been very well pleased to hear those who would detract from the Author of it observe, that the Letters which are sent to the

Spectator are as good, if not better, than any of his Works ... I have heard several of these unhappy Gentlemen proving, by undeniable Arguments, that I was not able to pen a Letter which I had written the Day before.

(*Spectator* 542)

The attribution of the *Spectator* letters involves the question of literary fame. Correspondents are both readers and writers, and Mr Spectator suggests that some readers believe that they have at least as much literary talent as the editors. Many contemporary novelists claim to be merely editors of journals or letters – Defoe depicts himself as the editor of Moll Flanders's autobiography; Samuel Richardson poses as the editor of Clarissa and Lovelace's letters – yet it is unlikely that these claims were taken seriously. Here, however, the question of how to ascribe authorship is more complicated.

Many correspondents claim to be writing to the *Spectator* in search of literary fame. Timothy Stanza, who sends in a poem to his mistress, writes candidly, 'You cannot imagine how much Service it will do me with my Fair one, as well as Reputation with all my Friends, to have something of mine in the *Spectator*' (*Spectator* 473). As one correspondent puts it, 'It is no Wonder if all Mankind endeavours to get somewhat into a Paper which will always live' (*Spectator* 78). Steele describes the *Guardian* as 'a kind of Nursery for Authors' where a writer can see 'if his Parts and Talents are to the publick Taste' before embarking on a more ambitious work (*Guardian* 98). Mr Spectator imagines his neglected correspondents as 'Writers, who impatiently long'd to see them [their contributions] appear in Print, and who, no Doubt, triumph'd to themselves in the Hopes of having a Share with me in the Applause of the Publick' (*Spectator* 442). Boswell reports that in the early part of the century 'there were several people alive in London, who enjoyed a considerable reputation merely from having written a paper in "the Spectator"' (1964–71: 3.33). Books sometimes claim, on no evidence, to have been written by contributors to the *Spectator*. Donald F. Bond cites the *History of Providence; or, the Six Days Work of the Creation* (1723), advertised as 'by the Author of several Spectators' (D.F. Bond 1965: lvii).

Johnson satirizes these pretensions to literary fame in 'The Idler', where he explains that 'he that is known to contribute to a periodical work' may 'grow considerable' at very small expense and 'by a single paper, may engross the honour of a volume', attributing this to the jealousy of readers who will allow literary merit to their fellow-readers, but not to the paper's editor: 'The standing author of the paper is always the object of critical malignity. Whatever is mean will be imputed to him, and whatever is excellent be ascribed to his assistants' (no. 2).[26]

The fame these would-be authors lay claim to is an extremely limited and dubious one. The final issue of the first *Spectator* series lists only seven corre-spondents by name: as for the rest, the editor has 'not been able to trace Favours of this kind, with any Certainty' (*Spectator* 555). All the letters in the periodical are printed anonymously or pseudonymously. The authors of the letters in Lillie's collection also sign their epistles with colourful sobri-quets such as Jonathan Telltruth (1725: 1.10), Obadiah Clumsey (*ibid.* 1.119) and Fungoso Stich (*ibid.* 2.214). The only way to prove authorship of a piece in the *Spectator* must have been either to show the manuscript to friends before sending it in or to insert personal details which would be recognized. Many letter-writers tell the editor that they have included these personal markers, particularly when their contributions are designed for the eyes of a wayward spouse or lover. 'They tell me', Mr Spectator writes of these correspondents, 'The Persons to whom they [their letters] are addressed have Intimations, by Phrases and Allusions in them, from whence they came' (*Spectator* 204). Of course, the correspondents would have had no way of knowing whether Addison and Steele would retain these distinguish-ing marks when they edited the letters for publication. These letter-writers' literary repute must, then, have been confined to a very narrow circle or based solely on hearsay and unsubstantiated bragging.

In the *Englishman*, Steele ascribes the *Spectator*'s popularity to its corre-spondence: 'The great Success of a former Paper was owing to this Particu-lar, that from the Plan of it, it lay open to receive the Sentiments of the rest of the World into it' (*Englishman* 16). Addison and Steele *do* occasionally print complaints from readers at the sheer volume of letters and their uneven quality. One reader begs the editor 'to pardon us such Letters of your Corre-spondents as seem to be of no Use but to the Printer' and to substitute advertisements in their stead (*Spectator* 310), while another notes 'that those *Spectators* which are so prettily laced down the Sides with little c's [quotation marks], how instructive or diverting soever they may be, do not carry with them that Authority as the others' and urges the editor to 'bestow one Penful of your own Ink' upon the malefactors he is writing in to complain about (gentleman who drive coaches as a hobby) (*Spectator* 526).

These protests, however, are exceptions. Mr Spectator is far more fre-quently occupied in pacifying disgruntled correspondents angry at the omis-sion of their letters. 'My Correspondents take it ill', he tells us, 'if I do not from Time to Time let them know I have received their Letters' (*Spectator* 48). Even if he is unable to print these missives, he sometimes offers brief answers to them within the periodical, even when these are not of any inter-est to his general readership. In *Spectator* 581, the editor proposes dedicating one paper a month to acknowledging correspondence received and offers brief answers to some of the letters, even though he warns that these notices will be cryptic to most of his readers: 'Though I appear abstruse to most

People, it is sufficient if I am understood by my particular Correspondents'. Mr Spectator perceives a duty to deal with his correspondents – 'I think my self obliged to take some Notice of them' (*Spectator* 566) – even at the expense of his general audience, almost as though these were personal letters which it would be rude not to answer.

Addison and Steele repeatedly appeal to norms of polite social interaction in this context. 'It would be Arrogance to neglect the Application of my Correspondents', we are told (*Spectator* 168). In a entire number dedicated to soliciting new correspondents, Mr Spectator begins by asserting that 'it is an impertinent and unreasonable Fault in Conversation, for one Man to take up all the Discourse' (*Spectator* 428), and in another paper he explains that 'it is reckoned a Piece of Ill-breeding for one Man to engross the whole Talk to himself' (*Spectator* 613). The choice of metaphor implies that the letter-writers and the editor are engaged in a social relationship, one modelled on conversation, that is, personal, face to face, verbal interaction. It is a relationship characterized by mutuality, equality, sociability and civility: rather like the relationship between Mr Spectator and his fictional club.

This idea that an editor has a moral obligation of some kind to respond to correspondents in print is a common one among periodical writers. In his essay-series 'The Idler', Johnson comments that, in most publications, 'in a short time, apologies have become necessary to those ingenious gentlemen and ladies, whose performances, though in the highest degree elegant and learned, have been unavoidably delayed' (no. 2). This seems an odd convention, however. Why should Mr Spectator acknowledge or publish letters which are boring, irrelevant to the topic of the day or simply superfluous? Defoe's attitude in the *Review* seems far more understandable. He claims wearily to have 'thrown by a monstrous Heap of such Letters, wholly un-answer'd' (4 October 1711).

We need to examine why Mr Spectator makes such a merit of reacting promptly to his correspondence, particularly since many later editors were to imitate this focus on letters. In the *Review*, Defoe vividly describes the pressures facing an author inundated with correspondence. He tells his readers that he has been '*Letter baited by Querists*' (*Review* vol. I, Preface), forcing him to dedicate half his publication to answering their queries, even though such a project was 'as remote from his Thoughts, when he began this Paper, as making a Map of the World in the Moon' (*Supplementary Journal*, September 1704). Mr Review has even taken to writing '*civil, private Answers*' to these letters (vol. I, Preface), even though some correspondents try to bribe him into printing their contributions, 'with the *Prevailing Argument* of *Money* inclos'd' (*Little Review* 1, 6 June 1705). The *Examiner* also notes that 'some Wit, and much Leisure, have made it a Fashion among ingenious Persons, to send Letters . . . to us Weekly Writers' and claims that the editor has been 'rather burthened than relieved by those Intelligences', especially since readers take offence when he neglects to print their missives (48, 28 June 1711). He feels an obligation, however, 'to do what lies in my Power, towards introducing into the World, the Works of these *Anonymous* Persons who are so fond of being Authors' (*Examiner* 48).

The *Spectator*'s correspondents base their entitlement to publication on four different kinds of claims. They claim a right to a hearing of their complaints and appeals against injustice; they offer to further the editor's knowledge by bringing his attention to new species of people and new kinds of behaviour; they demand answers to queries; and they use the paper as their only possible means of communicating with others to whom they urgently need to convey a message.

It is striking how many of the letters to the *Spectator* are protests and lamentations. One of Lillie's letter-writers aptly describes the periodical as 'the common repository of complaints' (1725: 2.195). Like Dunton's Athenian Society, Mr Spectator serves as a confidant to the troubled. The frontispiece to Charles Gildon's *History of the Athenian Society* (c.1693) shows desperate readers clutching knives and nooses and holding up petitions to the periodical's editors to save them from their despair (Figure 3.1). Mr Spectator also has his share of unhappy readers. He comments:

> Were I to publish all the Advertisements I receive from different Hands, and Persons of different Circumstances and Quality, the very Mention of them, without Reflexions on the several Subjects, would raise all the Passions which can be felt by the humane Mind. As Instances of this, I shall give you two or three Letters; the Writers of which can have no Recourse to any legal Power for Redress, and seem to have written rather to vent their Sorrow than to receive Consolation.
>
> (*Spectator* 402)

While the editor alludes here to 'all the Passions of the humane Mind', the letters he prints in this issue highlight human suffering, in particular a letter from Sylvia whose mother wishes her to prostitute herself to a friend of her husband's. She urges the editor to print her letter, 'if you have any Compassion for Injured Virtue'. While none of the *Spectator*'s correspondents are suicidal, many express a profound sense of injustice, such as the female shopkeeper subjected to continual sexual harassment who tells the editor:

> The Chearfulness of Life which would arise from the honest Gain I have, is utterly lost to me from the endless, flat, impertinent Pleasantries which I hear from Morning to Night. In a Word, it is too much for me to bear.
>
> (*Spectator* 155)

Figure 3.1 Frontispiece of Charles Gildon's *The History of the Athenian Society* (c.1693).

Numerous correspondents complain of pettier annoyances, such as people who speak the priest's part of divine service along with him – 'a Thing extremely offensive' to the writer – (*Spectator* 236); a man who sings and dances in a coffee-house, disturbing the other customers (*Spectator* 148); or a beautiful young woman who distracts the men from their devotions at church (*Spectator* 503). The writers appeal to Mr Spectator since 'the Offence does not come under any Law' (*Spectator* 503).

Some correspondents justify their contributions both because they are legitimate complaints against others and because of their novelty value. The *Spectator* is often presented as a collection of pen-portraits of different anti-social characters, a sort of reference work of folly. Mr Spectator explains that 'when I meet with any vicious Character, that is not generally known ... I draw it at length, and set it up as a Scarecrow' (*Spectator* 205). Correspondents sometimes sound almost gleeful at having unearthed new prey for the editor. 'As you have somewhere declared [in *Spectator* 108], that extraordinary and uncommon Characters of Mankind are the Game which you delight in', writes one, 'I thought this Discovery would not be unacceptable to you' (*Spectator* 371).

Some readers participate enthusiastically in the project of classifying Londoners, which is such a prominent feature of the *Tatler*. 'You have in some of your Discourses described most sort of Women in their distinct and proper Classes, as the *Ape*, the *Coquet*, and many others [see *Spectators* 209 and 247]; but I think you have never yet said any thing of a *Devotée*', writes one, sending in a description of a woman who is immersed in gloomy piety (*Spectator* 354). Other letter-writers claim that the characters they describe are unique. One complains of his wife, who has become obsessed with needlework and cookery to the point of locking her children away in a remote corner of the house, to prevent them disturbing her in her housewifely pursuits. 'I believe this is the first Complaint that ever was made to you of this Nature', he tells the editor (*Spectator* 328). The *Spectator* demonstrates a keener interest in these originals and less of a concern with sorting and cataloguing social types than the *Tatler*. Mr Spectator also relies far more heavily on his correspondents for his information than Isaac Bickerstaff did.

In particular, since Mr Spectator is a bachelor, and the members of his club also appear to be unmarried – there is certainly no mention of club members' wives – he relies on his readers for accounts of married life, a very frequent topic in the paper. As one correspondent puts it, 'There are very many things which you cannot possibly have a true Notion of, in a single Life, these are such as respect the married State' (*Spectator* 176). Mr Spectator also condemns sexual immorality on many occasions and dedicates a number of papers to the subject of prostitution.[27] His knowledge of sexual licentiousness is drawn not primarily from conversation with Will Honeycomb but from his correspondents: 'My Reader must not make uncharitable Inferences from my speaking knowingly of that sort of Crime which is at present treated of [debauching women]. He will, I hope, suppose I know it only from the Letters of Correspondents' (*Spectator* 182).

Despite Mr Spectator's lack of personal experience of marriage, a number of correspondents write in to ask the editor's advice on love matters, particularly on the choice of a partner. One correspondent alludes to Mr Spectator's reputation as 'the Ladies Philosopher' dispensing 'pretty Advice' (*Spectator* 380), while another calls him 'the universal judge of all those that cannot bring their causes before any other court' (Lillie 1725: 2.206). The letters on courtship often resemble similar queries in the *Athenian Mercury*, which is full of letters from readers seeking love guidance, but Addison and Steele's treatment of these love cases differs from Dunton's in certain important regards. Dunton's correspondents are confronted with complex and tricky dilemmas, some of which seem to have been invented to test the editors' ingenuity. One reader asks, for example, whether he should marry the woman he loves, in opposition to a promise made at his father's deathbed (*Athenian Mercury* XIII.5, 20 February 1694); while another wonders whether he should betray a friend's confidence by warning his parents that he is in love with '*a notorious Jilt of the Town*' (*ibid.* XIII.20, 14 April 1694); and a third enquires about the ethics of breaking a rashly-made vow (*ibid.* VIII.16, 22 October 1692). Urmi Bhowmik has shown that the *Athenian Mercury* can be seen as a journalistic extension of a seventeenth-century Protestant casuistical tradition that included the work of divines such as Jeremy Taylor, Robert Sanderson, William Perkins and Richard Baxter (2003). The *Athenian Mercury*'s editors lay claim to an authority which is almost sacerdotal.

The love queries sent to the *Spectator*, however, are less complicated. Most correspondents are simply torn between love and avarice. B.D. asks Mr Spectator whether she should marry a handsome but poor lover, whose main qualifications are shining eyes and skill on the dance floor (*Spectator* 475); Biddy Loveless is 'very amorous and very covetous' and cannot decide between her rich lover, Will, and her handsome lover, Tom (*Spectator* 196); and an unnamed male correspondent wonders whether to marry a young woman whom he loves but who has no fortune (*Spectator* 254). These are typical examples. The letters are frequently so schematic that it seems likely that many of them were written by Addison and Steele themselves to serve as exempla, rather than sent in by actual readers.

Unlike a modern agony aunt, and unlike Dunton's Athenians and their imitators, Mr Spectator usually leaves these queries unanswered. His response to B.D. is typical: he considers her 'ripe for asking Advice' but unlikely to pay any attention to his admonitions and therefore decides to 'communicate the Letter to the Publick, without returning any Answer to it' (*Spectator* 475). In Steele's later periodical the *Lover*, the editor, Marmaduke Myrtle, also receives a number of love queries. As one reader puts it, he 'plays the Casuist' (*Lover* 31). Myrtle tells us that 'I must confess I did not sufficiently weigh the great Perplexity that I should fall into, from the vast Variety of Cases, when I undertook my present Province' (*Lover* 22). Strikingly, however, he rarely publishes any responses to the love cases sent in by correspondents. Unlike the missives sent in to the *Athenian Mercury*, these letters do not require any answers: any right-thinking reader will quickly deduce what the correct course of action would be. Mr Spectator and Marmaduke Myrtle are very different editor-personae from Isaac Bickerstaff, with his Court of Honour and the Athenians, with their authoritative pronouncements. Bickerstaff and the Athenian Society seem far more like 'universal judges' than Mr Spectator. Mr Spectator's readers are not expected to wait with baited breath for his answers to correspondents' questions, but to know the answers and be amused or entertained by the letter-writers, a response they share with the editor. While the Athenian Society is an exclusive club of especially knowledgeable men who answer questions, Mr Spectator's readers are part of his club and share his values.

In addition to those correspondents who write to gain Mr Spectator's sympathy or advice or to obtain a place in his famous paper, there are many who use the paper primarily as a means of communicating with other readers. Some letter-writers hope that wayward spouses, lovers or friends will be reformed by recognizing their pen-portraits in the *Spectator*. This phenomenon is also alluded to in the *Athenian Mercury*, where we are told that one cruel husband, on reading the depiction of himself in the paper, '*is convinc'd, and almost converted from* Brute *to* Man: *He has look'd at his picture so long that he now loaths it*' (XIX.23, 14 January 1696). Many readers hope that Mr Spectator's moral authority will convince, where their own pleadings have failed. A wife, whose husband is prone to fits of rage in which he breaks her crockery, asks the editor to publish her letter: 'My Husband having a great Veneration for your Writings, will by that Means know you do not approve of his Conduct' (*Spectator* 563). A woman who is plagued by the insults of a rude houseguest tells the editor, 'Your Printing this Letter may perhaps be an Admonition to reform him: Assoon [*sic*] as it appears I will write my Name at the End of it, and lay it in his Way' (*Spectator* 508). A husband hopes that his negligent wife will change her ways on recognizing herself in the *Spectator*'s pages, since 'she reads you, and there is a Phrase or two in this Letter which she will know come from me' (*Spectator* 194). The most elaborate of these endeavours to use the *Spectator* as an instrument of moral amendment is henpecked husband Anthony Freeman's attempt to tame his domineering spouse, a woman whose behaviour is so outrageous that he tells the editor that she would 'afford you for some Months at least Matter enough for one *Spectator* a Week' (*Spectator* 212). Freeman plans to have his friend Tom Meggot read a *Spectator* containing a detailed character sketch of Mrs Freeman in her presence and promises to report the results of this experiment. Several days later, Meggot describes Mrs Freeman's reaction: 'raging, swooning, railing, fainting, pitying her self, and reviling her Husband' (*Spectator* 216). He fears that even the *Spectator* cannot reform her: 'We are upon a thing we have not Talents for' (*ibid.*).

Some correspondents use the *Spectator* not to complain about their lovers or to try to reform them, but simply to communicate with them. For

women readers, in particular, the periodical provides a possibility of addressing their lovers frankly without forfeiting their modesty. One impecunious
suitor asks his mistress to take this means of reassuring him of her affection.
He promises to look out for 'any Hint in any future Paper of yours she gives
me the least Encouragement' (*Spectator* 304). The correspondent Statira
encloses a letter to her lover, who is reluctant to declare himself because, she
suspects, he would rather marry a wealthier woman and take Statira as his
mistress. Her letter, she tells the editor, is 'a Declaration of Passion to one
who has made some feint Addresses to me for some time' (*Spectator* 199) – a
declaration which would surely not have been acceptable if made directly –
and she has chosen to address him through the pages of the *Spectator* since it
is both public and private at once: 'I can be at once revealed to you, or, if
you please, lye concealed' (*Spectator* 199). The self-confessed jilt Amoret
sends in a letter to her lover, apologizing for her previous treatment of him.
She claims to have chosen this method of communication, since her lover has
demanded that she 'contrive a way to make your Recantation as well known
to the Publick, as they are already apprized of the manner with which you
have treated me' (*Spectator* 401). A cheeky postscript reveals that the correspondent's remorse is disingenuous, however. Amoret, who is probably a
creation of Eustace Budgell's, asks Mr Spectator to 'assure him [her lover]
that I know nothing at all of the Death of his rich Uncle in *Gloucestershire*'
(*ibid.*). Mr Spectator proclaims himself 'not at all displeased that I am
become the Courier of Love' and is happy to provide a vehicle for messages
from lovers, even at the expense of other readers. 'As to the Reader's Entertainment', he explains, 'he will, I hope, forgive the inserting such Particulars
as to him may perhaps seem frivolous, but are to the Persons who wrote
them of the highest Consequence' (*Spectator* 204).

   The later issues of the *Spectator*, in particular, contain the beginnings of an
inter-readerly sociability: readers who are interested in the views and writings of correspondents and who wish to communicate with each other
through the paper. The periodical does not resemble the democratic free-for-
all of a modern unmoderated Internet discussion group: readers still appeal
primarily to Mr Spectator and seek the editor's opinions and sanction, rather
than asking other readers directly for information. However, readers of the
Spectator were involved in a relationship which was not just two-way –
between editor and reader – but also between readers. The periodical fosters
a feeling of belonging, of clubbability, within its pages. It is a club that is,
of course, both exclusive – composed of people of particular discernment –
and open – to feel part of this club you only need to regard yourself as a
regular *Spectator* reader. The shift from fictional club members to correspondents within the *Spectator* also reflects a wider trend in the development of
the periodical: from the gossipy essay-periodical, which initially appealed to

a small, select London audience, to the magazine with its nationwide audience and its heavy reliance on readers' letters and contributions.

Finally, the shift from club to correspondents is symptomatic of the increasing divergence between the aims and strengths of the periodical and those of the novel. While novelists explored the personalities of their often eponymous heroes and heroines in ever more precise detail, journalists turned away from the character sketch. Addison and Steele describe letters as the ideal way of revealing personality. 'I have ever thought', remarks Mr Spectator, 'Men were better known, by what could be observed of them from a Perusal of their private Letters, than any other way' (*Spectator* 27). He feels confident that he 'may pronounce their Characters from their Way of Writing' (*Spectator* 124), since 'nothing discovers the true Temper of a Person so much as his Letters' (*Spectator* 284). While novelists also employ letters to reveal disposition, they do so in order to explore the thoughts and feelings of their central characters in depth. In the periodical, letters are used rather differently. They serve as extensions of the journalistic alter ego, as when Addison confesses to 'casting his Thoughts into a Letter' (*Spectator* 542) in order to express himself in ways that would not be appropriate to Mr Spectator, and as depictions of the periodical's readership. We are always uncertain whether letters are fiction or fact, the work of the editor or a reader. The letters present us with a dizzying array of speakers. The periodical reminds one correspondent of a magic box which contained only one face painted on it

> that by pulling some Pieces of Isinglass over it, was chang'd into a grave Senator or a *Merry Andrew*, a Patch'd Lady or a Nun, a Beau or a Black-a-moor, a Prude or a Coquet, a Country 'Squire or a Conjurer, with many other different Representations very entertaining . . . tho' still the same at the Bottom.
>
> (*Spectator* 134)

The *Spectator*'s increasing focus on correspondence foreshadows the development of the periodical as a whole from a preoccupation with eccentric editor-personae and their small fictitious clubs to the heterogeneity we see in the later magazines. In the *Spectator*, however, this variety is still under strict control. Unlike some of those later magazines, the *Spectator*'s content is miscellaneous, but not jumbled. The correspondents do not form a cacophony of competing voices, each appealing to only a small segment of the paper's readership. Nor does the paper stake its reputation on the authenticity of its readers' letters. Behind the isinglass, the physiognomy of Mr Spectator is always visible. Both club members and correspondents serve ultimately to illustrate and validate the editor's views.

4 'Faction and Nonsense'

The rivalry between *Common Sense* and the *Nonsense of Common Sense*

One area of early eighteenth-century public life in which women are almost always conspicuously absent is the political essay-periodical. Despite Delarivier Manley's fiercely Tory essays for the *Examiner* in 1711,[28] very few of the contributors to such papers have been identified as women, and the papers touch on issues of specifically feminine concern only infrequently. Lady Mary Wortley Montagu is the only woman known to have edited a political essay-journal in London before 1770. In her journalism, she addresses the question of women's involvement in politics and of their representation in the most popular political essay-paper of the 1730s, *Common Sense*. Attitudes towards women in the two periodicals – whether condescending, hostile and misogynist, or chivalrous and even feminist – are an important indicator of the editors' journalistic aims. Sometimes the editors choose to emphasize their role as political commentators, their involvement in a sphere in which women and their interests are marginal, and at other times they choose to portray themselves as witty and literary essay-writers in the tradition of Addison and Steele. In such a tradition, women readers and female concerns are central.

For a brief few months at the turn of the year 1737–8, Montagu entered the public sphere of politics as a journalist.[29] Unlike almost all the major literary figures of her generation, she chose to defend Robert Walpole's administration. Montagu wrote anonymously in the guise of a humble male hack, scribbling her copy, she tells us, in 'my *Garret*' (*Nonsense* 1), and she particularly cautioned her printer to ensure that the writer's identity remain unknown: a caution that was to prove all too successful for more than two centuries. The paper ran for only nine issues, at irregular intervals, between 16 December 1737 and 14 March 1738. Only two incomplete print runs have survived and the paper was not reprinted until the mid-twentieth century (Montagu 1947). There is no mention of the *Nonsense of Common Sense* in Montagu's letters of this period, and none of her contemporaries appear to have been aware of her authorship of this paper.

Montagu had made two previous brief forays into journalism. A letter of hers had been printed in the *Spectator*: a playful description of a club of widows and the husbands they have buried (*Spectator* 573). She also contributed a letter to the *Flying-Post* (13 September 1722), in the persona of a Turkey merchant, recommending the inoculation practices against smallpox which Montagu had observed in Constantinople (Montagu 1993: 95–7). Montagu's excursion into political journalism was the only time in her life when she was directly involved in the publication of her own work. Her attitude to publication was highly ambivalent. She warns her friend Lord Cornbury 'that it was not the busyness of a Man of Quality to turn Author, and that he should confine himselfe to the Applause of his Freinds and by no means venture on the press' (Montagu 1967: 3.37). Montagu's perception of publication as unfitting for an aristocrat makes it even more surprising that she chose to edit a political periodical. As Isobel Grundy notes, 'This was writing under the sign of Grub Street', which was 'an odd milieu for a lady of rank' (1999: 372). Montagu tells her daughter, Lady Bute, in 1753 that, although 'no body ever had such various provocations to print as my selfe', she has never done so, 'having never aim'd at the Vanity of popular Applause' (Montagu 1967: 2.39). Towards the end of her life she assures her:

> I hope you have not so ill opinion of me as to think I am turning Author in my old age. I can assure you I regularly burn every Quire as soon as it is finish'd and mean nothing more than to divert my solitary hours.
>
> (Montagu 1967: 3.19)

On the other hand, she circulated her poems, essays and letters in manuscript and allowed friends to take copies. As Lady Bute was to complain in later life, 'Everything got into print sooner or later' (Montagu 1993: 19). Montagu might well have secretly agreed with Sheridan's creation Lord Sneerwell in *The School for Scandal* who claims that it is 'very vulgar to Print, and as my little Productions are mostly Satires and Lampoons on particular people I find they circulate more by giving copies in confidence to the Friends of the Parties' (Sheridan 1975: 233–4).

Montagu's attitude towards politics was equally ambivalent. Only a few months after the last issue of the *Nonsense*, she writes to her friend Lady Pomfret that she had always been merely 'a humble spectator' of the political scene and that she wonders why Chesterfield's increasing physical frailty does not induce him to 'quit the stage' on which he plays 'an under-part in a second-rate theatre'. She apologizes for boring her friend with such a 'trifling subject' as politics and describes contemporary political writing as 'profoundly dull' (Montagu 1967: 2.126–7). Her most intimate letters – those written to Francesco Algarotti in the early months of 1738 – do not mention her journalistic activities directly, but hint at a profound weariness and disillusion with politics. Montagu writes that she is unable to distance herself from the 'Noise, croud and Division' of London, and, in an indirect allusion to the title of her paper, she tells Algarotti that only the remembrance of him can soothe and palliate 'the rough impressions of Faction and Nonsense' (Montagu 1967: 2.115).

Why, then, did Montagu enter the journalistic fray? On her manuscript copy of the *Nonsense of Common Sense* she wrote, 'All these wrote by me M.W.M. to serve an unhappy worthy man', i.e. Robert Walpole (Montagu 1993: 105). Since Walpole's victory in the general elections of 1734, the Opposition had been in some disarray. Bolingbroke returned to France in 1735 and Pulteney took an increasingly less active part in Opposition politics in the House of Commons. The government launched the *Daily Gazetteer* in 1735, combining most of the ministerial writers in one paper, which was distributed free in large quantities by Walpole's henchmen at the Post Office. In 1737, there was a dramatic change in the political climate when Frederick, Prince of Wales moved into open opposition, providing a powerful figurehead for all those opposed to Walpole. In February 1737, Pulteney proposed a motion in Parliament to increase the Prince's allowance. Also, on 5 February, the new Opposition paper *Common Sense* was launched, edited by Charles Molloy, probably financed and backed by the Old Pretender, and containing contributions by Chesterfield, Lord Lyttleton and other prominent Opposition figures (Goldgar 1976: 156–7). On 31 March, Henry Fielding's dramatic satire on the Robinocracy *The Historical Register for the Year 1736* opened at the Little Theatre in the Haymarket to huge popular applause. *Common Sense* borrows its title from the figure of Queen Common-sense in Fielding's popular play of the previous year, *Pasquin*. In May, Pope's vicious satire *The First Epistle of the Second Book of Horace Imitated* appeared and the Opposition launched a new periodical attack with the *Alchymist: or, the Spirit of Fog Reviv'd*, which was promptly indicted by the Grand Jury of Middlesex as a 'Scandalous, Seditious and Treasonable Libel' (Harris 1987: 125). Walpole responded to these literary sallies with a tougher stance towards the journalists, a campaign of harassment and prosecutions and the introduction of the Theatre Licensing Act in June, triggering fears of similar measures to place journalistic literature under the control of a censor. In November, however, with the death of his ally Queen Caroline, Walpole's position was further weakened. One month later, Montagu, the close friend of both Walpole's mistress, Maria Skerett, and his chief supporter in the House of Lords, Lord Hervey, took up the journalistic cudgel on his behalf.[30]

An early eighteenth-century journalist writing in a political periodical who wished to address the concerns of women had several options. Some editors chose to satirize women's undue influence in political debate or their frivolous and uncomprehending interest in party politics. In the *Spectator*, for instance, Addison ridicules those women who patch according to party (*Spectator* 81). The Whig ladies, the right-hand sides of their faces spotted with black, glare at their feminine political rivals in the opera boxes opposite them. For them, politics is a game: a fashion and a feminine vanity. In the *Jacobite's Journal*, Fielding mocks the Jacobite women's party rage, which he opposes to the moderation of female Whigs:

> May you not often pass a whole Day in the Company of a Whig-Lady without knowing her political Principles, unless indeed that her Silence on that Head declares her not to be of our Party [the Jacobites]? Whereas, with our Women, it is hardly possible to sit an Hour.
>
> (2, 12 December 1747)

The editor John Trott-Plaid tells his readers that he will be assisted in writing the *Jacobite's Journal* by his wife, who is pictured in the paper's frontispiece, ludicrously mounted behind him on an ass. He tells us that his wife will write 'a very considerable Part of this Paper', dedicating herself to the concerns of her female fellow-travellers (*Jacobite's Journal* 2). She is qualified for this office by 'a most masculine Spirit', as well as by her mendacity, drunkenness and stupidity (*ibid.*). The portrait is a damning indictment of female political journalists as well as women readers of political papers, even though the promised issues by Mrs Trott-Plaid were never forthcoming. The *Gray's Inn Journal* warns its women readers that an interest in politics tends 'to inflame the Ladies with Party-Rage, to cause Heats in the Face, and to occasion those Vibrations of the Fan, Bitings of the Lips, and Fidgets on the Chair, which greatly discompose the whole Form', making it a more formidable destroyer of female beauty than 'a Spotted-Fever or the Small-Pox' (6 October 1753).

Other editors take the approach of separating issues dealing with women and their foibles from those dedicated to political questions. Women, for them, have no connection with politics and no interest in the subject. The correspondent Omphale in Fielding's *Champion* assumes that women are uninterested in political journalism. She complains that 'out of so many Daily, Evening, and Weekly Papers, not one, that we ever hear of, meddles with any Concerns of ours. – All are devoted to Politics, nothing but Politics' (327, 15 December 1741). She defines women's periodicals as those modelled on the *Tatler* and the *Spectator* and argues that similar publications might prevent women from satisfying their thirst for printed material by 'devouring those crude, injudicious Things in the Novel and Adventure-

Way' (*ibid.*). Political periodicals are liable only to induce 'such a Fit of the Vapours, as Hart's Horn, Sal-volatile, or Assa foetida itself, can hardly cure' (*ibid.*).

Politics was, however, sometimes, though not frequently, regarded as a fitting topic for both female editors and readers. The *Orphan Reviv'd* (1718–20) followed a political essay-leader with foreign and domestic news, 'Printed and Sold by ELIZ. POWELL', and letters were addressed to 'Mrs. Powell' and 'Madam', although Elizabeth Powell's persona remains undeveloped. In the *Friendly Writer* (1732–3), news is reprinted with commentary in the voice of an elderly Quaker woman. The frontispiece shows the paper's editor, Ruth Collins, dressed in the distinctive garb of her sect, sitting writing at a desk, with a rather severe expression on her face (Figure 4.1). She defiantly claims, '*I shall despise those who take occasion to scoff at my Manner of Writing, and scorn the Work of a weak Woman*' (1732, Preface). The Dissenting tradition has always included women preachers and prophets and female Quakers can speak at a meeting if the spirit moves them. Ruth Collins seems to claim some of this authority for her political journalism, employing evocatively religious diction: '*Doth it much rejoice my Spirit, that the Work of a poor weak Woman should find Grace and Acceptance among the Men of the World*' (February 1732). Despite the colourful language – news is reported in a Quaker idiom throughout – Ruth Collins does not appear to be a figure of derision, since the paper sincerely represents Dissenting interests. The issue for February 1732, for instance, is followed by an unironic pamphlet seeking the repeal of the Test and Corporation Acts. The *Parrot* (1728) contains discussion of news under the auspices of a Mrs Prattle. The editor complains that 'nothing will now go down among the Women but what is somewhat relating to State and Politicks' (3, 9 October 1728). Eliza Haywood's later paper of the same name (1746), written by 'the AUTHORS of the FEMALE SPECTATOR', incorporates a news section called the 'Compendium of the Times' in the form of a letter from a gentleman to his friend in the country.

In papers specifically addressed to female readers, politics was frequently presented in dialogue form, 'as the most easy, familiar, and natural Method for all Capacities' (*Lady's Weekly Magazine* 1, 19 February 1747). Mrs Penelope Pry's *Lady's Weekly Magazine*, 'calculated intirely for the Service and Amusement of your *Sex*' (*ibid.*), communicates foreign affairs in the form of a conversation between the well-informed editor and two female friends, as well as printing domestic news under place headings, in the conventional way. The editor's young friend Miss Bloom tells her readers that women should follow political developments: 'I like to know what is doing in the world, as it will furnish me with knowledge useful in conversation and pleasing in Society' (*ibid.*). Jasper Goodwill's *Ladies Magazine* presents news in the form of 'A History of England by Question and Answer' as the

Figure 4.1 Ruth Collins of the *Friendly Writer* (1732–3).

leading essay of each issue in 1751. Women were also sometimes depicted as readers of more mainstream political essay-sheets. A correspondent of the polemical *Mist's Weekly Journal* tells the editor that 'nothing has made your Paper more agreeable, than the carrying it home to our Wives and Daughters, who us'd frequently to read you with Pleasure' and warns that 'if you disoblige the Women . . . Your Sale will never pay Paper and Press' (73, 3 May 1718). An elaborate satire on Walpole in Henry Fielding's *Champion*, citing Quintillion, Aeschines and Horace, is 'sign'd by a Woman, a Spinster . . . BELINDA' (334, 31 December 1741).

In the *Freeholder*, Addison argues that 'Ladies are always of great use to the Party they espouse, and never fail to win over Numbers to it' (no. 4). In accordance with this doctrine, he devotes a number of the periodical's issues to attempts to persuade his female readers that loyalty to the Hanoverian succession is in their best interests. Women enjoy greater liberties under a Protestant than a Catholic government, he argues (*ibid.*); men who harbour a wish to betray their monarch will be equally unfaithful to their wives (*Freeholder* 8); and the spouses of disaffected Tories are denied the pleasure of attending Court (*Freeholder* 26). He encourages the Whig ladies to express their support for the cause by such feminine means as flirting with Whigs and scorning Tories, barring non-Jurors from their basset tables (*Freeholder* 8) and sporting fans decorated with motifs 'both of Despotick Power and of Male Tyranny', such as 'a Nunnery of lively black-Eyed Vestals, who are endeavouring to creep out at the Grates' or 'a *Turk* dropping his Handkerchief in his Seraglio' (*Freeholder* 15). Addison urges the ladies to form a voluntary association and suggests that in their constitution they should promise to use their feminine charms – 'our Tongues and Hearts, our Eyes, Eye-Lashes, Favourites, Lips, Dimples' – in the service of King George (*Freeholder* 8).

The *Freeholder* essays addressed to women are bristling with double standards. The early issues are chiefly concerned with inciting the Whig ladies to display their political loyalties and urging them to become active in national politics. In the later issues, however, the editor concentrates on dissuading Tory women from those same activities and demonstrating how unfeminine it is to engage in political debate. While the Whig ladies are shown fluttering fans and eyelashes, the Tories are depicted as red-faced shrews, bursting their stays with fury: expressing 'the most masculine Passions', while their bosoms are 'heaving with such Party Rage' (*Freeholder* 26). They forget their domestic duties: they 'are so conversant in Matters of State, that they wholly neglect their private Affairs' (*ibid.*). In his paper, Addison claims that he wishes to 'treat our Women as Members of the Body Politick' (*Freeholder* 32), but his oscillation between praise for Whig women's political activities and denigration of female Tories as 'polemical Ladies' (*ibid.*) raises doubts about how seriously we should take this political address to women. It seems more likely that these papers are designed as comic relief from more serious political debate, since 'no Periodical Author, who always maintains his Gravity, and does not sometimes sacrifice to the Graces, must expect to keep in vogue for any considerable Time' (*Freeholder* 45). Addison describes female interest in politics as one of 'several Objects that may very innocently be ridiculed' (*ibid.*) and concludes his papers on female Whigs and Tories with the hope that women may soon revert to their customary lack of interest in politics and that 'the Discoursing on Politicks [among women] shall be looked upon as as dull as talking on the Weather' (*Freeholder* 38). Women's involvement in politics, he tells us, has led to 'the Ruin of good Houswifery' and the 'visible Decay of the National Beauty' (*ibid.*). Party rage, he warns, unsexes both female Tories and female Whigs.

Montagu may well have written the *Nonsense of Common Sense* partly in response to similar satires on women and politics. The more immediate impetus for the paper may have been provided by the 10 December 1737 issue of *Common Sense*, which contains a letter from 'NONSENSE, a Terrestrial Goddess' who, in a phrase which neatly unites misogyny and Opposition politics, claims to have 'the Ladies, the Poetasters, and the M– [ministry] on my Side'. Like Addison and the editors of *Common Sense*, Montagu is concerned to expose and correct the misplaced political influence of women, but unlike them she sees women's political activity as not simply restricted to an addiction to nonsense or to such fashion statements as anti-Papist pictures on fans.

In the very first issue of her paper, she displays her political allegiances by criticizing those who opposed compulsory mourning for Queen Caroline. The targets of her attack are those Opposition peers who were reluctant to display full mourning for their sovereign because they had disliked her political alliance with Walpole. In Montagu's essay, however, it is the women who are too vain to wear black and who also refuse to support the domestic wool industry, preferring French fripperies to British manufacture: 'Our Ladys, who are so accustom'd to shiver in silks, that they exclaim on the Hardships of Warmth and Decency' (*Nonsense* 1).[31] She appeals to their vanity in her attempts to persuade them to buy British:

> I can assure them it would be highly advantageous to their complexions. Many cold Faces that I have seen at the Opera ... would have had an agreeable glow ... if their Bodys had been cover'd with the warm product of our sheep.
>
> (*Nonsense* 1)

Montagu even makes the tongue-in-cheek suggestion that the intervention of women is responsible for the war with Spain. She tells her readers that fine ladies, who visit the opera regularly to swoon over the celebrated castrato Farinelli, have indirectly started the clamour for war. Farinelli's departure from London for Spain is, writes Montagu, 'one of the Reasons we have for going to War, and the principal one with all polite Ladies and Gentlemen' (*Nonsense* 3).

The second issue of *Nonsense* is devoted to the proposal to reduce interest on the sinking fund to pay off the National Debt from 4 to 3 per cent – incidentally proving that the paper is not simply a vehicle of party rage, since this was an Opposition policy, not a Whig one (Grundy 1999: 373). As Grundy points out, Montagu is unusual in considering the effects of a political measure specifically on the lives of women (1999: 373). Montagu argues that the reduction in interest may lead fathers to apprentice their daughters to trades, rather than relying on an income from the stock market (*Nonsense* 2). She also describes the opposition to the measure as symptomatic of women's ability to influence parliamentary measures. Women who have refused suitable, but humble, matches in their youth out of pride are now forced to live on the interest of their savings and therefore oppose the rate cut. Montagu suggests that these ladies should simply retire to the country, instead, to save the money they spend at the London diversions (*ibid.*).

Commenting on women and politics, Montagu writes wryly:

> I have allways been an Humble Admirer of the Fair Sex ... and ... am glad they can find in the imaginary Empire of Beauty, a consolation for being excluded every part of Government in the State. But ... I am shock'd when I see their Influence in opposition to ... the common Welfare of the Nation ... their ... Tattle has had force enough to put a stop to the most reasonable Design that has appear'd in public for a long time ... I am persuaded that the British Mothers, sisters, and mistrisses ... have exerted their Authority on this occasion and have met with astonishing Success.
>
> (*Nonsense* 2)

Montagu's paper is not a misogynistic attack on her sex's ill-informed meddling in a subject which they cannot understand. Instead, it is an attempt to re-educate women politically and engage them in her own political causes. Her political rhetoric is implicitly addressed to a female readership and presupposes that they can play a major role in national politics: they have an 'Authority' which they can exert with 'astonishing Success', especially when they act in unison. It is the 'British Mothers, sisters, and mistrisses' to whom she appeals to put aside merely private and personal considerations and become disinterested, politically-informed subjects and, potentially, a powerful unofficial lobby. Furthermore, at the same time as awakening the political conscience of her female readers and citing their ability to influence politics, Montagu is also alerting them to their own powerlessness in the public sphere. In a bitter aside, she professes that she is 'glad they can find in the imaginary Empire of Beauty, a consolation for being excluded every part of Government in the State' (*ibid.*). Many periodicalists before Montagu had wished to educate women, to inspire them with greater moral seriousness and exhorted them to turn from beautifying their persons to ornamenting their minds. Montagu seems to have been the first to suggest that women might turn from dressing-tables and *billet-doux* to a greater involvement in public life. She wishes them to realize the injustices of the patriarchal system, to exercise the power which they do possess for 'the common Welfare of the Nation' and to increase their own status.

For the writers of *Common Sense*, on the other hand, women are scarcely accessible to political reasoning. 'I have', the editor tells us, 'in order to be of some Use to them, stipulated with my Stationer, that my Paper shall be of the properest Sort for pinning up of their Hair' (*Common Sense* 5 February 1737). The joke that women use periodicals only to curl their hair is repeated by Mr Fitz-Adam of the *World*: 'Very few ladies of condition could spare time . . . to read over a paper . . . but . . . I contented myself with knowing that I was every week adorning their heads, though I could not be permitted to improve their understandings' (171, 8 April 1756). Yet, as early as issue 4, the editor of *Common Sense* handles a topic of specifically feminine interest: dress. He addresses his paper on fashion to women, 'as Dress is more immediately the Province . . . of the fair Sex' (26 February 1737).

Despite attitudes towards women which are at best dismissive and at worst deeply hostile, the editors of *Common Sense* often claim to be appealing to a mixed audience, of which female readers are not the least significant group. The paper's statements of editorial purpose always stress the importance of its female readership:

> I was resolv'd . . . to make this Paper entertaining as well as Instructive . . . As to the Design of this Paper, it is to take in all Subjects whatsoever . . . the *Quicquid agunt Homines* is my Province, and *Homines* comprehends not only all Men but all *Women* too . . . the Conduct of the fair Sex will therefore come under my Consideration.
>
> (*Common Sense* 11 June 1737)

The *Spectator* 'of moral and facetious Memory' is the editor's avowed model: 'Whenever I take up the *Spectator*, I am ready every Minute to break out . . . *they have stolen all my fine Thoughts*' (*Common Sense* 11 June 1737). *Common Sense* is presented as an essay-series, like the venerable *Tatler* and

Spectator, on diverse topics, both political and literary: the editor borrows the *Tatler*'s motto '*Quicquid agunt homines*'. The paper is to appeal to women as well as to men: that is, to be entertaining, as well as instructive. Women, who are so difficult to comprehend and so inaccessible to the dictates of political common sense, may be attracted by the paper's variety and by the entertainment it promises. The advertisement for the forthcoming publication of *Common Sense* in volume form announces grandly that 'the Essays in this Collection . . . have had the good Fortune to make their Way into the Closet of the Ingenious, as well as to the Toilet of the Fair . . . they have been the Amusement of the Grave and the Gay' (11 March 1738). The editors 'cannot help bragging of the Pleasure it has given us to think, that the finest Eyes in *Great Britain* should be every Week employ'd in reading these Papers' and make the rather surprising claim that a future historian of the press, when he or she finds extant copies of *Common Sense*, will be most struck by the fact that 'this Work was chiefly patronized by the Women' (*ibid.*).

The pose of Spectatorial editor, writing on manners and morals, was common among political journalists who were attempting to avoid the accusations commonly levelled at newspapers that they were both mendacious and boring. In the *Jacobite's Journal*, Fielding supposes that 'few Readers will, I believe, imagine it Presumptuous in any Author to enter the Lists against . . . Newspapers; since his Talents must be very indifferent, indeed, if he is not capable of shining among a Set of such dark Planets' (1, 5 December 1747). The *Gray's Inn Journal* characterizes the foreign news section of newspapers as 'dull Letters from the *Hague*, and fictitious Advices from the *Swede* and *Turk*' and views the domestic news as even more dreary and irrelevant:

> I could never conceive, what Kind of Advantage can redound to a rational Creature, who can receive neither Instruction or Entertainment, in reading that Mr. *Such-a-one* died at his Country House, when perhaps the Gentleman is in perfect good Health; and if *Squire Rent-Roll* is arrived in Town with a grand Retinue, I apprehend it in no way interesting to any Man breathing, except his Taylor.
>
> (29 September 1753)

Political journals often tried to escape these accusations of dullness by including some of the topics and apparatus of the essay-periodical in their papers. *Applebee's Original Weekly Journal* combined foreign and domestic news with 'agreeable Letters on several Subjects' (12 March 1720). *Applebee's* 'Muses Gazette' became a regular feature in 1720. It contains theatre reviews, '*Secret History*' in the style of Delarivier Manley and tales of love and gallantry. *Mist's Weekly Journal* includes a number of humorous articles, such as the journal of the sailor Simon Fore-Castle (12, 2 March 1716) and a soothsayer's prediction whose elaborate framing device recalls the subtitles of Delarivier Manley's novels: it is said to be 'the Relation of an ancient Jew, as it was printed at Rome, and sent from the Hague to a merchant in London' (19, 20 April 1717). The title of the *Medley* suggests a wide variety of subjects. As the editor points out, 'I can properly make use of any matter whatsoever, whether invented by myself, or given, or lent' (2, 11 October 1710), although the paper does not live up to its promise of diversity, being mostly dedicated to attacks on the *Examiner*. Manley defends the *Examiner* against the charge of tedium by telling readers that 'my Business was to *Instruct*, I would not descend to *Divert*' and 'I did not so much as pretend to *Wit*' (no. 51). These claims are somewhat undercut, however, by her claim that 'among all the Men of Wit, who are in the Interest of the present Ministry, I know not one who hath escaped some Report or Suspicion of being the Author' (*ibid.*). The *Craftsman* adopts an *eidolon*, Caleb D'Anvers, with many Spectatorial characteristics. His age (66), 'ancient family' and independent fortune, inconspicuous manners and preference for a 'a retired life', education at Westminster and Oxford and 'natural inclination to the politer arts' all recall Bickerstaff and Mr Spectator (1, 5 December 1726). This presentation of Caleb D'Anvers as a disinterested, leisured gentleman serves to distance him from what Haywood describes scornfully as 'Hackneys for the Publishers of News-Papers, who, by their Writings, would fain influence . . . low and unthinking . . . Readers' (*Parrot* 4).

The pretence of genteel amateurism was adopted by a number of political writers. The editor of the *Old Whig; or, the Consistent Protestant* hopes that his paper will render ecclesiastical topics 'Enquiries for Gentlemen', rather than 'Controversies for Schoolmen and Divines' (160, 30 March 1738). The *Daily Gazetteer* taunts its rival the *Daily Post* with the accusation of being the work of a hack: 'The Publick must judge between you and I . . . who writes most like a Gentleman' (2, 1 July 1735), while even an exclusively political paper like the *Remembrancer* is keen to point out on its title page that its editor is 'George Cadwallader, *Gent.*'. This obsession with gentility is partly a reflection of the contemporary conviction that only someone with a stake in their country – in the form of landed property – can legitimately hold a political opinion, a conviction which justified the fact that only those with real estate could vote. This belief also affected the credibility of political journalists, who waste a great deal of ink bandying about mutual accusations of poverty. As Addison puts it in the *Freeholder*,

The Arguments of an Author lose a great deal of their Weight, when we are persuaded that he only writes for Argument's sake, and has no real

Concern in the Cause which he espouses. This is the Case of one, who draws his Pen in the Defence of Property, without having any; except, perhaps, in the Copy of a Libel, or a Ballad. One is apt to suspect, that the Passion for Liberty, which appears in a Grub-street Patriot, arises only from his Apprehensions of a Gaol.

(1, 23 December 1715)

The editor anticipates that his readers 'will conceive a Respect for the Author of this Paper, from the Title of it; since, he may be sure, I am so considerable a Man, that I cannot have less than forty Shillings a Year' (*Freeholder* 1).

For the editors of *Common Sense*, this pose of gentility requires a certain obligatory amount of what Swift, writing of Addison, described as 'fairsexing it' (1974: 2.482). This journalistic gallantry has dual implications. On the one hand, the issues which address topics of specifically feminine interest are not central to the periodical but allow the editor to display his or her essayistic virtuosity. The more trivial the writer's theme, the greater the skill involved in producing a witty and stylish essay: 'Writers, of such universal Talents, may draw something that is useful and entertaining from the most barren Subject in Nature. – The *Spectator* . . . has been very learned upon Dancing' (*Common Sense* 11 June 1737).[32]

On the other hand, to address oneself to the concerns of manners and morals, rather than the sphere of politics, was to discuss topics of special interest to women and in which women were especially important. To treat of such feminine topics – and hence attract a large female readership – was to tread in the hallowed footsteps of Addison and Steele, to write a paper of literary value, to handle topics of perennial interest, as well as of contemporary political relevance, and to ensure a long posterity in leather-bound volumes on library shelves. It was to distance oneself from starving hacks and paid hirelings and to aspire to a lofty political disinterestedness. A writer with interests wider than politics was also thought to have a clearer and more objective attitude towards contemporary political issues.

There is no evidence to suggest that *Common Sense* really had an especially large number of female readers. There are no letters signed with women's names in the first 66 issues of the periodical, and women are addressed specifically very infrequently. Indeed, the tone of the writers of the paper, particularly Lord Chesterfield's, is hardly the decorous and respectful tone of gentle rebuke adopted by Steele. Women are treated to some of the paper's most bitter satire. Sexual innuendo is never far from the surface. One writer tells us, with tongue-in-cheek smuttiness, that he wishes to emulate the *Spectator*'s treatment of women: 'As to the Fair Sex, he handled them from

Head to Foot; not a Part about a fine Lady was left untouch'd' (*Common Sense* 11 June 1737).

The editors frequently hint at the physical monstrosity and masculinity of intellectual women and suggest, with glee, that ugly women 'may more properly be call'd a Third Sex, than a Part of the Fair one' and that if they 'should endeavour to be honest good-humour'd Gentlemen, they may amuse themselves with Field Sports and a chearful Glass; and if they could get into Parliament, I should for my own Part, have no Objection to it' (*Common Sense* 26 February 1737). In a later issue, Chesterfield makes the impish suggestion that all the women who have played significant roles in history were in fact hermaphrodites:

> All the reputed Female Heroes of Antiquity were of this Epicene Species … the greatest Monarch that ever fill'd the *British* Throne … was Queen *Elizabeth*, of whose Sex we have abundant Reason to doubt … thus much is certain, that she thought it improper for her to marry a Man … I therefore require that those Women who insist upon going beyond the Bounds allotted to their Sex, should previously declare themselves in Form Hermaphrodites.
>
> (*Common Sense* 10 October 1737)

Coupled with this enjoyment of the freakishness of those women who overstep the bounds prescribed to femininity is a deeply cynical attitude towards the sexual and moral laxity of women in general. Addressing his essay ostensibly to the fine ladies who are forced to leave the delights of London for the *longuers* of a country existence, the author of another issue recommends the perusal of amatory fiction to pass the time agreeably. In the French romances a lady can find all the amusement she requires:

> If intruding Nature breaks in with warmer Images, she will … find … suitable and corresponding Passages. The pleasing Tumult of the Senses, the soft Annihilation, and the expiring Sighs of the dissolving happy Pair, may agreeably recall the Memory of certain Transactions of the foregoing Winter, or anticipate the expected Joys of the ensuing one.
>
> (*Common Sense* 9 September 1737)

Montagu was quick to accuse the writers of *Common Sense* of lewdness and indecency. She portrays herself as the champion of women, defending them against the unjust accusations of her rival writers:

> I have allways … profess'd my selfe a Freind thô I do not aspire to the character of an admirer of the Fair sex; and as such I am warm'd with

Indignation at the barbarous treatment they have receiv'd from ...
Common Sense.

(*Nonsense* 6)

For Montagu, defence of women is part of her heritage as a writer of a literary essay-periodical in the mode of Addison and Steele. She disingenuously
claims to be the author of 'short essays of Morality, without any touch of
Politicks' and, as such, will leave 'puns and ordures' to the lewd authors of
Common Sense (*Nonsense* 7). Her papers, instead of being addressed to amateur
politicians, have a wider appeal, she claims, to 'honest Men and modest
Women' (*Nonsense* 5), whilst the authors of *Common Sense* are only interested
in raising mirth 'at the expence of Decency or morality' (*Nonsense* 7).

For Montagu, contemporary journalism has become inextricably linked
with indecency. She reports with indignation in one issue the (probably fictitious) story of her attempts to get her paper published and claims that it
was rejected by both Court and Opposition printers as too politically
neutral. The Court printer suggests that, if the writer's taste lies not in politics, he or she might try a little pornography instead:

> If you are obstinately bent not to be read by the politicians ... you
> should try to please the Ladys and the fine Gentlemen ... I ... told
> him, my Intention was to write to ... Honest men and modest Women
> ... However ... the Tuesday following ... my Ingenious printer had
> thrown in a little Bawdy at the end of a Paragraph, that no way led to
> any Idea of that sort [see *Nonsense* 2] ... I ... immediately sent for the
> Fellow ... 'I'll assure you, Sir', (said he in a Heat) 'I have done all I
> could for the service of your paper; but 'tis a damned ministerial thing
> ... all the Bawdy in the Dunciad won't carry it off ... (pulling the
> Common Sense of December 31. out of his pocket) 'I'll engage this shall
> be read all over the Kingdom'.

(*Nonsense* 5)

In fact, the issue of *Common Sense* in question (31 December 1737) contains a satirical mock-obituary of Orator Henley's wife, which Montagu
attacks as a heartless insult to Henley's sincere grief. The issue is certainly in
poor taste, but it is not at all bawdy. Montagu is deliberately eliding the
distinction between pornography, political hack-work, libel and sensational-
ism. 'Honest men and modest women' are presented as almost synonymous
terms; modesty comes to stand in for political integrity and financial
independence. Montagu is not alone in her accusation that *Common Sense* is
both indecent and ungentlemanly, which she employs as roughly synonymous terms. The editor of the *Miscellany* also complains that the editor of

Common Sense, 'though reputed a *Gentleman,* an essential Part of whose Character is *Good-breeding*, has so superlatively offended by the *fulsome Lewdness* of his Images, that it is impossible for any one, not *wholly prostituted* . . . to be *pleased* with him' (269, 17 February 1738). Montagu admits that there may be a place for lewdness in political satire, but she warns the editors of *Common Sense* that only a great deal of wit and skill can carry it off and tells them to leave such methods to the petty hacks:

> Leave then to the miserable writers for Daily Bread the two pences that they collect by such little arts . . . old Hugh Spencer, first minister to Edward the second . . . confesses that he us'd to mix Bawdy in his politick conferences . . . But . . . he gave orders to all his Authors in pay never to talk Bawdy without mixing a great deal of Wit with it . . . If you . . . would make the same Resolution, I am persuaded that all your Future papers thô they might be very dull, would at least be very decent.
>
> (*Nonsense* 7)

The writer of a non-political essay-periodical is above such lewdness, Montagu implies. She takes Steele as her model of a chivalrous champion of women and an essayist whose papers could not raise a blush in a virgin cheek. Her predecessor frequently describes himself as a 'Knight-Errant to the Fair Sex',[33] placing his eloquent pen at their service, and Montagu also adopts this metaphor to describe her own stance:

> As I profess my selfe a protector of all the oppressed I shall look upon them as my peculiar care. I expect to be told, this is downright Quixotism . . . But however, I shall keep up to the character I have assum'd, of a Moralist, and shall use my endeavours to releive the distress'd.
>
> (*Nonsense* 6)

She wishes to revive the age of Steelian fair-sexing:

> that taste which was once universal when Sir Richard Steele entertain'd, before he appear'd attach'd to any party, but that of Virtue and good sense. That Gentleman had the Glory of pleasing without the assistance either of Lewdness or Malice.
>
> (*Nonsense* 7)

The indecency with which women are treated in *Common Sense*, Montagu appears to imply, is a measure of how far the editors have wandered from the Steelian ideal of objective, witty, decorous, moral and, indeed, apolitical, writing. By attacking them for their disrespectful treatment of women, she is also suggesting that they have no claims to the literary heritage of the *Tatler* and *Spectator* and are merely hacks, engaged in a paper war with periodicals of different political persuasions, fighting dirty with the weapons of bad language, scatological jokes ('ordures') and pornography. She suggests at one point that they keep a prostitute by them to help to provide ideas for their papers: 'A Girl that understands her trade ... will furnish new hints' (*Nonsense* 7), a suggestion especially apt as a literal reading of their political and literary prostitution, as they sell their pens to the Opposition. She herself aspires to the character of 'a Moralist', as Richard Steele was before he ventured into political journalism, 'before he appear'd attach'd to any Party'.

Montagu, the first woman known to have edited a political essay-paper, looks back wistfully to an imaginary golden age of journalism, before political rivalries. This enables her to suggest an alternative treatment of women: one which is chivalrous, but not gallant – rational, rather than based on erotic desire or admiration of beauty. She is 'a Freind' to women without 'aspiring to the Character of an Admirer', distancing herself loftily from politics as the domain of 'miserable writers for Daily Bread' (*Nonsense* 7). She suggests that instead of 'amuseing them with triffles', writers should regard women as 'capable of makeing ... the most Estimable Figures in Life' (*Nonsense* 6) and begins herself by abandoning flattery and attempting to re-educate her female readers in politics.

5   Inventor or Plagiarist?
Edward Cave and the first
magazine

The title under which Edward Cave chose to launch his new periodical in 1731, the *Gentleman's Magazine; or, Trader's Monthly Intelligencer*, itself announces Cave's self-consciousness about the status of his publication as an example of a new genre: he is the first to use the term *magazine*, which previously meant 'a place in fortified towns, where all sorts of stores are kept' (Chambers 1738) or, more generally, a 'storehouse' (Johnson 1755), to refer to a periodical. In addition, the title suggests both a preoccupation with class and a confusion of traditional class boundaries, which, for many historians and critics, characterized mid-eighteenth century English society.[34] In this chapter, I will be arguing that these two aspects of Cave's project are connected: the publication's format as a compilation and the new social and literary role assumed by Edward Cave, a role which rejects easy classification.

Debates over copyright, sparked by the Copyright Act of 1710, led in the early eighteenth century to a re-examination of the nature of authorship and in particular to the question of whether a translation, adaptation or abridgement could be considered an original work and fall under the protection of the act. There was no copyright on periodical material and, indeed, the *Gentleman's Magazine* was explicitly an anthology of articles 'collected chiefly from the Public Papers', as its title page announces.[35] Yet whilst Cave borrowed much of his material from other sources, he certainly considered himself the originator of a new form of publication, and he regarded the attempts of others to imitate his successful formula as piracy. Cave was not the author of the material in the *Gentleman's Magazine*, nor was he the *Magazine*'s editor (Samuel Johnson, John Hawkesworth and others filled that role), but on the other hand he was much more than simply a bookseller financing a project overseen by others. The *Gentleman's Magazine* was overwhelmingly associated with the individual Edward Cave. The periodical was well known to be his brain-child and his business venture, his invention and his obsession. Cave was widely believed to exercise personal control over every aspect of the *Magazine*.[36] He blurs the boundaries between the writer-editor and the bookseller-publisher, between literature and the commercial venture. In doing so, his publication raises important questions about the nature of literary property, legitimate and illegitimate borrowing and authorship in this period.

In one sense, Cave's publication was not designed to have a character of its own, but simply to reflect contemporary interests and concerns. Johnson defines a magazine as 'a miscellaneous Pamphlet' (1755), and the strength of the *Gentleman's Magazine* lay precisely in its heterogeneity: 'greater Variety than any Book of the Kind and Price', as its title page announces. Cave refused to associate his publication with one particular kind of material, political stance or target readership and, as a result, the *Magazine* combines many features that had previously been present only in separate periodicals. The strength of Cave's formula lay in its flexibility, as he himself stresses: 'Our Magazine ... must necessarily bear the stamp of the times, and the political, historical, and miscellaneous parts, dilate or contract in proportion to ... the reigning taste' (*Gentleman's Magazine* XVII, 1747, Preface).

Cave's most striking innovation in the *Gentleman's Magazine* lay in his insistence that it was not a vehicle for his own interests and opinions, but a selection of the writings of others. Journalistic plagiarism in itself was no novelty in 1731. Newspaper editors made a merit of having gathered their information from as wide a variety of printed sources as possible. The first daily paper, the *Daily Courant*, promises that 'at the beginning of each Article he will quote the Foreign Paper from whence 'tis taken', without adding any 'Comments or Conjectures of his own' (11 March 1702). Miscellanies such as the *Monthly Chronicle* printed summaries of the foreign and domestic news, drawn from the month's press, whilst the *Grub-Street Journal* reprinted passages from the daily newspapers, together with caustic commentary on their accuracy and prose style. Annuals like the *New Miscellany* reprinted letters and poems from other publications. In addition, ruthless, unacknowledged borrowing had increasingly come to characterize the periodical press. Cave, however, was the first journalist to make a positive feature of his lack of originality. In the 'Advertisement' carried in his first issue, he envisages the editorial task as one of simply abridging and collating. Newspapers

> are of late so multiply'd, as to render it impossible, unless a man makes it a business, to consult them all ... This consideration has induced several Gentlemen to promote a Monthly Collection, to treasure up, as in a *Magazine*, the most remarkable Pieces.
>
> (*Gentleman's Magazine* I, 1731, Preface)

Thus many of Cave's articles were plagiarized from other papers, usually with acknowledgement and without supplementary commentary. Cave's editor Samuel Johnson acknowledges this in 1741: '*All the share of Applause we now claim, is from a diligent . . . Endeavour to exhibit a well chosen Variety of Subjects*' (*Gentleman's Magazine* XI, 1741, Preface).

The editor depicted here is wedded to no particular political party, cause, academic or literary interest. The collective implied by the vague pronoun 'we' and the allusion to 'several Gentlemen' in the initial advertisement suggest a business enterprise rather than a writer. Their aim is to 'promote a Monthly Collection', to 'make it a business' to consult the current publications and to join in a '*diligent . . . Endeavour*'. The impersonal tone of such statements is mirrored by the paucity of our knowledge about the decision-making structures of the *Gentleman's Magazine*. It is difficult to identify any consistent principles of selection underlying Cave's heterogeneous collection of monthly articles. The character of the publication changed considerably during Cave's lifetime, and Albert Pailler has identified no fewer than five separate phases of the *Magazine* in the period 1731–54 (1975: 1.453–4). We do not know who was behind the *Magazine*'s changes in direction and focus. This obscurity is the result of a deliberate strategy on Cave's part and is heightened by the use of the sobriquet Sylvanus Urban to refer to the editor of the *Gentleman's Magazine*. The *Gentleman's* is always described as the work of Sylvanus Urban, but 'Urban' is not a pen-name adopted by a writer in the way that Isaac Bickerstaff is Richard Steele's pen-name in the *Tatler*. Urban is a composite figure: Cave himself uses the sobriquet, but so do Johnson, John Hawkesworth, John Nichols and other editors both during and after Cave's own lifetime. Urban is a personification of the *Magazine* itself, a kind of journalistic *genius loci*. It is often impossible to tell who is behind a particular contribution signed by 'Urban'. The vagueness is deliberate: it allows Cave as 'Urban' to assume the roles of bookseller, printer, editor and author simultaneously.

Cave's claims for his publication are based not so much on the high quality of the contents, but on the originality of the concept. He prides himself on the invention of a self-consciously new genre of periodical. The *Magazine*'s enormous success inspired numerous contemporaries to adopt the same formula. Pailler estimates that between 1732 and 1756 there were at least 18 London papers calling themselves *magazines*, although not all of them adopted Cave's format (1975: 1.492–3). Miscellanies, *museums* and *palladia* also attempted to muscle in on Cave's success. Cave regarded the term *magazine* as his trademark and was careful to distance his production from its myriad progeny. Johnson's poem 'Ad Urbanum' depicts an editor selflessly devoting himself to literature, in studied indifference to a host of mercenary parasites:

What mean the servile, imitating crew

. . . .

Ne'er seek; but still thy noble ends pursue,
Unconquer'd by the rabble's venal voice.
Still to the Muse thy studious mind apply,
Happy in temper as in industry.[37]

(*Gentleman's Magazine* VIII, May 1738)

The 'rabble' here refers to Urban's rival editors and publishers, a set of unscrupulous imitators ready to plagiarize his ideas. Plagiarism is portrayed as the hallmark of Grub Street.

This vision of Urban *contra mundum*, struggling for 'noble ends' against the world of commercial publishing, can be seen most clearly in the accounts of the rivalry between the *Gentleman's* and the *London Magazine*. Founded only a year after the *Gentleman's*, the *London* followed Cave's plan and layout very closely, as the account in the *Grub-Street Journal* admits:

The *London Magazine* . . . tho' he ridiculed his elder brother, yet . . . he endeavoured to establish his own credit and reputation . . . by passing for him. To this end . . . he called himself the *London Magazine; or, Gentleman's monthly intelligencer; containing greater variety, and more in quantity, than any monthly book extant*; only inverting his brother's words; and taking *Multum in parvo*, instead of *Plurimum in parvo* for his motto.

(168, 15 March 1733)

This social impostor, a younger brother attempting to pass as the first-born heir, is portrayed by Urban as the product of a vulgar, money-grabbing book trade. Johnson's 'An account of the life of the late Mr. Edward Cave' describes the *London* in similar terms as 'supported by a powerful association of booksellers, and circulated with all the art, and all the cunning of trade' (*Gentleman's Magazine* XIV, 1754: 57). The *London* was founded by a group of publishers and booksellers, including John Wilford, Thomas Cox, John Clarke and Thomas Astley (Sullivan 1983: 202–6). Urban is quick to dismiss the 'powerful association' of booksellers in a Popeian vision of Grub Street:

Printers and hungry Booksellers unite
Their little Wits to show one common Spite.
Dully they trace the Author's Various Quill
And feintly imitate his well-known Skill.

(*Gentleman's Magazine* II, 1732, Preface)

In this description, only the *Gentleman's Magazine* has the literary dignity of being the work of an 'Author'; the proprietors of the *London* are simply impoverished and 'hungry' garret-dwelling hacks, morally corrupted by 'the art, and . . . cunning of trade' and living off servile plagiarism. While Urban is portrayed as a single figure – an 'Author' – his parasites are legion, united in their 'common Spite'.

The *London* retaliates by focusing on the ironies of defending the originality of a concept which is itself dependent on plagiarism:

> Your assurance . . . is very extraordinary, in reflecting upon us for compiling a book from the public papers, in several of which we have a property, when you have not a share in any one of them; which makes your work little better than a downright piracy.
>
> (*Grub-Street Journal* 124, 18 May 1732)

Of course, the *London*'s editors had no legal basis for their 'property' in 'the public papers', as there was no copyright on periodical material. Anyone, Urban retorts, can own a share in a paper or reprint what he or she pleases:

> Our Right to set up and carry on a Monthly Book from old News-Papers having been ridiculously question'd; we take this Liberty to assert it, as the common Privilege of Authors, and if the Freedom of the Company of Stationers can add thereto . . . that is not wanting. The Objection – if a Man is not a Proprietor in the News-Papers, therefore he has no Right to abridge them – is too ridiculous to deserve a serious Answer; it being in any one's Power . . . who has a few spare Guineas, to qualify himself upon that Footing.
>
> (*Gentleman's Magazine* II, 1732: 732)

The contrast here between the proud dignity of the 'Freedom of the Company of Stationers' and the implicit snobbery in the claim that anyone with 'a few spare Guineas' can own a share in a periodical is striking. Cave attempts to have it both ways: both to portray himself as an author defending 'the common Privilege of Authors' against the mercenary practices of booksellers and to assert his right as a bookseller and a member of the Stationers Company to print what he pleases. He is asserting both a moral (author's) and a legal (stationer's) right to his copy. Both these rights are extremely dubious. Cave is evoking the Licensing Act, which granted members of the Stationers Company a monopoly on printing; the act had lapsed in 1695. It is perhaps for this reason that Cave falls back on the idea of his rights as an 'Author'.

The imprint of the *Gentleman's Magazine* states that it is 'printed for the AUTHOR', and when Cave writes a poem defending his *Magazine* and attacking the *London* he signs the poem as 'the Author and Printer of the *Gentleman's Magazine*' ('To Mr. Bavius on his Last Paper', *Grub-Street Journal* 169, 22 March 1733). In his *Dictionary* (1755), Johnson defines an *author* as 'he to whom anything owes its original' (sense 1) and 'he that effects or produces any thing' (sense 2) as well as the 'first writer of any thing; distinct from the *translator* or *compiler*' (sense 3) and 'a writer in general' (sense 4). Cave is certainly the author of the *Gentleman's* in the first of Johnson's senses, but he also profits from the unclear distinctions here between projecting a literary work, producing a compilation or creating original literary material. In his biography of Johnson, Sir John Hawkins uses the word *author* in a similarly general way, describing Johnson's own literary ambitions:

> He had entertained a resolution to depend for a livelihood upon what he should be able, either in the way of original composition, or translation, or in editing the works of celebrated authors, to procure by his studies, and, in short, to become an author by profession.
>
> (1787: 27)

The indeterminacy of the term *author* is reflected in contemporary debates about the copyright status of translations and abridgements. In 1715, in the case of *Burnet* v. *Chetwood*, when a group of booksellers argued that an English translation of a work previously published in Latin 'may in some respects be called a different book, and the translator may be said to be the author', the judge supported this claim, finding that a translation was 'not within the provision of the [1710 Copyright] act'.[38] Similarly, in the case *Giles* v. *Wilcox* in 1740, Lord Chancellor Hardwicke ruled that an abridgement could constitute a new work in the terms of the act (Rose 1993: 50).

Cave uses the term *author* to suggest that his *Magazine* is the lone upholder of literary values, battling against cabals of mercenary booksellers and printers. He often poses as a genteel, disinterested editor in contrast to his money-grubbing bookseller rivals. In the preface to the 1732 volume, we are told scornfully that one imitator was 'behind a Counter hatch'd', whilst Urban, by contrast, publishes his paper as a favour to the public, 'tho' small Emolument to him accrue'. The following year, the preface claims loftily that 'no views of Gain the *Editor* excite'. Cave was not alone in this pretence, of course. The editors of the *Grub-Street Journal* claim a similar distinction, reporting that their paper was successful despite being 'continually opposed and denigrated by the generality of Book-sellers, and their hackney authors' (*Memoirs of the Society of Grub-Street* 1737: 1.xi).

Urban returns to the issue of the plagiarism of his concept in the preface to the volume for 1738, which is split between a condemnation of the *London Magazine* and a defence against a recent attack on the *Gentleman's* in *Common Sense* (11 March 1738). In a vivid piece of conspiracy theory, the editors of the *London* are portrayed as a motley band of mercenary opportunists:

> *A Knot of enterprising Geniuses, and sagacious Inventors, assembled from all Parts of the Town, agreed ... to seize upon our whole Plan ... Some weak Objections were indeed made by one of them against the Design, as having an Air of Servility, Dishonesty and Piracy; but it was concluded that all these Imputations might be avoided by giving the Picture of St Paul's instead of St. John's Gate* [as a frontispiece].
>
> (*Gentleman's Magazine* VIII, 1738, Preface)

Stealing a rival's concept betrays a total disregard for business ethics and lack of literary and personal integrity. The phrase '*enterprising Geniuses, and sagacious Inventors, assembled from all Parts of the Town*' suggests not only booksellers and printers, but a far more heterogeneous and disreputable group of projectors, ready to involve themselves in any shady dealings which might generate capital. In their '*Servility, Dishonesty and Piracy*' and their silencing of the '*weak Objections*' of the only man among them with a conscience, they almost resemble a criminal fraternity.

If 'the execution of another man's design' is treacherous and base, the theft of individual examples of his or her writing is the prerogative of a gentleman and a scholar, and the victim should be flattered by his or her inclusion in the periodical. The editor of the *Gentleman's* answers the complaints of *Common Sense* (11 March 1738) that he has reprinted their essays without permission:

> *We are sorry that by inserting some of his Essays, we have filled the Head of this petty Writer with idle Chimeras of Applause, Laurels and Immortality ... Should any Mention be made of him or his Writings by Posterity, it will probably be in Words like these: 'In the* GENTLEMAN'S MAGAZINE *are still preserved some Essays under the specious and inviting Title of* Common Sense. *How Papers of so little Value came to be rescued from the common Lot of Dulness, we are ... unable to conceive, but imagine that personal Friendship prevailed with* URBAN *to admit them.*
>
> (*Gentleman's Magazine* VIII, 1738, Preface)

In this grand vision, the *Magazine*'s survey of the month's press has been transformed into a treasury of the best periodical writing of the age. *Common Sense* survives for posterity only by being reprinted in the *Magazine*, just as

Pope's dunces could never have attained lasting fame, had they not been immortalized in his mock-epic. This suggestion is voiced within the *Magazine* by a correspondent who tells Urban to disregard a 'rival's envy':

> The cunning Ape for this would urge your rage,
> To get himself recorded in your page.
> (The sons of *Bathos* are remember'd yet,
> Not for their own, but for the *Dunciad*'s wit.)
>   (*Gentleman's Magazine* VIII, March 1738: 156)

Urban is motivated not by 'rage', like Pope, however, but by charity and 'personal friendship' to assist a struggling, second-rate writer with a place in his *Magazine*. Inclusion in the *Magazine*'s pages is represented here as a reward conferred on a sycophant by a patron.

The role of a latter-day Maecenas was one in which Cave was very comfortable. He offered prizes for four poetry competitions in the *Magazine* in the 1730s (Pailler 1975: 1.163–214), and Samuel Johnson's own debut in the *Magazine* was the elegant Latin tribute 'Ad Urbanum' cited above, which, as Robert DeMaria has pointed out, alludes to a neo-Latin ode by the Polish writer Maciej Kazimierz Sarbiewski, addressed to Pope Urban, which earned Sarbiewski a Papal laureateship (1993: 46). In the same package in which he submitted his Latin poem, Johnson sent Cave a copy of *London* (1738), soliciting his aid – as a person noted for his 'generous encouragement of literature' – for the poem's author, a 'friend' for whom Johnson claims to be merely the agent. He flatters Cave with the suggestion that he will 'reward it in a manner different from the mercenary bookseller', implying that Cave is a patron, not a businessman, a kind of journalistic Pontiff (Johnson 1992: 1.14). Cave responded appropriately: he printed part of the poem in the May 1738 issue of the *Gentleman's*, as well as arranging its publication with Robert Dodsley.

When Cave was threatened with prosecution for reprinting extracts from Joseph Trapp's *Four Sermons* (1747), he chose to describe his pilfering as that of a scholar disseminating learning: 'We need not tell our Readers what useful Volumes the World must have been deprived of, had it been reckoned unjust . . . in the Compilers of . . . Literary Journals, to make Extracts from Books' (*Gentleman's Magazine* XVII, 1747, Preface). One of the most common contemporary arguments against awarding authors a perpetual copyright of their works was that it would, as John Locke argues, prove 'very unreasonable and injurious to learning' (qtd. Rose 1993: 33). Johnson prepared a kind of legal brief in defence of Cave's abridgements of Trapp, in which he argues that abridgements benefit readers 'by facilitating the attainment of knowledge, and by contracting arguments, relations, or descriptions into a narrow compass' (*Gentleman's Magazine* LVII, July 1787: 555–7). Although he acknowledges that an abridgement may damage the sale of the original, Johnson regards abridgements as not merely legitimate, but praiseworthy enterprises: 'A tedious volume may ... be lawfully abridged, because it is better that the proprietors should suffer some damage, than that the acquisition of knowledge should be obstructed with unnecessary difficulties'. As specific examples of the uses of abridgement, he cites the abridgement of the 44-volume *Transactions of the Royal Society* and books which provide 'general systems of sciences'. Clearly, Johnson chooses examples here that help to dignify Cave's own publication, but elsewhere he defends the necessity of abridgements that serve a less exalted purpose: the labours of the 'abridger, compiler and translator' help to convey important information to those incapable of appreciating the original work. Men whose 'eyes are offended by a glaring light ... will gladly contemplate an author in an humble imitation, as we look without pain upon the sun in the water' (*Rambler* 145).

Cave's publication had some of the same aims as grander projects like the *Transactions of the Royal Society*. Cave often presents the *Magazine* as a kind of historical reference work or encyclopaedia. He is not the first editor to do so: Daniel Defoe hopes that the collected volumes of his *Review* 'will compose a Compleat History of *France*' (19 February 1704). The *Gentleman's Magazine* also contains cross-references and an index, which 'will be extremely convenient for those who may have occasion to look for any Occurrence' (I, 1731: 508). Sylvanus Urban describes the *Magazine* as 'an exact and impartial history of the times' that 'will be consulted by the curious to the latest posterity' (*Gentleman's Magazine* XV, 1745, Preface) and prove, as a correspondent puts it, 'an authentick Collection for Historians to refer to' (*Gentleman's Magazine* II, April 1732, Verso of title page). In his monthly review of books, Cave accordingly ranges the *Magazine* under the heading 'History', rather than with other periodicals, which are registered as 'Miscellanies'.[39] The editors of the *London Magazine* were to claim a similar dignity for themselves: 'All transactions of a Month's standing are ... recorded in the Secretary of State's Office ... and all future Recitals of them, fall under the proper and only Denomination of History' (*London Magazine* II, May 1733). Any attempt to impose stamp duty on the monthly magazines, they write, 'might as well include *Josephus*, *Rapin's History* and *Baker's Chronicle*' (*ibid.*).[40] Many of Cave's rival publications also claim to provide encyclopaedic knowledge, as titles such as the *Universal Magazine of Knowledge and Pleasure* (1747–1815) suggest.

In the 1750s and 60s, the number of magazines became so great that collections began to appear that plagiarized at second hand, drawing their material exclusively from the magazines themselves: publications such as the

Magazine of Magazines (1750–1), *Grand Magazine of Magazines* (1758–9) and *Beauties of All the Magazines Selected* (1762–4). After 1746, in response to these collections, the *Gentleman's* began to shift focus. The reprinted articles from the month's press became less important, and more space was dedicated to original material and to readers' letters and contributions. At the same time, the debate about originality and plagiarism also changed tack as the *Gentleman's* increasingly accused other periodicals of plagiarizing its own articles, prompting a debate in the contemporary press over what constituted legitimate and illegitimate borrowing.

After 1746, the *Gentleman's* no longer contains defences of the *Magazine's* practice of printing abridgements from the month's press. Borrowing articles from other journals *per se* appears to have become a widely accepted practice: largely, perhaps, because of the precedent set by Cave himself. The important issue was now the question of whether or not such borrowings were acknowledged. The *Grub-Street Journal* succinctly defends 'Abbreviations of the daily News Papers':

> There is nothing of *Plagiarism* or *Pyracy* in it. For the former is a surreptitious taking Passages from an Author, without naming him; and the latter, printing another's Property to his Detriment. But neither can be charged upon a Work which constantly quotes the Author.
>
> (reprinted in *Gentleman's Magazine* IV, January 1734: 3)

In a similar vein, the editors of the *London Magazine* protest that they '*shall never . . . pretend to palm upon the World any* printed *Pamphlet, Poem, or Paper, by way of an* original Manuscript *of our own*' (IV, 1735, Preface). If they were to do such a thing intentionally, '*the Loss of all our Customers would be the least Resentment we could expect*' (*ibid.*).

In the 1740s and 50s, the *Gentleman's Magazine* attempts to woo readers with the boast that it contains more original pieces than any of its competitors. With so many rival magazines on offer, Cave is no longer able to market his publication on the basis of the originality and utility of its concept alone. He is still keen to emphasize the idea that the *Gentleman's Magazine* is an original and his competitors merely pale imitations: now, however, these rivals have shifted from copying the *Magazine's* plan to plagiarizing its contents. Urban claims:

> We have been so fortunate as to exhibit . . . many excellent productions. The merit of them is in some degree shewn, by their being every month carefully copy'd into various collections, tho', for the most part, without any acknowledgment of their obligation.
>
> (*Gentleman's Magazine* XIX, 1749, Preface)

From being a collection of the work of others, the *Magazine* has become a source of material. An ample supply of original material is, in fact, a prerequisite for a successful magazine, according to Urban, who writes with scorn of those whose magazines are simply scissors-and-paste operations. Such publications, we are told, are 'often the last effort of disappointed writers, whom the publick has rejected under every other appearance, and who hope, that in a Magazine the contributions of others will supply the defects of their own inability' (*Gentleman's Magazine* XXIV, 1754, Preface).[41] Other magazine editors also stress the originality of their material. Mrs Penelope Pry of the *Lady's Weekly Magazine* assures her readers that 'our Essays shall be all original' (1, 19 February 1747). Mrs Stanhope of the *Lady's Magazine; or, Polite Companion* boasts of 'having her essays copied over in almost every other periodical publication' (II.1, Preface).

The periodical press in the mid-eighteenth century presents the modern reader with a dizzying number of accusations and counter-accusations of plagiarism. Articles, letters and poems are printed and reprinted, with and without acknowledgement, sometimes with such frequency as to make it difficult to ascertain their original source. Tracking an article through its changes and abridgements can feel like taking part in a game of Chinese whispers. Periodical material is, by its nature, more difficult to copyright, as it is often anonymous or pseudonymous and frequently collaborative writing.

Contemporaries also often claim that the writing itself is not of a high enough quality to merit legal protection. The *Grub-Street Journal* is typical in its contention that '*no Man can assume to himself a Property by employing Persons to collect a Heap of trivial, ridiculous, and false Paragraphs of News, and then publishing them*' (210, 3 January 1734). Lord Camden comments in 1774 that copyright should, of course, not be extended to 'Scribblers for bread, who teize the Press with their wretched Productions, fourteen Years is too long a Privilege for their perishable Trash' (qtd. Rose 1993: 154). Copyright confers a kind of literary dignity, a stamp of respectability denied to periodical writing.

Magazine editing, in particular, was frequently regarded as a purely manual activity. For Johnson, the 'abridger, compiler and translator' are 'manufacturers of literature' (*Rambler* 145); the *London Magazine* refers scornfully to '*Dr. Urban, and his fellow* Handicraftsmen, *as they may properly be called, for the Head seems to have very little Share in any Thing they publish*' (VI, 1737, Preface); whilst the *Universal Spectator* derides those who '*collect, transcribe, abridge*, and raise *Magazines* from the Productions of others' and whose writings are 'entirely *Manufacture*; for they are the Works of the *Hand* more than the *Head*' (24 August 1734). Clearly, there can be no rights to intellectual property where there is a general belief that there has been no intellectual activity, where a production is seen as purely mechanical, manual labour. There are few acknowledgements that editing a periodical – selecting materials judiciously – could be a creative activity in itself. The correspondent who praises Urban for these skills is a rare exception: '*You have generally the good Fortune, it must be confessed, in sorting your Materials, to mix the* Useful *with the* Agreeable; *which, indeed, is* HORACE'*s Praise of a* good Writer *and belongs to you as a* Good Compiler' (*Gentleman's Magazine* IX, November 1739: 601).

The Copyright Act fixed the copyright of new material at 21 years and of existing material at 14 years: the same lengths of time as those specified for the patenting of inventions. As Rose and Zionkowski have shown, this led to interesting debates about the ways in which literary work differed from scientific invention (Rose 1993; Zionkowski 1992). Edward Cave, however, attempted to blur these distinctions. Denied the literary dignity of authorship, he sought the distinction of having added to the store of human knowledge by the invention of a new literary genre. Cave asks us to value his *Magazine* for its originality and success as a concept. By doing so, he added a significant new dimension to the eighteenth-century copyright debate and a new category of intellectual property.

In his *Biographia Britannica*, Andrew Kippis describes Cave as 'the inventor of a new species of publication, which may be considered as something of an epocha in the literary History of this Country' (1778: 3.315). However, most of Cave's contemporaries may well have been reluctant to allow him the prestige of an inventor. The status of current journalistic material is rarely discussed in mid-eighteenth century debates about copyright. This silence is an eloquent one. It is probable that many contemporaries ranked Cave among the 'the manufacturers of literature' whom Johnson describes as an 'order of men which deserves our kindness, though not our reverence' (*Rambler* 145). For most, he may have been merely a humble plagiarist.

However, with its enormous popularity, the *Gentleman's Magazine* exerted a significant influence on the course of subsequent literary history. Unable to use copyright legislation to protect original pieces – at least partly because of Cave's own pioneering use of extensive plagiarism in the *Gentleman's* – magazine editors in the decades after Cave's death increasingly relied on the anonymous unpaid contributions of their readers, contributions often so bad that they justify Johnson's acerbic remark that 'no man but a blockhead ever wrote, except for money' (Boswell 1964–71: 3.19). The lack of copyright protection for current journals in the eighteenth century may also have helped to create the widening gulf between the poetry of the Romantic period, with its premium on originality, and journalistic writing. Whilst journalism was later awarded copyright protection, it was never to achieve the same literary cachet as fiction, poetry and drama. To return to the question posed by the title of this chapter: was Cave a plagiarist or an inventor? He was both. He was the inventor of a new kind of plagiarism and, ironically, his novel approach helped to ensure that journalism was popularly associated with second-hand material and thought to be lacking in fundamental originality and, within Cave's lifetime at least, unworthy of the dignity of copyright protection.

6 Polite, genteel, elegant

The *Female Spectator* and the editor's pretensions to gentility

Eliza Haywood's periodical the *Female Spectator* opens with the statement that 'it is very much, by the Choice we make of Subjects for our Entertainment, that the refin'd Taste distinguishes itself from the vulgar and more gross' (bk I: 2.17).[42] In this chapter, I will explore ideas of social and cultural refinement in Haywood's periodical. Critics since Jürgen Habermas have associated the periodical with middle class culture, regarding it as a public forum for bourgeois debate (see Clery 1991). In the *Female Spectator*, however, Haywood aligns her periodical with a far more socially exclusive group, which she variously defines as polite, leisured, genteel, elegant, tasteful and 'gay'. This chapter focuses on the ways in which a preoccupation with social class influences Eliza Haywood's literary strategies within the *Female Spectator*: in her choice of persona, her depiction of her readership and her selection of material. The chapter is divided into three sections. In 'A polite editor', I examine Haywood's use of the fiction of the editor as a genteel lady of leisure who does not write for profit. In 'Genteel readers', I turn to Haywood's depiction of her readership. Finally, in 'Elegant entertainments', I focus on Haywood's prescriptions for women's leisure pursuits and education, which are characterized by an acute concern with social exclusivity.

A polite editor

At first glance, the title of Eliza Haywood's *Female Spectator* appears to allude to its editor's gender, but not her social class. It suggests that the periodical will be a female version of Addison and Steele's earlier paper, a *Spectator* written by a woman writer or one designed for women readers. The title is deceptive, since Haywood's heterogeneous monthly publication and the concise essays of her male namesakes have little in common, either structurally or thematically. Despite these dissimilarities, Haywood is keen to stake her claim to an Addisonian inheritance. Thirty years after the demise of the original *Spectator*, she alludes loftily to her 'learned Brother of ever precious Memory' (bk I: 2.17), as though nothing significant had been published in the interim.

Haywood follows Addison and Steele's example by introducing the reader to the editor and her associates in the opening number of her periodical. She promises 'in imitation of my learned Brother [Mr Spectator]' to 'give some Account of what I am, and those concerned with me in this Undertaking' (*ibid.*). The reader, the Female Spectator suggests, would only wish to read a paper written by an editor who would be respectable enough to qualify as a potential acquaintance. She declares, 'I, for my own part, love to get as well acquainted as I can with an Author, before I run the risque of losing my Time in perusing his Work' (*ibid.*). Of course, since the *Female Spectator* was published anonymously, the reader is not made acquainted with 'an Author', but with a fictitious persona. The polite introduction of editor to reader serves to establish the playful pretence of mutual gentility which Haywood will maintain throughout the publication.

Haywood's editor is a reformed coquette who has known high society and plans to share her insider knowledge of the social elite with her readership. A colourful past as a social butterfly is her main qualification for writing:

> I have run through as many Scenes of Vanity and Folly as the greatest Coquet of them all . . . My Life, for some Years, was a continual Round of what I then called Pleasure, and my whole Time engross'd by a Hurry of promiscuous Diversions. . . . With this Experience, added to a Genius tolerably extensive, and an Education more liberal than is ordinarily allowed to Persons of my Sex, I flatter'd myself that it might be in my Power to be in some measure both useful and entertaining to the Publick.
>
> (bk I: 2.17–18)

Haywood makes the incongruous transition from socialite to journalist appear natural and inevitable. Too old to shine in society, the editor is forced to seek attention and admiration through her writing. She has turned to journalism for amusement, not for gain. Ironically, the same vices and follies against which the editor was repeatedly to warn her female readers, particularly an inordinate love of 'Dress, Equipage and Flattery', have helped to qualify her for authorship: she is well acquainted with both the pleasures and the dangers of affluent society. The emphasis here is not on the Female Spectator's folly, but on the breadth of her experience and her corresponding broad-mindedness. Her knowledge of company has been 'general' and not selective, her intelligence is 'tolerably extensive', her education has been 'more liberal than is ordinarily allowed to Persons of my Sex', and her giddy career has provided her with 'Knowledge of many Occurences'. The editor's youthful flightiness accounts for the fact that she is acquainted with most strata of society, even though she herself is of a genteel background. Haywood adopts a similar persona in the *Parrot* (1746), whose editor has 'experienced almost as frequent Vicissitudes of Fortune as there are to be found in the Climate, having been . . . in no less than fifty-five Families of vastly different Ranks and Dispositions' (no. 1). Like the Female Spectator, the Parrot is prepared to 'as freely lay open my Errors, as I am willing to publish my Perfections' (*ibid.*), since these 'Errors' – talkativeness and inquisitiveness – are what qualify him for authorship.

The Female Spectator describes herself as having been 'caught up in a Hurry of promiscuous Diversions', referring to balls, routs, masquerades and other amusements fashionable with the leisured classes. This promiscuity also, however, reflects the myriad and rapid transitions from one topic to another within the periodical itself. Varied entertainments or 'promiscuous Diversions' form the subject matter of the eighteenth-century periodical *per se*, its vaunted *multum in parvo* (many things in a small space) or what one correspondent refers to as 'your agreeable Miscellany of beneficial and entertaining Topics' (bk XX: 3.275). In John Hill's contemporary 'Inspector' papers, the editor promises to 'search . . . Routs and Assemblies . . . Masquerades and Ridottoes . . . Operas and . . . Playhouses', in order to 'bring Entertainment from the Parties of the Great to People less exalted above the common Level of Mankind' (*London Daily Advertiser* 1, 1751). In a similar fashion, the *Female Spectator* provides vicarious thrills by allowing its readers a taste of 'promiscuous Diversions' at second hand.

What little we learn about the editor's background in the course of the periodical confirms her gentility: she claims an acquaintance with families 'of Condition and Figure' (bk XI: 2.385), fine ladies (bk XIII: 3.5), the daughter of 'a dignified Clergyman' (bk XXIV: 3.412) and with the former prime minister Robert Harley (bk XI: 2.400). The Female Spectator demonstrates an easy familiarity with the trappings of gentility, describing with confidence the library holdings of 'some of the ancient Nobility and Gentry of this Kingdom' (bk XII: 2.435) and alluding to her possession of servants (bk II: 2.54), expensive imported 'Ornaments of Dress and Furniture' (bk XV: 3.98) and a greenhouse, complete with a gardener to tend it (bk XIX: 3.247). When the correspondent John Careful describes the editor as 'a Person who knows the World perfectly well' (bk VIII: 2.280), he is referring both to her colourful past and to her experience of high life, or, as the editors of the contemporary periodical the *World* put it, 'that part of the human species which calls itself the WORLD' (1, 4 January 1753).

By choosing a genteel persona, Haywood was following a well-established journalistic tradition: one which was particularly prescriptive for women.

Whilst some male editors, such as Oliver Goldsmith, could be defiantly frank about their commercial motivations for writing (see Chapter 10), those who wrote under female pseudonyms almost universally adopt a pose of gentility. The male hack was a rather suspect figure, but the female hack was beyond the bounds of propriety. When Goldsmith writes as a male journalist, he poses as an 'Indigent Philosopher', but the contemporary editor of the *Lady's Magazine* (1759–63), who has sometimes been identified with Goldsmith, writing in a female guise, adopts the sobriquet of the Hon. Mrs Caroline Stanhope.[43] Phrases like 'the prostitution of talents' carried all-too-literal connotations when used to describe women journalists. Instead, female editors claimed to write out of vanity, coquetry and the desire to please. Women editors denied the pursuit of profits, but still represented writing as a para-sexual activity: as flirtation, rather than prostitution. The editor of the *Lady's Magazine* tells her readers, 'She is actuated by a more noble principle [than profit], the love of applause, from which she has felt the most pleasing sensations' (II.1, 1760).

The *Female Spectator* claims to be the work not of an individual, but of a club. We are introduced to the Female Spectator's 'club' in the first issue of the periodical: the witty and genteel wife Mira; 'a Widow of Quality, who ... continues to make one in all the modish Diversions'; and Euphrosine, 'the Daughter of a wealthy Merchant' (bk I: 2.19). Haywood's club may be modelled on Addison and Steele's club in the *Spectator*, but its members are far less individualized and differentiated than the memorable eccentrics Will Honeychurch, Sir Roger de Coverley *et al*. They represent different aspects of womanhood – wife, widow, maid and spinster[44] – as well as both the wealthy mercantile classes and the fashionable denizens of the West End (Figure 6.1).

The club fiction serves an important purpose. It bridges the gap between writing as an organized, professional activity and the civilized conversation of genteel society, establishing a cosy pretence of social, rather than financial, relationships, both among editors and between editors and readers. The Female Spectator repeatedly refers to her club as a 'society'. The trope of sociability originates with the *Tatler*, whose editor Isaac Bickerstaff wishes to amend what he suggestively refers to as 'the Conversation-Part of our Lives' (*Tatler* 56). Editorial clubs were to remain popular. The editors of the *Court Magazine* are characteristic. They are described as 'a Society of Gentlemen'. In playful acknowledgement of the convention of editorial affluence, the writers insist 'we are all gentlemen ... and every day in the week salutes us with ... a clean shirt' (I [for 1761], 1763, Preface). The closing issue of Haywood's *Female Spectator* promises a continuation by a club composed of men and women (bk XXIV: 3.423).

The female equivalent of the gentleman's club night is the lady's visiting

Figure 6.1 The *Female Spectator* club.

day. The title of the *Female Spectator* recalls the *Female Tatler* (1709–10), which was set in the editor Mrs Crackenthorpe's drawing room amid the gossip of guests at her visiting day and then at the visiting days of an elegant 'Society of Ladies'. Haywood employs a similar device in her pamphlet *The Tea-Table* (1725), whose subtitle announces its elevated social context: 'A Conversation between some Polite Persons of both Sexes, at a LADY'S VISITING DAY' (Haywood 2000b). Like Mrs Crackenthorpe, the central figure, Amiana, occupies a position in high society: she is 'always encompass'd with a Crowd of the great World' (Haywood 2000b: 71). As women, Mrs Crackenthorpe and Amiana cannot make forays into London coffee-houses to eavesdrop on the capital's inhabitants. Instead, they invite society to come to their own well-appointed drawing rooms. They therefore interact with a much more restricted social group than Isaac Bickerstaff and Mr Spectator: their observations and remarks are drawn from an exclusive circle of 'Persons of a very elegant Taste' (Haywood 2000b: 3). Amiana's area of expertise is therefore high-society gossip. Published in the same year as Haywood's infamous *roman à clef Memoirs of a Certain Island* (1725), the pamphlet promises its readers similar fare: 'Where have the Curious an Opportunity of informing themselves of the Intrigues of the Town, like that they enjoy over a TEA-TABLE, on a Lady's *Visiting-Day*? (Haywood 2000b: 3).

Haywood tantalizingly suggests, in the opening issue of the *Female Spectator*, that she will provide her readers with scandal from political and social high life. She invites them to read the *Female Spectator* as a periodical *à clef* by ironically cautioning them *not* 'to make what they call a Key to these Lucubrations' (bk I: 2.20). By choosing a genteel editor-persona, Haywood suggests that she has first-hand knowledge of the upper echelons of society, which she will be able to share with her readers. When the correspondent Curioso Politico rebukes the editor in a later issue for not having elucidated the 'Mysteries of the *Alcove*, the *Cabinet*, or *Field*' (bk VII: 2.295), he does so in class terms. He rebukes her with being 'an idle, prating, gossiping old Woman, fit only to tell long Stories by the Fire-side' (bk VII: 2.293), presenting an image very different from that of the elegant hostesses Amiana and Mrs Crackenthorpe. He dismisses her 'Lucubrations' as only suitable for an unsophisticated country readership: 'They are fit Presents for Country Parsons to make to their young Parishioners; – to be read in Boarding-Schools, and recommended as Maxims for the well regulating private Life; but are no way fit for the polite Coffee-Houses' (bk VIII: 2.294).

As Curioso Politico's remarks suggest, for contemporaries the type of material that a periodical contained, its target readership and the social class of its editor were closely connected. The figure of Haywood's editor remains underdeveloped within the periodical. The Female Spectator is neither an idiosyncratic, loveable and eccentric character, offering a refreshing new perspective on events, nor a character in an elaborate frame narrative chart-ing the editor's adventures in novelistic fashion (by contrast with Mary Sin-gleton of the *Old Maid*, for example). Instead, Haywood's adoption of the persona serves primarily to establish the periodical's tone and subject matter as one suitable to a genteel author. The pretence of gentility was more ubiq-uitous in journalism than in any other literary form in this period – prob-ably because journalism was a more disreputable genre than any other, more likely to be associated with the meretricious trash produced by Grub Street hacks than with the august tones of Addison and Steele. To write in the persona of a genteel woman was to raise the expectation that the periodical's readership would be equally genteel. This suggestion of mutual gentility must have been particularly flattering to Haywood's readers.

Genteel readers

Little is known about the actual readership of Haywood's periodical. At a cost of between 1 and 3s., Haywood's novels were beyond the price range of those 'of scanty means' (Blouch 2000b: 308). Haywood's former lover the poet Richard Savage describes Haywood's novels as designed to 'teach young Heiresses the Art of running away with Fortune-hunters and scandalising Persons of the highest Worth and Distinction' (qtd. Whicher 1915: 125–6). Young heiresses and persons of 'Worth and Distinction' – however scandal-ized – are the subjects of many of the *Female Spectator*'s tales and figure largely in the editor's depictions of her audience.

These descriptions of Haywood's readership are, at best, conjectural, and they refer in any case to Haywood's novels, not her journalism. However, since the *Female Spectator* retailed at 1s. per book – making a total cost for the 24 books of £1 4s – it was more expensive than many other periodicals and must have been unaffordable to many. Furthermore, Haywood distances the *Female Spectator* from other periodicals: referring to its issues as 'Books' and her readers as 'Subscribers'. By calling her readers 'Subscribers', she links the periodical with large-scale, lavish publications boasting a substan-tial aristocratic readership. There is no external evidence to suggest that the *Female Spectator* was actually published by subscription. However, by bor-rowing her title from the century's most famous periodical, yet neither num-bering nor dating her issues, but instead referring to them as books, Haywood may be trying to have it both ways. She is simultaneously exploit-ing the literary cachet of writing in the genteel tradition of Addison and Steele and dissociating herself from other journalists.

In order to understand Haywood's preoccupation with gentility more clearly, we need to turn to the representations of her readership in the *Female Spectator*. The most explicit depictions of the periodical's audience are the descriptions of its correspondents. Although it is impossible to know whether this correspondence is real or fictional, the readers' letters serve an important purpose within the periodical by bridging the gap between literary professionalism and genteel amateurism. They suggest that the periodical is a forum for the polite and civilized to communicate with each other. The Female Spectator claims in book XVIII that she would have ended the periodical after three volumes, had it not been for her eminent correspondents:

> That we have changed our Minds, and continue the *Spectatorial* Function yet a little longer, is owing to some Hints we have lately received from Persons of the most distinguished Capacities, on Subjects universally interesting ... who assure us, they would transmit their Sentiments to the World by no other Canal.
>
> (bk XVIII: 3.207)

Whether real or fictitious, Haywood's correspondents are overwhelmingly genteel. Most date their letters either from fashionable West End addresses – Cavendish Square, Bedford Row, St. James's Street, Hanover Square, Pall Mall and Haymarket – or from the more upmarket coffee-houses: Giles's, the Bedford and White's Chocolate House.[45] The *Female Spectator* prints a number of contributions from those in high life. The correspondent Antiquarius, for example, sends in a series of (spurious) letters between Caesar and Livia Drusilla, which have been given to him by 'a certain noble Earl' (bk XX: 3.275).[46] The rich nobleman Veritatus flatteringly rebukes the editor for deciding to abandon her publication 'just at the Time its Reputation is established; and when not only myself, but a great many others had resolved to send you something to employ it' (bk XXIV: 3.406). By the time the Female Spectator ends her publication, it has become the chosen vehicle for the contributions of people of learning, affluence and high society, thus establishing the publication's impeccable social and intellectual credentials.

In her opening number, the Female Spectator claims that, in writing the periodical, 'my Ambition was to be as universally read as possible' (bk I: 2.18). At first glance, the readership she envisages does appear to be broad: it includes men and women, inhabitants of the City and the West End and urban and rural readers. Almost all of them, however, share a certain gentility. The periodical's audience includes 'modish fine ladies' (bk XX: 3.256), 'readers of a polite Taste' (bk XX: 3.257) and people 'who shine in what they call High-Life' (bk XXIV: 3.394). When the editor advises her female readers to bear their husbands' infidelities with patience she offers the somewhat dubious consolation that 'few Men of any Condition are gross in their Amours' (bk X: 2.348), a remark which assumes that her readers' husbands are men 'of Condition'.

In the final number of the *Female Spectator*, Haywood reflects on the nature and aims of her periodical. She acknowledges that she has intentionally disappointed her readers' expectations of the publication:

> Many of the Subscribers to this Undertaking, I am told, complain that I have deviated from the entertaining Method I set out with at first – That since the Second or Third Book I have become more serious. – That I moralise too much, and that I give them too few Tales.
>
> (bk XXIV: 3.411)

She explains that she hoped to lure her audience with 'such Things as I knew would please them: Tales, and little Stories to which every one might flatter themselves with being able to find a Key' and only gradually reveal her moral purpose, in order to attract a readership of 'the Gay and Unreflecting, who are indeed those for whom this Work was chiefly intended, as standing in most need of it' (bk XXIV: 3.412). The phrase 'Gay and Unreflecting' implies both a moral condition and a class status. Her readers are able to be 'Unreflecting' because they are neither burdened by financial worries nor obliged to earn their own livelihoods. They are 'Gay' because they participate in the diversions considered appropriate to their rank. To reach this audience, the Female Spectator has to disguise her moral purpose. As Mira reminds the editor, 'People, especially those of Condition, are more easily *laughed out* of their Follies than *reasoned out* of them' (bk XIII: 3.34). When the Female Spectator refers to her time as 'this laughing, hoydening, careless Age' (bk XXIV: 3.410) and fears 'growing too grave for the Generality of my Readers' (bk XIX: 3.233), she is alluding not just to her readers' taste in literature but also to their class.

For Haywood, the upper classes are an important audience not only because of their perceived need of moral guidance, but also because of their influence over the behaviour of others: 'As all Modes, whether good or evil, are originally form'd by the great World, and gradually descend to their Inferiors, *there* must the Rectification begin, if we would hope to see any Amendment' (bk XII: 2.422). The editor is sharply critical of the imitation of aristocratic manners. In this, she follows the example of Addison and Steele, whose aim in the *Tatler* was 'to attack prevailing and fashionable Vices' (*Tatler* 271), although she expresses her concerns in a tone of more extreme disapproval. The Female Spectator cautions that 'whatever is done by Persons of Quality presently becomes the Mode, which every one is ambitious of apeing let it suit ever so ill with their Circumstances' (bk V: 2.157). Combating the pernicious influence of fashionable great ones lies at the heart of the *Female Spectator*'s moral enterprise.

The Female Spectator attempts to improve her readers' morals by making her own publication fashionable. Her correspondent S.S.S. claims that the *Female Spectator* could make even Bible reading into a modish occupation. The periodical, he tells us, is 'read with Pleasure by several fine Gentlemen and Ladies, who would be ashamed to be seen with a Bible in their Hands' (bk XXIV: 3.393). If the editor were to recommend the book, they would soon be convinced that the Bible is full of 'such beautiful Compliments, such elegant Address, and such high Strokes of Politeness, as are not to be outdone in the most refined and accomplished Circles of Conversation' (*ibid.*).

The *Female Spectator*'s appeal to women readers was an integral part of its status as a fashionable periodical. In eighteenth-century periodicals, addressing a female readership and including topics considered particularly appropriate for women was considered a sign of literary and social gentility. Kathryn Shevelow has noted that the expression 'leisured woman' is 'almost . . . a tautology' in contemporary journalism (1989: 55). The *Lady's Museum*, for example, describes its female readers as 'undisturbed by the affairs of business; unburthened with . . . political entanglements' (*Lady's Museum* 1: II.129).

Almost nothing is known about the gender composition of the *Female Spectator*'s actual contemporary readership. Whether or not the *Female Spectator*'s audience was largely female, however, the editor frequently addresses her remarks to 'the Female Subscribers and Encouragers of this Undertaking' (bk XVII: 3.175). She promises the correspondent Philoclites that she will 'set [his letter] before the Ladies at the very first Opportunity' (bk XVIII: 3.208). She tells her readers that it is 'the Ladies (for whom I must confess myself the most concerned)' (bk XII: 2.414), using a term that neatly combines class and gender.

The Female Spectator's conception of her readership as female serves to distance her publication from contemporary newspapers. When the correspondent Curioso Politico writes in to complain that the periodical does not contain enough politics, the editor replies tartly, 'I never proposed . . . that these Lucubrations should be devoted merely to the Use of News-Mongers: — A Change-Broker might, I think, have as much Cause to resent my taking no Notice of the Rise or Fall of Stocks' (bk VIII: 2.295). The Female Spectator associates political coverage with disreputable 'News-Mongers' and mercenary change-brokers: with the grubby male world of professional politics and finance. While newspaper readers are associated here with tradesmen and stockjobbers, newspaper writers are portrayed as impecunious hacks. A letter from L.D. defends newspapers on the grounds that they 'put Bread into Mouths which otherwise would want it. – Many a wretched Author must starve in his Garret if Extracts of pretended Letters from Abroad did not support him' (bk XXIII: 3.355). The *Gray's Inn Journal* offers a further reason for the insalubrious reputation of newspapers: they usually carried an advertising section, absent from Haywood's publication, with puffs for patent medicines, especially those that treated syphilis. Charles Ranger expresses a reluctance to 'hand up Advertisements to a Gentleman's Wife or Daughter, which are only fit for an Hospital or a Brothel' (*Gray's Inn Journal* 29 September 1753).

When Haywood does introduce political debate into her periodical, it is in a feminized and gentrified form. In response to Curioso Politico's attack in book VIII, book IX features a debate on Great Britain's relationship with Hanover. The piece is contributed by the correspondent A.B., who writes from the fashionable address of St. James's Street and claims to have overheard the debate 'at a polite Assembly, compos'd chiefly of Ladies' (bk IX: 2.301), at which the behaviour of debaters and audience alike was impeccable. The topic gave the ladies 'an Opportunity of exerting, in a very great Degree, that Good Sense and Eloquence they were both possess'd of', while 'the rest of the Company took too much Pleasure in hearing them, to offer any Interruption, by taking the Part either of the one or the other' (bk IX: 2.302). Here, the *Female Spectator* introduces an alternative to the male genre of the newspaper – a mercenary, commercial publishing enterprise – in the form of an assembly of ladies, characterized by social exclusivity and good manners. The debate itself is couched in class terms: England is described as 'a Woman of an illustrious and ancient Descent, beautiful in her Person, unblemish'd in her Honour, and Heiress of immense Wealth', while Hanover is 'a little Mistress he [the King] had before enjoyed' (bk IX: 2.312).

Elegant entertainments

The activities of the political debating society largely made up of women reported by A.B. provide one model of an ideal activity for genteel women. In this final section, I'd like to turn to the leisure pursuits that the *Female Spectator* recommends to its female readership. The periodical comments extensively on fashionable amusements such as Ranelagh, Vauxhall, masquerades, operas, gambling and private parties. It also offers a model for a system of female education. These projects are intricately linked: the editor, together with her correspondent Philenia, advocates combining pedagogy with diversion. Haywood not only addresses her readership as genteel, but also provides a model for genteel behaviour. I will end by looking at the ways in which the periodical itself offers an education in miniature to its female readers.

Book I of the *Female Spectator* is full of dire warnings against the dangers of frequenting pleasure gardens and masquerades. The Female Spectator relates, for example, the cautionary tale of Flavia who attracts the attention of a pimp on a visit to Vauxhall in the company of some female friends and is later exposed to the machinations of the vicious nobleman Rinaldo (bk I: 2.45–51). Haywood's interest in this subject probably reflects the increasing number of pleasure gardens and open-air entertainments available in mid-century. Vauxhall Gardens enjoyed a revived popularity after extensive restoration work in 1737; Marylebone Gardens were opened to the public in 1738; Ephraim Evans erected his open-air orchestra in Cuper's Gardens in Lambeth in 1740; and the famous Rotunda at Ranelagh Gardens was erected by William Jones in 1741 (see Sands 1987 and Wroth and Wroth 1979).

Haywood is at pains to point out that it is the commercial character of these entertainments – not the pursuits themselves – that renders them dangerous. The Female Spectator assures us that there is no harm in those masquerades held by 'some great Families' at their country retreats for the benefit of themselves and 'a select Company' (bk I: 2.33). What the editor deplores are 'mercenary Entertainments' where 'the most abandon'd Rake, or low-bred Fellow, who has wherewithal to purchase a Ticket, may take the Liberty of uttering the grossest Things in the chastest Ear' and where respectable women are forced into proximity with prostitutes. 'I wonder', she exclaims, 'Ladies can reflect what Creatures of their own Sex they vouchsafe to blend with in these promiscuous Assemblies, without blushing to Death' (*ibid.*).

Most of the visitors at Vauxhall and Ranelagh, the editor tells us, are motivated primarily by 'the Vanity every one has of joining Company, as it were, with their Superiors', the wish to boast of 'the Notice taken of them by such a Lord, or such a great Lady' and 'to descant upon their Dresses, their Behaviour, and pretend to discover who likes who' (bk V: 2.157). By taking part in these entertainments, the nobility make themselves the object of gossip and slander, spread by those 'by whom it is unbecoming of their Characters even to be mention'd' (bk V: 2.168). These social melting pots are particularly dangerous for women, for whom class and sexual reputation are intricately connected. The men at Ranelagh, the editor warns, 'look upon all those of our Sex, who appear too much at these public Places as setting themselves up for Sale, and, therefore, taking the Priviledge of Buyers, measure us with their Eyes from Head to Foot' (bk V: 2.171).

While the editor highlights the dangers of socially indiscriminate gatherings, she is anxious to ensure that young women have access to leisure pursuits suitable to their social rank. The cautionary tales of young women seduced at Ranelagh and Vauxhall are outnumbered in the periodical by stories of the dangers of denying women the pleasures their class status and wealth entitle them to. The expense of such diversions is not mentioned in the *Female Spectator*, nor is there any suggestion that men who accompany their wives or daughters to public amusements are losing valuable time in an office or behind a counter. The Female Spectator represents these diversions as not only harmless, but necessary. Patricia Meyer Spacks has argued that 'the governing idea of the *Female Spectator* is the urgency of *experience* for middle-class women' (1999: xiii). While I would take issue with Spacks's stress on the middle class here, the phrase 'urgency of *experience*' evocatively describes Haywood's preoccupation with the perils facing spirited young aristocratic women who are denied appropriate access to the society of their peers.

In Haywood's later periodical the *Young Lady* (1756), the editor censures those parents who 'debar them [their daughters] from a free conversation with the polite world' (6, 10 February 1756). In the *Female Spectator*, tales of the ill effects of such seclusion abound. The correspondent Sarah Oldfashion decides to cure her niece Biddy of her passion for Ranelagh by sending her to live with a remote aunt in Cornwall, where she is set the singularly inappropriate task of embroidering a hanging. Biddy rebels against this regime by marrying her aunt's groom (bk xv: 3.100). An even worse catastrophe ensues when Manilius refuses his wife, Sabina, permission to attend assemblies, card parties and 'Public Diversions' (bk x: 2.351). Sabina's resentment of this treatment makes her vulnerable to the attentions of a lover, with whom she elopes to France. The Female Spectator defends Sabina's conduct as the inevitable result of her husband's prohibitions, remarking 'it is Pity a Mind of itself not disposed to ill, should receive any Provocations to be so' (bk x: 2.354).

When Sarah Oldfashion asks the Female Spectator for advice on curing Biddy of her addiction to Ranelagh, the editor suggests that the best remedy for young ladies 'too much bigotted to any one Pleasure' would be to send them to 'that polite Country', France (bk v: 2.167). French aristocratic society is held up as a model because it is far more socially exclusive than English. In France, according to Haywood, balls, assemblies and masquerades take place 'in the Palaces of Princes, and Houses of Persons of the first Quality', by contrast with the English 'mercenary Places of Resort; where all, without Distinction, are admitted for their Money' (bk v: 2.167). Most importantly, Frenchmen, we are told, treat aristocratic women with respect and engage in lively, flirtatious conversation with them without ulterior sexual motives: 'without Danger to their Virtue, or Prejudice to their Reputation' (bk v: 2.169). The women respond to this intellectual and social freedom by behaving with impeccable sexual propriety:

> Tho' no Place affords Scenes of Gallantry equal to it in any Degree of Proportion, yet I believe there is none where fewer false Steps are made, or Husbands have less Reason to complain of the want of Chastity in their Wives.
>
> (bk i: 2.28)

Haywood repeats this assertion in the *Parrot*, where she tells us that French women 'give into a Spirit of Gallantry', yet remain 'free from those guilty Emotions which agitate the Mind of the more warm' (no. 7).

In French aristocratic society, mixed-sex socializing is not associated with sexual misconduct, and for this reason it provides an ideal model for female education. The correspondent Philenia sends in a letter on women's education in France, which echoes the Female Spectator's views on French society closely. She claims that in France 'all Men of Learning, Wit, and Genius, have not only a free access to the Ladies, but are received by them with particular Marks of Distinction'. The men provide them with continual tuition, in the guise of flattery and flirtation:

> All they say is a continual Round of Gaiety and sprightly Wit; yet is their very Raillery on such Subjects, as mingle Information with Delight; and I protest to you, Madam, I have been sometimes more edified by a single Sentence laugh'd out, than by a formal, stiff, pedantick Harangue of an Hour long.
>
> But this is the least Advantage a *French* Lady reaps from her Regard for Men of Learning. – Had she an Inclination to Philosophy, Theology, History, Astronomy, or in fine, any particular Study, she has only to make Mention of it, and is sure of receiving a Letter the next Day, in which is contained the whole Pith and Marrow of that Science.
>
> (bk XII: 2.417)

In this society, according to Philenia, learning forms an integral part of the leisure pursuits of both sexes of the upper classes. In the French salons, aristocratic women patronize men of learning and spend time in their company without compromising their sexual reputations.

The Female Spectator commends this idea, but comments wryly that similar customs could never be introduced into England: 'What in France is looked upon as no more than, what it indeed is, innocent Gallantry, might here be censur'd as unbecoming Familiarity' (bk XII: 2.418). A desire for learning would be misinterpreted, the editor warns, as sexual desire for the scholar himself. Haywood restates this idea in *Epistles for the Ladies*, where four women write to a scholar, asking him to send them each a letter on a different intellectual topic. He interprets this request as a 'pretty Stratagem ... contrived on purpose to catch the Secret of my Heart' and airily refuses to write to any of them (Haywood 2000a: 319).

While her readers may not be able to implement Philenia's suggestions, however, the Female Spectator herself does. The editor combines learning with sociability in a manner close to Philenia's Francophile ideal when she and her club visit Mira's husband's country seat. They take advantage of his extensive grounds to make botanical observations and conduct experiments on snails. The Female Spectator recommends the study of zoology to those of her own class: 'Ladies, and those Gentlemen who have many vacant Hours upon their Hands' (bk XVII: 3.163). The editor and her companions also visit a neighbouring gentleman's private observatory where the women view the planets through a telescope and listen to their male companions debate the possibility of extra-terrestrial life. The gentleman-astronomer promises to contribute a letter on astronomy to the *Female Spectator* (bk XVII: 3.175). The letter is never forthcoming, but the exchange neatly models Philenia's dual scheme of learning through a combination of polite conversation and more detailed letters.

In her description of French society, Philenia describes the scholars as 'industrious Bees, which suck the Sweets of many Author's Works, and having collected whatever they find worthy, present it in the most concise and briefest Manner possible to the Lady' (bk XII: 2.416). There is an implicit parallel here between these men of letters and the editors of magazines. The image of the editor as an 'industrious Bee . . . sipping honey from every flower' (*Universal Magazine* XXXVIII, Preface), buzzing among the monthly press and gathering the choicest articles, was a very common one. At least four periodicals of the first half of the eighteenth century chose to call themselves the *Bee*,[47] whilst beehives appear on the title pages of publications such as the *Orphan Reviv'd* and the *Compleat Library* (Figure 6.2), with its motto:

> All plants yeild honey as you see
> To the industrious Chymick Bee

In the *Female Spectator*, private correspondence between men and women has been replaced by a printed exchange, mediated by the author. The periodical offers a free commerce between the sexes that is both public and modest, free from the dangers of gallantry and flirtation.

Male correspondents introduce most of the scholarly subjects tackled in the *Female Spectator*. Philo-Naturae writes on botany and extra-terrestrial life (bk XV: 3.82–9 and bk XIX: 3.234–42), Acasto sends in a critique of Mark Akenside's recently published *Pleasures of Imagination* (1744) (bk XX: 3.257–62),[48] Antiquarius presents Classical correspondence (bk XX: 3.275–81) and Extratellus examines Lucretius's views on immortality (bk XXIII: 3.356–61). The *Female Spectator*'s women readers may not be able to request personal letters on subjects of intellectual interest, but they can read such letters in the periodical. The female editor has replaced the aristocratic salon hostess, and her correspondents are the learned men whom she patronizes by printing their contributions. The *Female Spectator* provides its readers

THE
Compleat Library:
VOL. II.

Containing several Original Pieces, with an Historical Ac
count of the Choicest Books newly Printed in *England*·
and in the Forreign Journals.

AS ALSO,

The State of Learning in the World.

To be Published Monthly.

DECEMBER, 1692.

By a *London* Divine, *&c.*

Sic nos non nobis mellificamus apes. | *Omnia in libris*

All plants yeild honey as you see
To the Industrious Chymick Bee

LONDON, Printed for **John Dunton** at the *Raven* in the
Poultrey. Of whom is to be had the **First Volume of the**
Compleat Library.

Figure 6.2 Frontispiece of John Dunton's *Compleat Library* (1692–4).

with a virtual salon, which forms a replacement for the French aristocratic society to which those readers had no access, allowing them to become members of high society by proxy. By doing so, Haywood makes her persona, her readers and her periodical genteel.

Haywood's persistent focus on gentility within the *Female Spectator* has wider implications for our understanding of class issues in eighteenth-century women's writing. Haywood was a seasoned writer with a subtle grasp of public opinion, and her literary strategies often indicate wider social and cultural trends. This appears to be true of her pretence of mutual readerly and editorial gentility within the periodical. Haywood's work can be read as a particularly interesting case study of the literary strategies open to those who chose to write journalism under female pen-names, strategies that were profoundly influenced by the necessity of maintaining female decorum. Haywood's periodical sheds interesting light on the ways in which women writers were perceived in mid-century and on their attempts to gain a new literary respectability. The *Female Spectator* is a particularly skilful example of the ways in which the feminization of the eighteenth-century periodical led also to its gentrification, as female writers laid claim to a form of writing – journalism – previously perceived as louche and disreputable and attempted to portray it as decorous and even socially exclusive. In a period which was increasingly anxious about the possible ill effects of women's reading habits, Haywood offers a form of reading matter which is entertaining and accessible, but which will not compromise her readers' morals or their social standing. Just as a woman's sexual reputation was fragile, so her gentility needed to be equally carefully defended. Haywood flatters her readers by implicitly including them among the upper echelons of society. For those who are not already part of this polite society, the periodical holds out the promise that reading the *Female Spectator* will make them genteel. The difference between the *Female Spectator*'s title and the title of Cave's *Gentleman's Magazine* reveals an important, but silent, assumption of mid-century journalism. Gentlemen may be a subgroup of male readers, but all female readers are ladies.

7 'Writing like a teacher'
Johnson as moralist in the *Rambler*

Few eighteenth-century journalists can have approached the writing of a periodical with a deeper sense of moral responsibility than Samuel Johnson, a feeling evidenced by the prayer recorded in Johnson's diary on beginning the *Rambler*: 'Grant, I beseech thee, that in this my undertaking ... I may promote thy glory, and the Salvation both of myself and others' (1969: 1.43). In the *Rambler*, Johnson attempts to use the literary essay-periodical, which – unlike the essay *tout court* – was traditionally the vehicle of wit, primarily as a means of moral instruction.

In this chapter, I will begin by examining the ways in which Johnson's conceptions of the duties of a moralist influenced his approach to the essay-periodical. The most important features of Johnson's publication all shed light on Johnson's moralism: the *Rambler*'s uniformity of tone; its adoption of a persona who is a representative figure, rather than an eccentric individual; its focus on the universals of human behaviour, rather than current affairs or the fashions and follies beloved of Richard Steele; together with its didactic tone. In the second half of this chapter, I will turn to an examination of Johnson's aims as a moralist and look at three specific groups of essays which illustrate this ethical programme. Both Johnson's methods and his message reflect his desire to unify a readership and a society which he saw as increasingly split into mutually hostile groups based on profession and class.

Uniformity

The most immediately striking difference between Johnson's periodical and those of Addison and Steele is its consistency of tone, presentation and subject matter. Johnson acknowledges that 'among the various censures, which the unavoidable comparison of my performances with those of my predecessors has produced, there is none more general than that of uniformity' (*Rambler* 107). The *Rambler* is Johnson's longest work, and only four of its 208 essays are by other writers,[49] while three contain further brief contributions.[50] Johnson makes no attempt to vary his style or disguise the fact that he frequently makes use of the editor's time-honoured privilege of writing to himself. The fictional letters, whether they are from educated gentlemen or giddy young girls, are all written in Johnson's unmistakable sonorous, polysyllabic prose, leading Boswell to regret that the style of the *Rambler*'s female correspondents is 'strangely formal, even to ridicule' (1964–71: 1.223).

Johnson's refusal to print readers' letters in his publication was a very unusual one for a mid-century journalist. Many editors presented their papers primarily as vehicles for publishing the letters, essays and poems of their readers. The *Gentleman's Journal* describes itself as 'chiefly a Collection of other men's Works' (1, February 1692), referring to its readers' contributions. Eliza Haywood promises that those who send contributions to her *Young Lady* 'may depend upon seeing them faithfully inserted' (1, 6 January 1756). Magazine editors, in particular, found it cheaper to accept the unsolicited contributions from readers that flooded their desks than to pay staff writers. Their critics feared that the work of professional writers might soon be crowded out altogether by the meretricious contributions of readers. Correspondents were eager to see their own work in print, but understandably less willing to read the productions of their fellow literary dilettanti. A reader of the *Lady's Museum* complains that 'without foreign assistance your Museum would be much more to the pleasure of your readers' (I.4: 290). A correspondent of the *Court Magazine* complains that 'the Magazine . . . is so crouded with . . . those authors who write . . . for the sake of indulging their vanity' that there is no room for 'the traders in real wit and genius' (September 1761). One writer to the *Covent-Garden Journal* sheepishly apologizes for his own contribution, since 'in this very learned and enlightened Age, in which Authors are almost as numerous as Booksellers, I doubt not but your Correspondents furnish you with a sufficient Quantity of waste Paper' (33, 25 April 1752). He hopes that he himself is not motivated by 'the same Sort of Vanity as other puny Authors have been, to desire to be in Print' (*ibid.*). Johnson notes this phenomenon in the *Adventurer*, where he describes his time as 'the Age of Authors', in which 'writers will perhaps be multiplied, till no readers will be found', making particular mention of 'the innumerable correspondents of public papers' (115, 11 December 1753). At several points in the *Rambler*, Johnson apologizes for neglecting his correspondents. He imagines 'the . . . sorrow, impatience, and resentment, which the writers must have felt' (*Rambler* 56) and warns them wryly not to expect better success in future.

The lack of stylistic variety in the *Rambler* is mirrored by a lack of thematic variety. In the *Spectator*, serious moral remonstrations on the evils of gambling jostle with disquisitions on dancing and deportment. Almost all Johnson's *Ramblers*, by contrast, focus on timeless and universal elements of human motivation and behaviour. He includes very little local colour, as well as very few explicit references to current affairs.[51] For Johnson, the moralist's view of life must be comprehensive, since 'there is scarce any … good or ill, but is common to human kind' (*Rambler* 60).

The universality of the human experience is a frequent theme in the *Rambler*. Johnson tells his readers that 'a few pains, and a few pleasures are all the materials of human life' (*Rambler* 68). This paucity of subject matter seems inimical to the periodical as a genre, with its aspirations of providing '*variety of the most entertaining Subjects*' (*Ladies Journal* 1). Richard Steele tells his readers that he chose to adopt the alter ego of Isaac Bickerstaff partially in order to 'allure my Reader with … Variety' (*Tatler* 271); the *Gentleman's Magazine* announces proudly on its title page that it contains 'greater Variety than any Book of the Kind and Price'. The *Gentleman's Journal* bears the same motto and emblem as Cave's publication: 'E Pluribus Unum' (many united in one) and a hand holding a bouquet, perhaps alluding to the idea of the publication as an anthology, which literally means a gathering of flowers. The *Literary Magazine* defines a magazine as a 'MONTHLY COLLECTION' consisting 'of many Articles unconnected and independent of each other' (I, Preface). The *Lady's Magazine* asserts that 'the most laboured performances, even of genius, are insipid when compared to that agreeable medley composed by a variety of talents and tempers' (II.1, November 1761).

Not only are the topics suitable for a moralist few in number. Even the treatment of these subjects, according to Johnson, 'can admit only of slight … diversities'. All moralists 'lament the deceitfulness of hope, the fugacity of pleasure … and the frequency of calamity; and … concur in recommending kindness … and fortitude' (*Rambler* 143). Clearly, the moralist will have difficulty making his work entertaining to his or her readership, since, as Johnson writes, 'Nothing can strongly strike or affect us, but what is rare or sudden' (*Rambler* 78). The moralist must precisely interest his or her readers in the duties of common life, in 'things which nothing but their frequency makes considerable' (*Rambler* 60).

The uniformity of the *Rambler*'s tone and subject matter does not simply reflect the narrowness of the range of topics and approaches available to the moralist. It is also the result of Johnson's attempts to reunite a society which he regarded as deeply divided. Addison and Steele's periodicals also aimed to provide a unifying focus for their society. By concentrating on manners and morals, rather than on partisan politics, they attempted to heal the deep political rifts caused by the aftermath of the Civil War and the Glorious Revolution. Johnson, by contrast, portrays a society divided not by political allegiances, but primarily by occupation.

The division of mankind into different professions leads to narrow-minded partiality: 'Most men', Johnson writes, 'have a very strong and active prejudice in favour of their own vocation, always working upon their minds, and influencing their behaviour' (*Rambler* 9). Johnson envisages a society of warring factions. The distinctive characteristics of each professional group, he claims, 'have been of great use, in the general hostility which every part of mankind exercises against the rest, to furnish insults and sarcasms' (*Rambler* 173).

The most dangerous result of this minutely subdivided society, for Johnson, is the erosion of fellow-feeling for those of a different background or lifestyle from our own. Friendship, writes Johnson, is rare for this reason:

> We are by our occupations, education and habits of life divided almost into different species, which regard one another for the most part with scorn and malignity. Each of these classes of the human race has ... cares which another cannot feel; pleasures which he cannot partake; and modes of expressing every sensation which he cannot understand.
>
> (*Rambler* 160)

In this nightmarish vision, the different segments of society are separated by a profound failure to recognize the marks of a common humanity in the experiences of others. Inability to comprehend others' 'modes of expressing every sensation' impedes friendship. It is as though a crucial faculty of sensory perception were missing or damaged. Just as John Locke's blind man cannot form an idea of the colour scarlet without comparing it to something from his own realm of experience, the sound of a trumpet (1975: 126), so each individual can only feel and comprehend the pleasures and pains incident to his or her own particular situation. Mr Rambler's correspondent Victoria makes a similar point: 'We can scarcely communicate our perceptions to minds preoccupied by different objects, any more than the delight of well disposed colours or harmonious sounds can be imparted to such as want the senses of hearing or sight' (*Rambler* 130). One of the moralist's most important tasks, then, is to translate the language of individual experience into terms which every reader can understand.

While this fragmentation of society renders the moralist's task more necessary, it also makes it more difficult. Johnson's potential readers are preoccupied by their own concerns. Even those who have the leisure and inclination to dedicate themselves to knowledge are generally only interested in one specific branch of learning: 'The naturalist has no desire to know the opinions or conjectures of the philologer: the botanist looks upon the astronomer as a being unworthy of his regard: the lawyer scarcely hears the name of a physician without contempt' (*Rambler* 118). Readers absorbed by their own specialized pursuits will afford only a 'cold reception' to the writer who attempts to interest them in questions not immediately relating to their 'favourite amusements' (*Rambler* 118).

While essay-periodicals attempt to appeal to the general reader (a reader who, in this society, scarcely seems to exist), contemporary magazines claim to appeal to many different sub-categories of readers. The *London Magazine* imagines different sections of the magazine appealing to different sectors of its readership: '*one apt to be taken with Politicks, another with History, another with Poetry; one with serious and grave Subjects, another with humorous and comical ones; they may find all these in this Collection*' (1732, Preface). The *Gentleman's Magazine* describes its readership as divided into separate special interest groups:

> The Scholar instructs himself with Advice from the literary World; the Soldier makes a campaign in safety . . . The Politician . . . unravels the . . . Intrigues of Ministers; the . . . Merchant observes the Course of Trade . . . and the . . . Shop-keeper . . . the Price of Goods.
>
> (vol. x, 1740, Preface)

Cave's publication carries a wealth of specialized and technical information on subjects ranging from politics to natural science, catering to coffee-house newspaper readers, as well as electrifiers of bottles. Magazines often define themselves as sources of vocational information for professionals. The *Universal Magazine*, for example, promises its readers that 'the adventurous *merchant*, the industrious *tradesman*, the skilful *mechanick*, the toilsome *farmer*, and the careful *housewife*, shall never want some helps in their respective stations', while the magazine also caters to the more scholarly with articles on '*natural* or *experimental philosophy, mathematical problems, poetry* or *musick*' (1747, Preface). The *Royal Magazine* promises that 'the Statesman may be here instructed, the Philosopher satisfied, the Merchant and Tradesman improved, and the Polite agreeably amused' (1, October–December 1760, Preface). The bulky magazines of the 1750s could run to as many as several hundred pages in length: clearly they were not designed to be read cover to cover. Each issue of the quarterly *Royal Magazine*, for example, is 480 pages long. In the miscellaneous contents pages of publications such as the *Grand Magazine of Universal Intelligence*, articles on the cultivation of pineapples and the treatment of equine illnesses jostle treatises on the nature of sin and dissertations on English property law (see June 1760). The magazines reproduce in print the fragmentation of Johnson's society and the isolation of each group from the others, as each reader only peruses the one section of the magazine which is of interest to them. The editor of the *Imperial Magazine* comments that writing a periodical 'is attended with circumstances of peculiar difficulty, to those who are either under a real or supposed necessity, of addressing themselves to a community, made up of such different jarring members' (March 1760: 143). He advises editors to address each segment of the readership separately, since 'universal approbation . . . is no more to be expected, than indeed it is to be wish'd' (*ibid.*).

By contrast with the editors of magazines, Johnson encourages his readers to define themselves primarily as members of a larger body, which he variously refers to as 'the great republick of mankind' (*Rambler* 81) and 'the great republick of humanity' (*Rambler* 136) and describes as united by 'the universal league of social beings' (*Rambler* 81), using the imagery of politics and law to suggest a relationship of co-operation and mutual interest. The enormous success of the magazines, coupled with the paltry sales of the *Rambler*, must have led Johnson to fear that by attempting to appeal to all readers, he would risk capturing the attention of very few.

The *Rambler* and its readers

One of the most striking features of the *Rambler* is Johnson's constant awareness of the relative ineffectiveness of the periodical as a vehicle for teaching ethics. Addison and Steele regarded the essay-periodical as a medium that would enable them to reach a relatively large audience that could be addressed more effectively from the press than from the pulpit. Dread of the editor's satire has more power over readers' imaginations, Steele tells us, than the fear of hellfire: 'Though Men [do not] regard any mention either of Punishments or Rewards, they will listen to what makes them inconsiderable or mean in the Imaginations of others, and by Degrees in their own' (*Tatler* 205). Addison and Steele's approach requires a light touch, an ability, as Addison expresses it in the *Spectator*, to 'enliven morality with wit, and to temper wit with morality' (*Spectator* 10). In the opening issue of the *Rambler*, Johnson wishes that an author might 'glide imperceptibly into the favour of the publick' (*Rambler* 1) – a phrase that could aptly characterize Addison's suave geniality – and he later advises the man who 'wishes to attain an English style' to 'give his days and nights to Addison' (Boswell 1964–71: 2.150). Johnson's own publication, however, is characterized by a solemnly didactic tone and by the use of 'so many hard words' that Marchioness Gray complained that she almost 'broke her teeth' when she attempted to read the *Rambler* aloud (Clifford 1980: 80). Boswell describes Addison as writing with 'the ease of a gentleman', while Johnson 'writes like a teacher' and 'dictates to his readers as if from an academical chair' (1964–71: 1.224). If Addison and Steele brought philosophy, as they claim, 'out of Closets and Libraries, Schools and Colleges, to dwell in Clubs and Assemblies, at Tea-Tables and in Coffee-Houses' (*Spectator* 10), Johnson reintroduces the spirit of 'Closets and Libraries, Schools and Colleges' into the essay-periodical.

Addison's gentlemanly ease stems partially from his conception of his persona. Mr Rambler is a writer; Mr Spectator, by contrast, is a genteel amateur, 'born to a small Hereditary Estate'. His name itself indicates that he is not a member of any profession, but 'a Spectator of Mankind . . . a Speculative Statesman, Soldier, Merchant, and Artizan, without ever medling with any Practical Part in Life' (*Spectator* 1). As a professional writer, Mr Rambler's social standing is lower than that of Mr Spectator. He complains that those whom he wishes to admonish for fashionable follies regard him as 'a wretch of low notions, contracted views, mean conversation, and narrow fortune', who wishes to hinder 'those whom their birth and taste have set above him, from the enjoyment of their own superiority' (*Rambler* 14).

Johnson's refusal to pander to the snobbery of readers by adopting a more genteel persona may also be a reaction against a growing trend in mid-century periodicals. Their editors frequently lay claim to an intimacy with polite society. The *Royal Magazine* promises to relate '*all the Affairs of the* Beau Monde' (I, October–December 1750, Preface), and the *Court Magazine* claims to provide an account of 'the transactions of the Court' (September 1761). The *Adventurer* mocks these hollow pretensions to gentility with a proposal for a 'a new paper calculated solely for high life', entitled 'The BEAU-MONDE: Or, The Gentleman and Lady's Polite Intelligencer', which is to contain reports from the horse races, masquerades, playhouses and gambling dens, obituaries of lapdogs and accounts of the fluctuations of fashion (35, 6 March 1753).

Mr Spectator, then, displays a confidence in his social status which Mr Rambler lacks. In addition, Addison's tone reflects a buoyant reliance on his ability to attract a substantial readership. In the *Spectator*, he envisages his readership as a listless and unoccupied group of Londoners: 'mere Blanks' until 'set a going by some Paragraph in a News-Paper'. They look to his publication to provide them with a raison d'être. 'Such Persons', he announces gleefully, 'are very acceptable to a young Author' (*Spectator* 4). Johnson, by contrast, imagines a London full of bustling people, wholly preoccupied by their own petty concerns. He depicts a young author going out to the coffee-houses to hear news of the reception of his publication:

> He . . . hears in one quarter of a cricket-match . . . is desired to read a ludicrous advertisement; or consulted about . . . a favourite cat. The whole world is busied in affairs, which he thinks below the notice of reasonable creatures, and which are nevertheless sufficient to withdraw all regard from his labours.
>
> (*Rambler* 146)

Johnson's readers, unlike Addison's, are too busy to pay attention to an essay-journal. Johnson's perception of the difficulty of finding a substantial, receptive audience for the *Rambler* reflects the contemporary status of the essay-periodical. By the time of the *Rambler*'s publication, magazines had eclipsed essay-periodicals in popularity (see Mayo 1962 and Taylor 1993). Very few essay series were published independently in the 1750s and 60s – I am not aware of any which were launched in the 1760s – and those that did appear were quickly appropriated by the magazines, which incorporated them into their pages, a practice which may have accounted for the *Rambler*'s own low sales figures. Issues of the *Rambler were*, in fact, reaching a very wide readership, though not in their original form, but reprinted in the magazines. Paul Korshin has pointed out that some of the individual *Rambler* papers were more widely distributed in the 1750s than the *Tatler* and the *Spectator* were during their original runs in the 1710s, when there were no magazines to reprint articles (Korshin 1989: 92–105; see also McKeen Wiles 1968: 155–72). Charles Ranger of the contemporary *Gray's Inn Journal* complains that, unlike other journalists, he has not 'stood well enough with the Conductors of our Magazines, to be admitted to the Honour of furnishing them with an Essay once a Month, in order to display some select Lucubrations to the great Multitude, who purchase those monthly Miscellanies' (21 September 1754). Johnson must have been aware that his essays were being reprinted in the contemporary magazines. The *Gentleman's Magazine*, with which Johnson himself had been closely involved, frequently reprinted *Rambler* papers.[52] However, even as the magazines were disseminating some of Johnson's work to a larger audience, these popular, bulky publications were driving his essay-paper out of business. While for Addison and Steele the essay-periodical was an exciting new medium of communication, for Johnson it was a moribund form competing in a crowded literary marketplace with other, far more successful forms of writing.

The character of Mr Rambler

Before we explore the nature of Johnson's moralism in greater detail, we need to consider the persona through which he chose to present his ideas. The use of a journalistic *eidolon* is one of the conventions of periodical writing which Johnson inherited from his predecessors. Mr Rambler is particularly reminiscent of Steele's Isaac Bickerstaff, another elderly and eccentric, but high-minded, bachelor. However, Johnson's treatment of his alter ego is subtly, but crucially, different from Steele's, and this difference in approach is symptomatic of Johnson's views on the function of the moralist.

Paradoxically, in the opening issue of the *Rambler*, Johnson appears to reject the convention of writing in the guise of a persona. He claims that 'the epic writers' have 'almost unanimously adopted the first lines of Homer', but that 'such ceremonial modes of entrance' do not exist for those writing outside the genre of heroic poetry (*Rambler* 1). 'The ostentatious and haughty display of themselves has been the usual refuge of diurnal writers', Johnson writes, rejecting the colourful sobriquets and fictitious personae of his contemporaries who wrote in the guise of hermits, devils, lovers, mountebanks, Quakers, whores and old maids (*Rambler* 1). However, as Johnson was aware, there *were* 'ceremonial modes' of introduction for essay-periodicalists, for whom Addison and Steele's example was almost as prescriptive as Homer's had been for the Classical poets. As Daniel Defoe puts it, *'when Authors present their Works to the World, like a Thief at the Gallows; they make a Speech to the People'* (*Review* vol. I, Preface). At a later stage in the publication, Johnson tells us that readers 'were angry that the Rambler did not, like the Spectator, introduce himself ... by an account of his birth and studies ... and a description of his physiognomy' (*Rambler* 23).

Johnson rarely invites us to focus on the idiosyncrasies of his persona. We are given very little explicit information about Mr Rambler, except that, like Bickerstaff, he is an old man. He has known his acquaintance Suspirius, we are told, for 'fifty-eight years and four months' (*Rambler* 59), and this unflattering friend describes the editor as 'tottering on the edge of the grave' (*ibid.*). Mr Rambler's age does not endow him with special wisdom. Old age is always depicted in the *Rambler* in strikingly uncomplimentary terms. Old men, Johnson tells us, are choleric, censorious, peevish, devoid of compassion, unfit for friendship, vulnerable to flattery and avaricious.[53] Johnson never invites us to blindly venerate the old, suggesting instead that 'age is rarely despised but when it is contemptible' (*Rambler* 50).

Mr Rambler is also, of course, in possession of an inextinguishable pessimism. The correspondent Florentulus imagines Mr Rambler, on receipt of his letter, 'snuffing his candle, rubbing his spectacles, stirring his fire ... and settling himself in his easy chair, that he may enjoy a new calamity without disturbance' (*Rambler* 109). The Mr Rambler depicted in Florentulus's letter is a carefully constructed comic persona, but also, with his gloomy temperament and ponderous style, a playful Johnsonian self-portrait. Johnson's writing here, as elsewhere, is profoundly, yet subtly, autobiographical; he repeatedly invites us to identify the writer himself with his alter ego.

It is when Johnson is describing the compositional process that we most frequently glimpse the author behind the mask. He appears to be confiding his own difficulties to us when he tells us that, for 'the authors of these petty compositions', 'The imagination ranges from one design to another, and the hours pass imperceptibly away till ... necessity enforces the use of those thoughts which happen to be at hand' (*Rambler* 184). It is clear that, despite the use of the third person, it is his own writing that Johnson is describing. The passage closely resembles the celebrated description of writer's block, in an issue on the theme of procrastination:

> I sat yesterday morning employed in deliberating on which, among the various subjects that occurred to my imagination, I should bestow the paper of to-day ... I grew every moment more irresolute, my ideas wandered from the first intention, and I rather wished to think, than thought, upon any settled subject; till at last I was awakened from this dream of study by a summons from the press.
>
> (*Rambler* 134)

The use of the first person gives the passage a confessional quality, while it also has a striking immediacy, reminiscent of Richardson's technique of 'writing to the moment'. It is the composition of 'the paper of to-day' which Johnson is describing, that paper which his readers have in their hands on that specific date. The words 'I was now necessitated to write' introduce the subject of the essay, the theme of indecision and delay: he passes from the description of his mental inertia to the actual writing in the main part of the essay, just as he passed from bewilderment to resolution in reality. We sense from the passage that it is Johnson, not Mr Rambler, who sits daydreaming over his copy, unable to think of a topic for that day's paper.

There are dangers, however, in identifying a writer with his or her didactic alter ego, as Steele acknowledges in the *Tatler*, where he tells his readers that Bickerstaff is able to attack vices 'with a Freedom of Spirit that would have lost both its Beauty and its Efficacy had it been pretended to by Mr. *Steele*' (*Tatler* 271). Clearly, to write a moral periodical is to expose oneself to the charge of hypocrisy. Within the periodical, Johnson repeatedly reminds his audience of the personal fallibility of the moralist. 'Few men', he writes, 'celebrated for theoretic wisdom, live with conformity to their precepts' (*Rambler* 77): in his or her private life, the moralist is to be found 'acting upon principles which he has in common with the illiterate and unenlightened' (*Rambler* 54) and even 'swelling with the applause which he has gained by proving that applause is of no value' (*ibid.*).

These repeated warnings of 'the manifest and striking contrariety between the life of an author and his works' (*Rambler* 14) keep the reader aware of the writer behind the mask. Johnson is constantly vindicating his action in assuming the mantle of the moral teacher, in a way that seems almost defensive. He tells us that 'nothing is more unjust ... than to charge with hypocrisy him that expresses zeal for ... virtues, which he neglects to practise' (*ibid.*). The writer's personal life, Johnson assures his audience, should not be permitted to detract from his or her writings: 'Argument is only to be invalidated by argument, and is . . . of the same force, whether or not it convinces him by whom it is proposed' (*ibid.*). By comparison with the easy charm and quirky and loveable eccentricities of Bickerstaff and Mr Spectator, the character of Johnson's *eidolon* is scarcely developed. The focus is not on Mr Rambler's personality, but on the arguments which he proposes.

Despite a few comic touches, we learn nothing about Mr Rambler's background and very little about his friends, associates and habits. Mr Rambler is a representative figure whose fears, weaknesses and failings are typical of humanity. Johnson is keen to emphasize that the moralist does not have access to superior strength of character, but understands, because he or she *feels*, the same temptations and perplexities as his or her readers. He speaks throughout the periodical most frequently in the second person plural. Even when he writes of moralists, he describes their work as 'a taper, by which *we* are lighted' (*Rambler* 77; my italic).

In matters of morality, according to Johnson, 'Men more frequently require to be reminded than informed' (*Rambler* 2). The moralist's task, in Johnson's vision, is to voice the reader's own inner convictions, to repeat the prompting of his or her conscience. For this reason, Mr Rambler is an everyman, in whose voice each reader should recognize a mirror of his or her own mind and to whose sentiments 'every bosom returns an echo' (Johnson 1905: 3.441–2). The reader's identification with Mr Rambler is crucial to Johnson's moral project; his aim is that the reader should find moral precepts not only reinforced, but should 'persuade himself that he has always felt them' (*ibid.* 3.441).

Creating empathy

Harnessing the power of empathy is one of Johnson's central concerns in the *Rambler*. Comedy of the form most frequently practised in the eighteenth century involves distance: the distance, for example, between the writer and his or her persona, between Swift and Gulliver, Steele and Bickerstaff, a distance far greater than that between Johnson and Mr Rambler. Johnson, instead, continually creates proximity, encouraging us to recognize our similarity with others.

Johnson paints a vivid pen-portrait of Suspirius the 'screech-owl' (*Rambler* 59), who tires out his friends with his ceaseless pessimistic whining. The paper's moral is not directed at the unfortunate Suspirius, however, but at us, in our haste to judge him. We are told that 'to hear complaints with patience, even when complaints are vain, is one of the duties of friendship' (*ibid.*). Hearing complaints with patience is, in the *Rambler*, one of the editor's most important tasks. Johnson's extensive use of correspondence is one of the features which most clearly marks his work as a periodical, rather than simply a collection of essays. Almost all Mr Rambler's correspondents write in a tone that is characterized, as one letter-writer admits, by 'lamentation and complaint' (*Rambler* 147). The letters allow Johnson to comment on the full range of human experience and to model for his readers a compassionate response to human suffering in every form.

This tradition of the distressed reader appealing to the editor for relief dates back to John Dunton's epistolary periodicals of the 1690s, in which the editors, in the guise of the Athenian Society, claimed to provide a resource for the suicidal and prevent the 'desperate Hand, which ... else might attempt upon the Breast' (Gildon c.1693: 5). Steele's Bickerstaff offers his paper as 'the Patron of Persons who have no other Friend to complain to' (*Tatler* 245), and other editors were to follow this model. The editor of the *Visiter* promises, 'Whoever is pleased to make a Friend of me, I shall consider their Sorrows as my own' (1, 18 June 1723).

What distinguishes Johnson's correspondents is that the sufferings which they describe would be more likely to excite risibility than commiseration. As Johnson reminds us, 'There are many vexatious accidents and uneasy situations which raise little compassion for the sufferer' (*Rambler* 176). One correspondent appeals to Mr Rambler for a sympathetic response to 'a ludicrous persecution', which, despite its seemingly petty nature, 'wears away my happiness' (*Rambler* 147). His complaint is that he is constantly teased about his lack of assurance by his more worldly uncle. While the pages of the magazines of the 1750s and 60s also contain many sorrowful letters to the editor, they are of a very different nature from those in the *Rambler*. A letter from Evander in the *Lady's Magazine* is characteristic: 'There is a satisfaction for which I cannot account, and that too not a small one, which results from imparting our distresses to a person who has sensibility to discern their poignancy, and humanity to compassionate the suffer [*sic*]' (July 1761). Evander's plangent tones echo those of many of Mr Rambler's correspondents, yet he is a far more obviously deserving object of readerly sympathy than the figures who inhabit Johnson's periodical. Evander is about to retire from the world on the death of his beloved wife, who died of grief after the demise of their only child, a 6-year-old boy.

In the *Rambler*, the satirical character-sketch, beloved of periodical editors since Addison and Steele, is often transformed by Johnson into a compassionate appeal for sympathy with the distresses of others. A witty paper on the bankrupt virtuoso Quisquilius (*Rambler* 82) is followed in the next issue by a more balanced appraisal of the activities of collectors as a group. Johnson warns that it is not easy 'to forbear some sallies of merriment ...

when we see a man wrinkled with attention . . . in the investigation of questions, of which, without visible inconvenience, the world may expire in ignorance' (*Rambler* 83). The editor discourages his readers, however, from regarding Quisquilius simply as a figure of ridicule. He points out that the virtuoso's pastime keeps him from idleness, brutality and vice. He later prints a letter from the fictional correspondent Vivaculus, satirizing the activities of a club of virtuosos, and follows it with the comment, 'It may . . . somewhat mollify his anger to reflect . . . that he who does his best, however little, is always to be distinguished from him who does nothing' (*Rambler* 177). Describing pedants, Johnson carefully analyses the various motives that may lead 'the harmless collegiate' to hold forth on academic topics in inappropriate situations. He explains that the pedant is always characterized, often unjustly, as 'arrogant and overbearing', since 'we are seldom so far prejudiced in favour of each other to seek out palliations' (*Rambler* 173). Rather than apportioning blame, the moralist's task, for Johnson, is to 'mollify' and 'seek out palliations'. As a moralist, Johnson sets out to investigate the motivations of the foolish or futile human behaviour, which most of us are inclined to condemn without examination.

Johnson asks us to empathize not only with those who seem to invite derision, but also with those who, like the prostitute Misella, are scorned by 'the rigour of virtuous indignation' and from whom it is even considered 'meritorious to withhold relief (*Rambler* 170). Johnson's descriptions of the sufferings of the most unfortunate members of society are written with force and passion. He exhorts us to oppose capital punishment, citing Herman Boerhaave's question on witnessing an execution, 'Who knows whether this man is not less culpable than me?' (*Rambler* 114).[54] Johnson depicts the plight of the London prostitutes, 'covered with rags, shivering with cold, and pining with hunger'. The prostitutes would not need an advocate, he writes, 'if none were to refuse them relief, but those that owe their exemption from the same distress only to their wisdom or their virtue' (*Rambler* 107).

Johnson's writings have little in common with the sentimental novels of Henry Mackenzie or Frances Brooke, whose aristocratic protagonists are moved to displays of sentiment or acts of charity by innocent or repentant victims of misfortune. He does not simply appeal to the reader's own good nature and pity, presenting spectacles of the deserving poor for the audience's edification. Instead, he points out his readers' kinship with some of the most hated and feared members of their society: prostitutes and condemned criminals.

Moderating desires

Johnson's tone of 'dolorous declamation', as a correspondent aptly describes it (*Rambler* 109), together with his unrelenting focus on human sorrow, are intrinsic parts of what he regards as the moralist's most important duty: teaching 'the art of moderating the desires' (*Rambler* 180). One crucial way of moderating desires, for Johnson, is to take comfort in our distresses by comparing our own state with that of those unhappier than ourselves: 'Few are placed in a situation so gloomy and distressful, as not to see every day beings yet more forlorn and miserable, from whom they may learn to rejoice in their own lot' (*Rambler* 186). At first glance, Johnson may appear here to be advocating a smug satisfaction bordering on *schadenfreude*, but in fact he is recommending a habit of mind which he regards as all too rare, since we always regard others as more fortunate than ourselves:

> If the general disposition of things be estimated by the representation which every one makes of his own state, the world must be considered as the abode of sorrow and misery ... If we judge by the account which may be obtained of every man's fortune from others, it may be concluded, that we are all placed in an elysian region ... since scarcely any complaint is uttered without censure from those that hear it.
>
> (*Rambler* 128)

Not only are Johnson's readers unable to appreciate the specific sorrows of others, but they seem unwilling even to acknowledge that anyone else has any 'troubles and distresses'. 'Complaint' of the kind so often voiced by Mr Rambler's correspondents meets only with 'censure' and impatient disbelief. While Johnson frequently portrays a society in which members of different genders, professions or age groups fail to understand each other's pleasures and miseries, in this vision society is even more deeply segmented. Empathy and compassion are impossible when each individual believes that he or she is the only one to suffer. The moralist can offer no mitigation of the very real sorrows experienced by his or her readers – Johnson is always sceptical of the Stoics' philosophy of the unreality of suffering – but 'the business of moralists', Johnson tells us, is 'to detect the frauds of fortune' and show that even greatness 'has far fewer advantages, and much less splendour, when we are suffered to approach it' (*Rambler* 58).

Comparison of our state with that of others, for Johnson, is almost always delusive and morally damaging. The erroneous belief that others experience a happiness denied to us leads to three different forms of behaviour explored extensively in the *Rambler*: indecision, competition and dependency.

Indecision, procrastination and idleness

We might expect a moralist to emphasize the necessity of exercising great care in all our choices: instead Johnson almost always stresses the dangers of long consideration. Polyphilus in *Rambler* 19 possesses a 'powerful genius, which might have … benefited the world in any profession', but he vacillates between a variety of different callings, dabbling in medicine, law, scholarship and the military by turns. His tale warns us, Johnson concludes, 'That of two states of life equally consistent with religion and virtue, he who chuses earliest chuses best' (*Rambler* 19). Johnson frequently cautions his readers against Polyphilus's error:

> To let loose the attention equally to the advantages and inconveniences of every employment is not without danger; new motives are every moment operating on every side; and mechanicks have long ago discovered, that contrariety of equal attractions is equivalent to rest.
>
> (*Rambler* 153)

As we have seen, in the *Rambler* Johnson portrays a society split along professional lines into warring factions. This conflict appears particularly futile in light of the arbitrary nature of most of our choices, including that of a profession. We are unable to comprehend any state of life which we have not experienced at first hand: 'Of the state with which practice has not acquainted us, we snatch a glimpse, we discern a point, and regulate the rest by passion, and by fancy' (*Rambler* 63).

Every situation, Johnson writes, has its attendant evils, yet we can understand and feel only the disadvantages of our own condition: 'No man is pleased with his present state' (*ibid.*). We are all engaged in a restless search for a condition of greater ease and happiness:

> Thus the married praise the ease and freedom of a single state, and the single fly to marriage from the weariness of solitude. From all our observations we may collect with certainty, that misery is the lot of man, but cannot discover in what particular condition it will find most alleviations.
>
> (*Rambler* 45)

The moralist, by depicting the miseries of every condition of human life, prevents us from wasting our lives seeking an amelioration which no change can bring, so that we may 'be freed from the temptation of seeking by perpetual changes that ease which is no where to be found' (*Rambler* 66).

While not everyone spends their life, like Polyphilus, frequently changing their career, for Johnson, the 'insatiable demand for new gratifications ... seems particularly to characterize the nature of man' (*Rambler* 80). While here Johnson associates the desire for novelty with a search for pleasure, he more often characterizes it as a desire to 'find alleviations', to avoid pain. The poet Abraham Cowley's longing to emigrate to America exemplifies this universal wish in one of its simplest forms, according to Johnson: 'The general remedy of those, who are uneasy without knowing the cause, is change of place' (*Rambler* 6).

While Cowley's emigration scheme is portrayed by Johnson as childish and futile, the search for novelty is not merely an example of human delusion. Pleasure, by its nature, Johnson claims, is evanescent, while pain is lasting:

> It seems to be the condition of our present state, that pain should be more fixed and permanent than pleasure. Uneasiness gives way by slow degrees, and is long before it quits its possession of the sensory; but all our gratifications are volatile, vagrant, and easily dissipated.
>
> (*Rambler* 78)

Our sensory organization only allows us to experience the advantages and beauties of any situation briefly. Only in a new situation are there real possibilities of pleasure.

The perpetual desire for novelty, together with the weariness which accompanies large enterprises, combine to make sustained work very difficult. Indecision can lead to a kind of mental paralysis which renders real achievement impossible, even for those of 'active faculties and more acute discernment': 'He to whom many objects of persuit arise at the same time, will frequently hesitate between different desires ... and harrass himself without advancing' (*Rambler* 134). Wide-ranging talents and insatiable intellectual curiosity often lead, for Johnson, to perpetual procrastination. 'Acute discernment' and 'active faculties' are at odds with each other: Johnson insists upon the shortness of the time apportioned us and the necessity for less thought and more action.

This focus on action, rather than thought, is an unusual one for a moralist. Moral writing usually invites us to consider potential outcomes carefully before embarking on a course of action. As Johnson points out, temerity has frequently been the object of censure, while few moralists have warned against timidity (*Rambler* 129). Yet, for Johnson, diffidence prevents many from undertaking anything at all, since 'whatever is proposed, it is much easier to find reasons for rejecting than embracing' (*Rambler* 39).

Idleness is, for Johnson, one of the most constant features of the human mind and possesses a force stronger even than desire: 'We every day ... find multitudes repining at the want of that which nothing but idleness hinders them from enjoying' (*Rambler* 134). Johnson describes idleness almost as if it were an impersonal physical force, defining it as 'the *vis inertiae*, the mere repugnance to motion' (*ibid.*). We are neither driven to idleness by the hope of pleasure or by the wish to avoid pain. It offers no clear benefits: 'To neglect our duties, merely to avoid the labour of performing them . . . is surely to sink under weak temptations' (*ibid.*). Here, as elsewhere in the *Rambler*, Johnson acknowledges the inadequacy of reason to explain human motivation. However weak the allurements which idleness offers, it is one of the strongest of our impulses: 'one of the general weaknesses, which . . . prevail to a greater or less degree in every mind' (*ibid.*). In the world of the *Rambler*, any action not outrightly criminal is preferable to this state of total inactivity.

Idleness, in the *Rambler*, is often accompanied by a retreat into daydreams and fantasy. Johnson diagnoses daydreaming as a 'formidable and obstinate disease of the intellect' and prescribes a strict regimen of constant activity as a remedy: '[It is essential that] no part of life be spent in a state of neutrality or indifference; but that some pleasure be found for every moment that is not devoted to labour' (*Rambler* 89). For Johnson, daydreaming represents a complete abdication of moral responsibility, a relinquishment of our duties as social beings and a retreat into a solipsistic mental universe. Johnson's language when describing daydreaming is extreme. It is a 'frigid and narcotick' condition (*ibid.*): to live in a world of fantasy and wish-fulfilment is, for Johnson, scarcely to be alive at all.

Many of the characters who inhabit the *Rambler* are afflicted with this mental malady. The unreliable Aliger is a particularly vivid example of the moral degeneracy of those who surrender themselves wholly to the power of their own imaginations: 'It was so pleasant to live in perpetual vacancy, that he soon dismissed his attention as an useless incumbrance . . . The hopes or fears felt by others, had no influence upon his conduct' (*Rambler* 201). Aliger defrauds his creditors, deceives his friends and jilts his bride, without premeditated malice, simply out of a kind of mental frigidity which prevents him from acknowledging that anything outside his own mental world could have a substantial reality.

A number of the *Rambler*'s correspondents live in a state of complete mental torpor. Euphelia, exiled to the country for the summer, gives a vivid description of this condition:

> I am forced to be awake at least twelve hours . . . I walk because I am disgusted with sitting still, and sit down because I am weary with walking. I have no motive to action, nor any object of love, or hate, or fear, or inclination.
>
> (*Rambler* 42)

Indecision, which often begins as the confusion of an active and intellectually curious mind, faced with a plethora of choices, can lead, in Johnson's world, to procrastination and idleness, the solipsistic world of fantasy and, finally, to this condition of mental vacuity.

Johnson offers an escape from this nightmarish trajectory in those *Rambler* papers which discuss the proper uses of time. 'The great incentive to virtue', Johnson tells us, 'is the reflection that we must die' (*Rambler* 78). The reminders of the brevity of life are designed to urge us to action. Always a practical, not a speculative, moralist, Johnson suggests that thinking too long or too deeply is liable to lead to moral confusion and mental lassitude. Indecision, for Johnson, is one of the greatest obstacles to the fulfilment of moral duties.

Competition, envy and fame

In the *Rambler*, Johnson portrays a world of fierce, relentless competition. The urge to continually compare our condition with that of others is not restricted to the consideration of whether others are happier or more fortunate than ourselves. According to Johnson, we are constantly measuring our accomplishments against those of others: 'All human excellence is comparative' (*Rambler* 127). Johnson uses the term 'excellence' in the *Rambler* to denote both great achievements in themselves and the act of surpassing others. As Isobel Grundy has shown in her book *Samuel Johnson and the Scale of Greatness* (1986), for Johnson, all who aspire to honour or reputation must battle with a horde of eager competitors.[55] For Johnson, 'Most of our enjoyments owe their value to the peculiarity of possession' (*Rambler* 66). Johnson portrays each of us as striving for a solitary eminence: we wish not just to be good, but to be the best.

Johnson uses the word 'distinction' in the *Rambler* in a similar manner to 'excellence': it conflates absolute and comparative merit. To be distinguished is precisely to be different from others, therefore 'distinction' is a scant resource. 'Every one wishes for the distinctions for which thousands are wishing at the same time', Johnson tells us. Life, in the *Rambler*, is a constant series of competitions:

> A great part of the pain and pleasure of life arises ... from the success or miscarriage of secret competitions. ... we seldom require more to the happiness of the present hour, than to surpass him that stands next before us.
>
> (*Rambler* 164)

Success, in itself, is inadequate if it is not accompanied by victory over others. The affluent trader Serotinus, on returning to his native town, finds his happiness soured by the death or absence of those before whom he hoped to flaunt his superiority. Their place, he tells us, has been 'filled by a new generation with other views and other competitions' (*Rambler* 165). Denied the taste of victory over old antagonists, Serotinus concludes that wealth 'conferred upon me very few distinctions in my native place' (*ibid.*). Seged the king also discovers how little success can be enjoyed without victory. He offers rewards to those courtiers who can provide the best 'festive performances', but awards the same prizes to everyone. His guests 'departed unsatisfied, because they were honoured with no distinction, and wanted an opportunity to triumph in the mortification of their opponents' (*Rambler* 205).

Since our own happiness bears an inverse relationship to the success of others, there are clearly many incentives to envy. Yet envy, for Johnson, goes beyond self-interest: 'The great law of natural benevolence is oftner violated by envy than by interest' (*Rambler* 183). Envy is 'mere unmixed and genuine evil; it . . . desires not so much its own happiness as another's misery' (*ibid.*). Every successful man 'will have many malevolent gazers at his eminence' (*Rambler* 172), and 'he that has given no provocation to malice, but by attempting to excel, finds himself pursued by multitudes whom he never saw with all the implacability of personal resentment' (*Rambler* 183).

The malice which envy inspires, in the *Rambler*, most often takes the form of calumny. Johnson catalogues the various means by which we attempt to damage the reputations of others in *Rambler* 44. The whisperers, roarers and detractors whom Johnson describes are very effective at propagating misery, since they strike at fame, the desire of which Johnson describes as 'the original motive of almost all our actions' (*Rambler* 193). For Johnson, fame is a commodity in limited supply. He tells us:

> There is never room in the world for more than a certain quantity or measure of renown.... When this vacuity is filled, no characters can be admitted into the circulation of fame, but by occupying the place of some that must be thrust into oblivion.
>
> (*Rambler* 203)

As Grundy (1986) has argued, we can become famous only by supplanting someone else, elbowing them out of a crowded space. Successive generations cannot add new names to the roll call of the famous: each accession to fame must be balanced by a loss in an act of aggression. While fame is difficult to obtain, its possession is also insecure.

While Johnson envisages a society in which most people are motivated by a struggle for renown in some form, he continually reminds his readers just how little fame anyone can obtain. In the highly specialized, divided and divisive society portrayed in the *Rambler*, each individual is too exclusively preoccupied with his or her own concerns, to think much of others:

> The truth is, that no man is much regarded by the rest of the world . . . While we see multitudes passing before us, of whom perhaps not one appears to deserve our notice, or excites our sympathy, we should remember, that we likewise are lost in the same throng.
>
> (*Rambler* 159)

Like other contenders for fame, writers are often neglected and ignored. They also, however, frequently arouse an active hostility on the part of their potential readers. The act of publication is a bid for fame and presupposes, on the author's part, a provocative confidence in his or her own abilities. Justifying his own criticism of Milton's faults, Johnson writes:

> He that writes may be considered as a kind of general challenger, whom every one has a right to attack; since he quits the common rank of life, steps forward beyond the lists, and offers his merit to the publick judgment. To commence author is to claim praise, and no man can justly aspire to honour, but at the hazard of disgrace.
>
> (*Rambler* 93)

As Mary van Tassel has shown, Johnson repeatedly uses military images to characterize the relationship between himself and his readers (1988: 461–71). The writer, like the candidate for fame, thrusts himself or herself aggressively upon potential readers' notice, challenges all who wish to read him or her to an intellectual battle. Issuing a general challenge implies supreme confidence in one's abilities to defeat all comers. Writers who fail in this bid for applause are exposed to the 'unbounded contempt' of readers, enjoying what they regard as 'an honest triumph over unjust claims, and exorbitant expectations' (*Rambler* 1).

By openly courting admiration, writers lay themselves open to a charge of arrogance. For this reason, even when a writer attains literary success, he or she is unlikely to enjoy personal popularity. In fact, Johnson suggests that the more we admire an author's work, the less we will enjoy his or her company, since 'few spend their time with much satisfaction under the eye of uncontestable superiority' (*Rambler* 188). Writers in the *Rambler* are often portrayed as arrogant. The successful author Misellus ascribes his unpopularity to envy: he is 'too eminent for happiness' (*Rambler* 16). When he describes his behaviour in company, however, it is clear that he treats others with contemptuous rudeness. Similarly, Didaculus, a malicious wit, makes himself universally feared and hated: 'The natural pride of human nature

rises against him, who by general censures lays claim to general superiority'
(*Rambler* 174).

'General censures' are clearly not the subject matter of the *Rambler*.
Johnson far more frequently explains or palliates, than outrightly condemns
behaviour. Nor does he lay claim to a 'general superiority', reminding us,
instead, that the moralist shares many of his or her reader's failings. Johnson
does, however, stake a subtler claim to a superiority over his readers, as he
has assumed 'the office of a periodical monitor' (*Rambler* 15). A monitor is
one who inspects and regulates the behaviour of others. The pen-portrait of
Nugaculus in *Rambler* 103 demonstrates how easily a monitor can become
trapped in 'the cobwebs of petty inquisitiveness'. Nugaculus has an interest
in human motivation which mirrors Mr Rambler's. He quickly degenerates,
however, into a busybody, a gossip and a 'a perpetual spy' (*Rambler* 103).

The duty of a periodical monitor is twofold: to detect faults and to offer
advice on their reformation. The giving of advice, Johnson writes, is a
particularly delicate task. To advise someone implies superior knowledge
and, like any other assumption of superiority, is liable to be rejected:

> Vanity is so frequently the apparent motive of advice, that we, for the
> most part, summon our powers to oppose it without any very accurate
> enquiry whether it is right. It is sufficient that another is growing great
> in his own eyes at our expence, and assumes authority over us without
> our permission.
>
> (*Rambler* 87)

The moral writer faces an insoluble dilemma. In order to learn from the
moralist, readers must 'not only confess their ignorance, but, what is still
less pleasing, must allow that he from whom they are to learn is more
knowing than themselves' (*Rambler* 3). They are unwilling to allow the
moralist's superiority to themselves – understandably unwilling, since, as
Johnson so frequently reminds us, moralists are as fallible as their readers.
On the other hand, in order to benefit from the moralist's teachings, they
must accept his or her authority: 'Men would not more patiently submit to
be taught, than commanded, by one known to have the same follies and
weaknesses with themselves' (*Rambler* 14). In the universal battle for precedence, the moralist is in competition with his or her own readers. The competitions, rivalries and struggles for superiority which Johnson sees as
characterizing human society are not only the targets of the moralist's criticism, but threaten to make that criticism itself ineffective.

Patronage and dependence

In the *Rambler*, Johnson portrays a society in which we are constantly comparing ourselves with others. While in the *Rambler* papers on competition, envy and fame he focuses on the comparative estimation of abilities, achievements and renown, in the papers on patronage and dependence Johnson examines the ways in which wealth and class are used as markers of superiority and inferiority in a society obsessed with status.

A number of *Rambler* papers portray the arrogance of the rich towards their social inferiors: Prospero (*Rambler* 200) and Trypherus (*Rambler* 98) are only particularly striking examples of a behaviour which Johnson finds almost universal: 'It is scarcely possible to find any man who does not frequently . . . indulge his own pride by forcing others into a comparison with himself, when he knows the advantage is on his side' (*Rambler* 98). Like fame, wealth is relative and, Johnson implies, cannot be fully enjoyed without the gloating satisfaction of seeing others poorer. The arrogant rich are continually undoing the moralist's work of moderating desires, as they encourage us to make our happiness dependent on our place in a scale of prosperity.

In this world of continual comparisons, friendship is a rare quality: 'The greatest part of mankind content themselves without it, and supply its place as they can, with interest and dependence' (*Rambler* 64). Friendships between rich and poor, in particular, are almost impossible. Even the most altruistic friendship is based, Johnson argues, on reciprocal benefits: 'We are desirous of pleasing others, because we receive pleasure from them'. We are unwilling to acknowledge the benefits which we have received from social inferiors: 'To be obliged, is to be in some respect inferior to another; and few willingly indulge the memory of an action which raises one whom they have always been accustomed to think below them' (*Rambler* 166). Even in friendship we are anxious to maintain or enhance our status. In the universal tendency to categorize others as inferiors or superiors, all relationships tend towards a model of patronage and dependence: 'We see every day men of eminence followed with all the obsequiousness of dependance, and courted with all the blandishments of flattery, by those who want nothing from them but professions of regard' (*Rambler* 166).

While these unequal relationships are so common, they are deeply damaging to the moral character of both parties. A number of *Rambler* papers vividly describe the misuse of power over others. The petty tyrants who inhabit the periodical's pages range from the terrifying to the despicable. Among the more egregiously wicked are the extortionate landlord Squire Bluster (*Rambler* 142) and Misella's wealthy guardian, who seduces and then abandons her (*Rambler* 170). Few of the characters portrayed in the *Rambler* display such extreme cruelty, however. Most content themselves with a continued series of small insults designed to keep the victim painfully aware of his or her own dependence. Hyperdulus describes this treatment vividly: 'petulance of accent, or arrogance of mien, some vehemence of interrogation, or quickness of reply, that recalls my poverty to my mind' (*Rambler* 149).

The pen-portraits within the *Rambler* are of representative, rather than extreme, characters. It is important that the reader should recognize his or her own failings in the behaviour of these oppressors, so that he or she may be shocked by 'the contemplation of his own manners' (*Rambler* 208) into reform. When Johnson wishes to remind us of the full human capacity for evil, he does so in an essay rather than a character sketch. In *Rambler* 148, Johnson portrays paternal tyranny. Within his own home, the father possesses a power far greater than that of even the most arbitrary rulers: 'Seldom any prince, however despotick ... [will] venture upon those freaks of injustice, which are sometimes indulged under the secrecy of a private dwelling' (*Rambler* 148). No possible motive of self-interest can explain why a father would be cruel to his children 'who can disturb him with no competition, who can enrich him with no spoils' (*ibid*.). A situation of dominance over others, for Johnson, has a power to corrupt which goes beyond rational explanation.

Although Johnson frequently portrays the oppressions of those in power, he also defends patrons against accusations of injustice. Portraits of negligent patrons (such as Liberalis's patron in *Rambler* 163) are balanced by Johnson's contention that many complaints of neglect are fictitious: 'Among wretches that place their happiness in the favour of the great ... nothing is more common than to boast of confidence which they do not enjoy' (*Rambler* 189). Many expect financial support who do not deserve it, Johnson argues. Johnson claims, for example, that when the behaviour of learned writers is 'impartially surveyed', it will be found that they 'seldom wanted friends, but when they wanted virtue' (*Rambler* 77). In Johnson's allegory of Patronage, he portrays the goddess's moral degeneration as simultaneous with the increasing impudence of those who do not deserve her favour and block the entrance to her palace from the more deserving (*Rambler* 91).

A number of *Rambler* papers depict the vices incident to dependency. All too often, Johnson claims, the dependent relinquishes moral responsibility, since his or her only rule of conduct is the desire to please: 'The greatest part of human gratifications approach so nearly to vice, that few who make the delight of others their rule of conduct, can avoid disingenuous compliances' (*Rambler* 160). One of the most dangerous of these compliances is flattery. The dependent, by contrast with the moralist, attempts to strengthen his or her patron's 'weaknesses and follies, regales his reigning vanity, or stimulates his prevalent desires' (*Rambler* 172). The dependent must therefore bear at least partial responsibility for his or her patron's vices. The ugly heiress Turpicula would never, Johnson tells us, have become vain, had she not been 'animated and emboldened by flattery' (*Rambler* 189).

The learned are far from immune to this almost universal tendency to court the favour of the great, Johnson argues. On the contrary, 'the most obsequious of the slaves of pride, the most rapturous of the gazers upon wealth ... are collected from seminaries appropriated to the study of wisdom and of virtue' (*Rambler* 180). Scholars, however, are singularly ill qualified to shine in company. Vivaculus exemplifies this social awkwardness. Years of solitary devotion to learning have left his mind 'contracted and stiffened' and his manners 'sullen and malignant' (*Rambler* 177). He goes to London to polish his social graces only to fall into the company of a society of antiquarians even more ill-mannered, morose and socially inept than himself.

Dusty pedants like Vivaculus are outnumbered in the *Rambler* by scholars who, like the frigid Gelasimus in *Rambler* 179, aspire to be wits. 'The airiness and jocularity of a man bred to severe science and solitary meditation' is more likely to provoke contempt than hilarity, Johnson tells us (*Rambler* 173). The wish to be regarded as a wit is a particularly misguided one. The wit, Johnson writes, is 'a character, which, perhaps, no man ever assumed without repentance' (*Rambler* 194). The wits portrayed in the *Rambler* are consumed by nervous apprehension, entering each company 'with a beating heart, like a litigant on the day of decision' and carefully calculating their nightly 'loss or gain of reputation' (*Rambler* 128). The wit's predicament is exacerbated by the fact that anxiety is incompatible with humour. Papilius, in *Rambler* 141, manages to retain an appearance of spontaneity only through painstaking study. Hilarius, in *Rambler* 101, however, finds that the ardour of his 'ambition of shining', coupled with his anxiety to maintain his reputation, combine to 'freeze his faculties'. The wit resembles the writer of an essay-periodical in the necessity that they are both under of providing regular entertainment and in their subjection to the never-ceasing 'call for novelty' (*Rambler* 141). We can sense, in these portraits of anxious wits, Johnson's consciousness that the essay-periodical as a form must have led his readers to expect twice-weekly specimens of wit. No wonder he describes journalism as 'the anxious employment of a periodical writer' (*Rambler* 208), a sentiment echoed in the *Gray's Inn Journal*, whose editor describes 'the anxious Character of a public Writer' (14 September 1754).

While Johnson never advocates assuming the role of a wit, he does recommend that scholars improve their social graces. He numbers 'an early entrance into the living world' (*Rambler* 137) as one of the most important qualifications for authorship. Johnson never recommends isolation or segregation. When scholars are gauche or boorish in company, they bring learning and moral wisdom into disrepute, leading most people to 'quickly shake off their reverence for modes of education, which they find to produce no ability above the rest of mankind' (*ibid.*). What is important for Johnson is not simply the intrinsic merit of a piece of writing, but its potential to reach an audience.

The *Rambler* was published at a time of rapidly changing patterns of ownership and control of periodicals, in which booksellers and printers, rather than writers, often determined the contents of publications. Essay-periodicalists were an increasingly endangered breed. In this context, the *Rambler* can be seen as an anachronistic project. The magazines ascribed their popularity to the heterogeneity of their contents, to the variety of their contributors and to their appeal to a segmented readership, divided by interest, profession and gender. Johnson, by contrast, wrote in a uniform tone, on a limited number of subjects, included very few readers' letters and attempted to appeal to a general readership.

Johnson's publication is a collection of his own moral ideas and a place in which to express his Christian ethics. While the *Rambler* is not a systematic treatise, the essays express a coherent moral vision. In the *Rambler*, Johnson attempts to combat the fragmentation of his society by diverting our attention from the specific to the general, from those things whose value is comparative to the fundamentals of human behaviour which we all share. He appeals to common interests and to a common culture which he regards as endangered. The essay-periodical had traditionally been written in the voice of the quirky individual, by cranks and spinsters who traced their lineage back to the loveable eccentricities of Isaac Bickerstaff. Johnson, by contrast, created in Mr Rambler a representative of humanity in whose essays he could voice the common concerns of all mankind.

8 'A becoming sensibility'

The *Old Maid* and the sentimental periodical

Anne Laurence claims that, during the eighteenth century, two thirds of adult women were single at any one time, many of them as widows, some as spinsters (1999: 56). However, as Bridget Hill has pointed out, society had 'no acknowledged place for the single woman' (2001: 11). Spinsters living alone were particularly financially and socially vulnerable: 'The most invisible women of all are the older unmarried women, with no family and less opportunity for employment in domestic service. Their disadvantaged status is emphasised by their high rate of early death' (Laurence 1999: 56). In addition to their social deprivation, old maids were the targets of some of the mid-eighteenth century's harshest satire. Contemporary old maids report being subjected to frequent public insults. The correspondent Constantia Issolea complains to the *Auditor*, 'If I walk in publick the Women cast a disdainful Stare at me; and the Men cry with Contempt, *What an old Hag*' (33, 1 May 1733). In similar fashion, a correspondent reports to the *Universal Spectator* that as she was passing two gentlemen in the Strand one commented, 'That is an Old Maid, poor Wretch! . . . in a sneering contemptuous Manner' (3 September 1737). Contemporaries often argue that the worst part of an old maid's situation is her exposure to 'the incessant impertinence of indelicate ridicule' (*A Philosophical, Historical, and Moral Essay on Old Maids* 1786: 1.17). 'Every one . . . knows', one writer claims, 'the sneers, the twits, the sarcasms, the toasts, and wishes that never fail accompanying an old maid upon all occasions' (*A Practical Essay on Old Maids* (n.d.): 33).

This chapter will focus on Frances Brooke's periodical the *Old Maid*, written in the persona of Mary Singleton, spinster. The paper was published weekly from 15 November 1755 to 4 July 1756: a total of 37 issues. As old maids were notorious for their peevishness and bitchy jealousy of other women, an old maid scarcely seems an appropriate choice of persona for the editor of an essay-periodical. The title of her publication must have led readers to expect satire and raised specific expectations about Brooke's treatment of her *eidolon*. The author of a proposal to establish a college for old maids acknowledges these preconceptions when he fears that '*the term* Old Maid *will probably be considered as a term of derision, and turn the serious reader away in disgust*' (*Considerations for Establishing a College for Old Maids in Ireland* 1790: 3). One of Brooke's readers contends that there is 'no character so generally the same, and concerning which the opinions of mankind do so perfectly agree, as that of an *Old Maid*' (*Old Maid* 6, 20 December 1755). In the first part of this chapter, I will examine Brooke's unusually sympathetic portrayal of female spinsterhood, by placing her depiction of Mary Singleton in the context of other contemporary representations of old maids.

Some essay-periodicalists before Brooke had chosen outré figures such as harlots, mountebanks and devils as their *eidolons*. These editorial personae were, however, either undeveloped or used as the objects of satirical attack; Brooke, by contrast, uses her periodical to elicit our sympathy for the figure of the spinster. Brooke's persona was probably not autobiographical. Born in 1724, she was 31 or 32 when she began writing the periodical and had married Henry Brooke at the latest by the end of the journal's run and probably at around the time she began the journal.[56] Mary Singleton, by contrast, is a spinster of at least 56.[57] Brooke chose a persona who would normally arouse readerly disdain and scorn in order to reinterpret the figure of the old maid and attempt to portray female celibacy in a more positive light.

It is not only her surprising choice of alter ego, however, that demonstrates Brooke's unusual approach to literary journalism. In the *Old Maid*, she combines features of the essay-periodical with those of fictional writing. Her frame narrative of the editor's niece, Julia, anticipates her later novels: not only in her use of character and plot, but also in the style and tone of her writing, which moves from journalistic suavity to the emotional language of the sentimental novel. In Brooke's paper, the older genre of the Spectatorial essay-periodical merges with the sentimental novel to create a new hybrid: the sentimental periodical. These two unusual aspects of her periodical – her choice of persona and her novelistic approach – are closely related. Writing in the style of sentimental fiction enables Brooke to champion female celibacy more effectively by placing her *eidolon* in a literary tradition in which empathy is more important than satire.

To appreciate my argument regarding Brooke, it is important to understand the satirical journalistic tradition in which she found herself, by examining the work of her close contemporaries Eliza Haywood, Christopher Smart and Bonnell Thornton. In some ways, an old maid is an obvious choice of persona for a female writer. Authorship and celibacy were often associated with each other, as eccentricity, irascibility and fierce pride were considered to be common to both. A male correspondent of the *Lady's Magazine* comments wryly, 'The greatest reproach of an old maid ... is her ill humour ... There is no race of men more apt to ... remit their natural good humour, than authors' (November 1761). The writer who has failed to attract readers and the old maid who has failed to attract men are depicted as suffering from a very similar disappointment, one particularly guaranteed to sour the temper: 'The fair sex may be considered as students in the most important and most delicate of all arts, the art of pleasing; and, of course, the Old Maid may be reckoned in the number of unsuccessful artists' (*A Philosophical, Historical and Moral Essay* 1786: 85). In this context, it is unsurprising that in her periodical the *Female Spectator* Eliza Haywood chose to portray her editor as a single woman who turns in middle age from attempts to attract lovers to attempts to please readers.

Brooke's choice of a female editor-persona may well have been influenced by Haywood's. Published in 1744–6, when Brooke was entering her twenties, Haywood's *Female Spectator* went through six collected editions by 1756 and is one of very few essay-periodicals known to have been written by women. Brooke may have also read the parody 'The New Female Spectator', published as a series in the *Spring-Garden Journal* (1752), which mimics Haywood's elevated moral tone and educational material. Haywood does not develop the character of her alter ego further in later issues of the periodical, however, nor is there any discussion of spinsterhood within the pages of the publication. The only account of incidents from the narrator's personal life we are given is a visit to the country (*Female Spectator* bk XVII: 3.161–75), in which her conduct is exemplary.

The Female Spectator's decorous behaviour and the moral focus of her periodical are all the more striking because it is precisely the former coquette turned old maid who attracts the harshest contemporary criticism and most clearly embodies the stereotype of old maidism: 'The superannuated beauty turns into the sharpest and most acrimonious Old Maid' (*A Philosophical, Historical and Moral Essay* 1786: 88–9). 'Involuntarily [*sic*] celibacy is principally occasioned by our own vanity and conduct, and too highly estimating the value of our personal accomplishments', the narrator of *A Practical Essay on Old Maids* tells her readers (p. 44). Cautionary tales of haughty beauties who have left hordes of weeping discarded suitors in their wake, only to be rejected in their turn, abound in the contemporary press. An anonymous poet who writes in to the *Gentleman's Magazine* envisages old maids in the afterlife remembering with bitter regret

> ev'ry youth that sought their love
> . . . .
> All whom a guilty pride and coy disdain,
> Frown'd from their arms, and doom'd to sigh in vain.

(XIX, March 1749: 131)

Contemporary attitudes towards the causes of female celibacy are succinctly summarized in the chorus of a late eighteenth-century popular song:

> no never nor cost a fond Lover a tear,
> 'Tis pity to die an old Maid.

(Willson 1795)

The underlying suggestion here that every woman has it in her power to
marry unless she is flighty or perverse is explicitly asserted by a number of
contemporary writers. The self-professed old maid Lucinda in *The Mysteries
of Virginity* tells us that 'there are no Women so ordinary, or ill shaped, but
there are Men as uggly, and deformed' (1714: 33). The author of *A Satyr
Upon Old Maids*, after describing the repellent physical characteristics of old
maids with a Swiftian attention to disgusting detail – 'rank Hide', 'putrid
Lungs', pestilential breath and 'pendant *Pearls*' of snot – goes on to assure
the spinsters that they can, nevertheless, find husbands (1713: 7–8). He or
she suggests night soil collectors, 'whose Nature is by Custom fed with
Stinks', as well as '*Lepers* and *Leachers* [*sic*]' and '*Zanies, Idiots, Dolts*' (*A Satyr
Upon Old Maids* 1713: 10–11). A contributor to the *Gentleman's Magazine*
has a further practical suggestion: the '*Tar* indelicate' will be pleased to
marry any willing white woman when he returns from India 'and negros
please no more' (XIX, March 1749: 131).

These caricatures of repulsive spinsters are less pernicious than the subtler
criticisms contained in works such as the *Philosophical, Historical and Moral
Essay on Old Maids* since, unlike the *Essay*, these works were clearly not
intended to be understood literally. In this context, however, an old maid
seems an odd choice of journalistic alter ego for Brooke who claims that her
periodical owes a debt to 'the admirable author of the RAMBLER' (*Old Maid*
26, 8 May 1756) and was written in emulation of the 'lucubrations of this
. . . genius', which she has 'studied . . . as a model of writing' (*Old Maid* 8, 3
January 1756).

Johnson's depictions of old maids within the *Rambler* may have influenced
Brooke's portrayal of Mary Singleton. Comments on older spinsters are rare
within the *Rambler* and express a careful mixture of criticism and praise.
Johnson asserts that those who grow old 'in a single state' are generally
'morose, fretful and captious', but this statement refers equally to men and
women (*Rambler* 112). In an essay on marriage and celibacy, he argues that
single women 'seldom give those that frequent their conversation, any
exalted notions of the blessing of liberty', but he goes on to enumerate the
miseries of an unhappy marriage (*Rambler* 39). He portrays the choice
between marriage and celibacy for women as a choice between Scylla and
Charybdis. There are only two pen-portraits of old maids within the periodi-

cal: the bad-tempered Tetrica and the sensible Tranquilla (*Ramblers* 74 and 119). Despite having been 'subject for many years to all the hardships of antiquated virginity', Tranquilla is cheerful, sensible and virtuous. She has chosen to remain single because she has never been courted by a man of sense and virtue and is later rewarded with marriage to the correspondent Hymenaeus (*Rambler* 167).

Johnson's balanced and sometimes sympathetic portrayals of old maids are characteristic of his treatment of those who were traditionally the victims of satire but they are very unusual in the context of mid-eighteenth century journalism. Most of the journalistic representations of spinsters in mid-century focus on the physical repulsiveness, pride, bad temper and moral turpitude of old maids. The editor of the *World*, to which Mary Singleton herself subscribes (see *Old Maid* 2, 22 November 1755), describes aged spinsters pooling their resources in order to afford to share 'a neat little house, a light-bodied coach, and a footboy' but in this struggle to maintain their gentility 'quarreling every day' (151, 20 November 1755). The barely disguised sexual rapaciousness of Martha Single is characteristic. A shrewish spinster of 55, she writes unconvincingly in the *Lady's Curiosity* of her determination to reject all offers and 'laugh with contempt on the prettiest fellow in *Great Britain*' (no. 8). Brooke's title would probably have reminded contemporaries less of Haywood's *Female Spectator* than of the grotesque and ludicrous creations of Christopher Smart and Bonnell Thornton.

Thornton portrays the editor of his *Drury-Lane Journal* (1752) as a widow who has turned to hack writing in desperation. While not strictly speaking an old maid, his *eidolon* Roxana Termagant, 'a female, and *witty*, and much above the age of eighteen' (*Drury-Lane Journal* 1, 16 January 1752) epitomizes many of the ascribed characteristics of the single woman journalist. The associations of women's writing with prostitution are underlined not only by her place of residence, a street infamous for its brothels, but also by the 'five wooden pictures, half-torn, of the *Harlot's Progress*' which decorate her walls (*Drury-Lane Journal* 3, 30 January 1752). Her own life, like the harlot's, is a cautionary tale. Her 'early propensity to learning' leads her to neglect feminine accomplishments and, in a parody of male education, she first becomes a school usher and is then taught the Classics for four years by her lover, a student at Cambridge. When she is deserted by her lover, she becomes first a bit-part actress and then the wife of a strolling player, before she is finally forced to enlist as a bookseller's hack (*ibid.*). Roxana's life is a course of progressive moral degeneration as she becomes first an actress, then an actor's wife and finally reaches the nadir of female respectability when she descends to journalism.

When Roxana dies, her niece Priscilla launches a new publication, the *Spring-Garden Journal*. Despite her youth, Priscilla is clearly an old maid in the making. The life of 'Vanity and Folly', which inevitably leads to old maidism in later life and which is only discreetly hinted at in the *Female Spectator*, is detailed here with relish. Like her aunt, Priscilla is characterized by her vanity and sexual notoriety. She writes her periodical from a room overlooking a park frequented by soldiers, above a subscription library, thus combining the dangers of female leisure, sexual over-exposure, literary ambition and indiscriminate novel-reading. The midwife Mrs Minnim has already offered to take Priscilla on as her apprentice, warning her that midwifery 'is likely to be my last and dernier Resort' (*Spring-Garden Journal* 4, 7 December 1752).

The associations of 'OLD MAIDISM' with female pretensions to learning, sexual promiscuity, poverty, prostitution and midwifery are manifest in Christopher Smart's periodical the *Student* (1750–1) in the figure of the 'Female Student'. Smart's alter ego has received a Classical education from her father, 'a grave fellow of a college' who sired her in a clandestine marriage (*Student* II: Polyhymnia).[58] Having 'made much greater progress in academical erudition, than many of your matriculated dons', she progresses sexually up the academic ranks, the mistress first of undergraduates, then of Fellows, and finally of a College Master (*Student* II: Calliope). When her charms fade, she is forced to take a lover without a degree, the bookseller Mr Brevier, publisher of Smart's periodical the *Midwife*, who, in a parody of a marriage proposal, has 'very lately honour'd *me* with the offer of a garret at the easy rate of writing sixteen hours a day' (*Student* II: Euterpe). Despite being 'a fusty OLD MAID', she assures the reader that she does not 'write out of pique, peevishness and resentment' (*Student* II: Polyhymnia). The implication, however, is clearly that she is a frustrated spinster, turning to scribbling for income when her sexual charms lose their force and writing attacks on men to revenge herself on those who have rejected her. The 'Vanity' which leads the old maid to flirt with men until it is too late to receive an honourable proposal is the same sentiment which leads her to value herself upon her education and her literary abilities; hence, the female writer is more likely to be an old maid than any other woman.

It is surprising, then, that Frances Brooke chose Mary Singleton as her *eidolon* when she launched her new periodical in 1755. Her publication demonstrates a deft awareness of the satirical tradition of scribbling old maids. How, then, does Brooke attempt to transform the hated and derided figure of the old maid into a persuasive spokeswoman for respectable values?

In her opening paper, Mary Singleton offers her readers a whimsical account of her motives for writing:

> In defiance of all criticism I will write: every body knows an English woman has a natural right to expose herself as much as she pleases . . .

since I feel a violent inclination to show my prodigious wisdom to my cotemporaries . . . [I] hope, by giving to the public the observations my unemploy'd course of life has enabled me to make, to obtain pardon for leading my days in a way so unserviceable to society.

(*Old Maid* 1, 15 November 1755)

Mary Singleton's vanity is apparent when she boasts of her 'prodigious wisdom' and the associations of women's writing with sexual looseness are underlined by the idea that editing a periodical is a form of self-exposure. Mary Singleton's tone, however, is confident – she defies criticism – and the writing of a periodical is depicted as a public duty. Her literary progeny compensates society for her biological sterility. The absence of marital responsibilities has enabled her to make observations which qualify her as a writer and her freedom from domestic cares leaves her the liberty to publish a periodical if she wishes. Her independence is highlighted: she 'feels an inclination' and is free to follow it, and she has 'a natural right' to launch her own periodical venture. There is no suggestion that the paper is written for financial gain; she is free, financially as well as morally, to dedicate herself to the service of the 'public'.

Mary Singleton does possess several of 'the follies of superannuated virginity' (*Old Maid* 36, 17 July 1756), although Brooke's depiction of them is mildly humorous, rather than ferociously satirical. Old maids were frequently satirized for their sexual desperation. The anonymous editor of the *Connoisseur* describes an allegorical dream-vision of the Temple of Marriage, in which an 'old woman, fantastically dressed . . . ran raving up to the Altar, crying out, that she *would* have a husband' (*Connoisseur* 95, 20 November 1755). Unable to persuade any of the assembled company to marry her, she seizes a bride cake and – 'furious with rage and despair' – crams it down the editor's throat, in token of their matrimony (*ibid.*). He wakes to find 'the nauseous taste of it still in my mouth' (*ibid.*). Published only five days after Brooke launched her periodical, the dream-vision may be an attack on the *Old Maid* and the sexually rapacious old woman, an image of Mary Singleton.

Brooke's *eidolon* bears only faint and disarmingly innocuous traces of the characteristics of the spinster as sexual predator, however. She delights in reading her love letters 'once a year on my birth-day, by the help of spectacles' (*Old Maid* 1, 15 November 1755) and the periodical enables her to receive male correspondence again. Her correspondent Virginius, who, as his name suggests, is '*an Old Maid of the masculine gender*' (*Old Maid* 6, 20 December 1755), relies on at long last seeing a letter in print which has been rejected by every other periodical. He rests his faith on 'that *obliging willingness*, with which Ladies of your *distinction* have always been observed to admit the addresses of those, who have the appearance of *any thing masculine* about them' (*ibid.*). Mary Singleton assures readers that, 'I shall expect to hear from [Virginius] again, with all the impatience of a virgin of fifty, who must not hope for civilities every day' (*ibid.*). To show him, however, that 'I have more than one string to my bow', Mary Singleton prints a letter from the 'jovial old Bacchanalian Batchelor' Tom Bumper, who sends her a poem inspired by her charms, together with 'a gallon of Claret', and promises to toast her at his club (*ibid.*). The editor is able to receive epistolary gallantries from male correspondents who cannot see her wrinkles. Nevertheless, Mary Singleton's tone is not one of sexual desperation: she light-heartedly teases Virginius and thanks Tom Bumper politely for his offer, but refuses the present of claret, as she is a teetotaller.

Little is known about the actual contemporary audience of Brooke's periodical. However, she prints a number of letters from old maids – whether real or fictitious – within the pages of her publication. Some of the old maids who feature in Brooke's paper closely resemble the misogynistic stereotypes depicted by Smart and Thornton. Brooke's most lurid creation is Sarah Whispercom, a nosy busybody who has grown a beard as a result of attempting to copy male behaviour by shaving her chin (*Old Maid* 24, 24 April 1756). Mrs Singleton's correspondent Cana Greypate, a 'maiden lady' living in Oxford, has many obvious similarities with Roxana Termagant and the Female Student (*Old Maid* 9, 10 January 1756). Cana had herself 'formed a design to entertain the public with periodical lucubrations' (*ibid.*). Cana's pride in her erudition does not disguise her sexual desperation – she wishes to change her condition 'upon the first offer' – or her volatile temper (*ibid.*). Her letter is blotted with the marks of 'vehemency of passion' (*ibid.*). Instead of publishing a moral periodical, Mrs Singleton advises her to find an equally sour old Fellow with whom she can descant in private on the vices of the age (*ibid.*). The elderly bachelor, the editor implies, will be as sullen and cantankerous as the old maid.

These negative images of the old maid are more than balanced in the periodical by more positive portrayals of female celibacy. Cana Greypate's letter is immediately followed by one from Marian Doubtful who wonders why Mary Singleton does not offer 'encouragement to your own sex to live single', since 'a single life must be much less disagreeable, than . . . union, with one, who . . . excite[s] . . . loathing and contempt' (*ibid.*). Another of her correspondents views the 'choice of a single life' as a natural response to 'generous indignation at the insolencies of modern husbands' (*ibid.*). The idea of the single life as the choice of a generous nature, rather than the result of rejection, is reflected in the comments of some of Mary Singleton's male correspondents. E.F. praises women 'like you, Madam', who, by remaining single, have been enabled to devote their talents to society and 'have passed their early time in improving themselves, and their latter days in improving others' (*Old Maid* 11, 24 January 1756).

The most striking vindication of the single life within the periodical is Mary Singleton's allegorical Choice of Hercules, a dream vision of the choice between marriage and celibacy (*Old Maid* 21, 10 April 1756). In her dream, Mary Singleton is restored to youth and beauty by the gods and allowed a second chance to choose her way of life. She is led to the fane of Marriage, fragrant with myrtles and orange blossom, but flees when she sees Care, Discord and Jealousy seated behind the goddess's throne. Celibacy's haunt at first appears dreary by comparison, and Neglect, Contempt and Derision support her train, but on a nearer approach she sees Tranquillity at her side. A captivating youth then approaches, whom Mary Singleton soon recognizes as Liberty, a companion more attractive to her than any other lover. She enlists as a votary of Celibacy and is conducted by Peace and Contentment to the Temple of Happiness, equidistant from the two deities. When Mary Singleton awakes:

> I have the satisfaction to find myself really accompanied by *Peace* and *Contentment* ... I am ... in a state generally attended with spleen and Illnature, one of the best tempered creatures breathing ... very inoffensively blotting paper in the service ... of my fellow citizens.
>
> (*ibid.*)

For Mary Singleton, the periodical is not a vehicle in which to vent the 'spleen and Illnature' generally seen as inseparable from an old maid's character, but a therapy to ward off depression and envy. Every old maid, she suggests, has something to contribute to society, in a public, if not in a domestic, capacity. The spinster Abigail Easy tells Mary Singleton that her depiction of the pleasures and freedoms of celibacy has convinced her that the editor is not, like Roxana Termagant and the Female Student, simply 'some fellow who had taken the petticoat in disguise', but 'one of the sisterhood' (*Old Maid* 23, 17 April 1756). She recognizes herself in the sensible and light-hearted editor, as she could not do in the monstrous satirical creations of earlier writers. Whilst 'growing daily more in love with that *liberty* and *independency* I made my choice, I am as chearful and happy a creature as yourself' (*ibid.*).

Brooke's positive attitude towards old maids not only characterizes her as 'a feminist with a strong sense of decorum' (McMullen 1983: 61). It also reflects her attitude to the periodical as a genre. Like Haywood, Brooke rejects the practice of making the periodical editor an outlandish comic figure. Mary Singleton is strikingly restrained, lacking in eccentricity and only mildly whimsical. As Min Wild has shown, she is a credible spokeswoman for the values of civic humanism (1998: 421–36).[59] Like Johnson's Mr Rambler, she functions far more as a representative of good sense than as a figure of fun. Although it incorporates elements of the periodical tradition which included an idiosyncratic editor-persona, Brooke's publication is not primarily a vehicle of satire, but instead shares many features with her later novels, in particular the novels of sensibility *The History of Julia Mandeville* (1763) and *The History of Emily Montague* (1769).

The *Old Maid* is exceptional among contemporary periodicals in the amount of space it dedicates to its frame narrative. Almost half the issues deal in some way with the Old Maid's personal life and the love affairs of her niece, Julia, and Julia's friend Rosara. She announces her design 'to present my readers . . . with such real events of my life, and the lives of my friends as are particularly interesting' and adds, almost apologetically, that 'I shall also think myself obliged to intermix with these such subjects as shall appear to me either useful or entertaining, tho' they have no connection with the affairs of Mrs. *Singleton*' (*Old Maid* 28, 22 May 1756). The 'affairs of Mrs. *Singleton*', the editor suggests, are to be at least as important as the miscellaneous 'useful or entertaining' subjects which usually comprise the bulk of an essay-periodical.

Mary Singleton's past is colourfully novelistic. Born to a fortune of £400 per year, she falls in love with a young man who 'had not a shilling'. They become secretly engaged and plan to marry on her father's death. When her lover inherits an estate, however, he immediately informs Mary Singleton that he is to marry the appropriately named Miss Wealthy. Less typically for the plot of a novel, Mary Singleton sends him a spirited reply and then goes on a four-year tour of the Continent with her sister and brother-in-law. She returns, heart-whole, to find that her lover has been ruined by his wife, an extravagant 'city fortune' corrupted by novel-reading into a love of gaming and intrigues. Two years after their return to England, Mary Singleton's sister dies in childbirth. Mary Singleton adopts her sister's daughter and decides to remain celibate for the child's sake. The penniless lover, sudden deaths, vicissitudes of fortune and poetic justice all recall the plots of contemporary novels. These plot twists also provide ample justification for the editor's marital status. Jilted by a mercenary lover, Mary Singleton's own behaviour has been irreproachable: circumstances, rather than temperament or behaviour, have made her an old maid.

Mary Singleton's maternal duties make her in some senses an exception to the general run of old maids and somewhat counteract her praise of the self-sufficiency of the celibate life. Within the periodical, Brooke champions celibacy as a choice, but, within the novelistic frame narrative, she makes it a question of duty, rather than inclination. In order to retain our sympathies for Mary Singleton, Brooke feels the need to explain the reasons behind her failure to get married. 'If any old maid is excusable', Mary Singleton tells us, 'I hope I am: for tho' I have not had the honour of being a mother, I have had all the cares of one' (*Old Maid* 1, 15 November 1755).

It is not merely in the description of Mary Singleton, however, that Brooke evokes the traditions of the novel. In the second issue of the *Old Maid*, Mary Singleton describes her niece, Julia, in explicitly novelistic terms, beginning with her appearance, 'as . . . it is the fashion to describe the persons of all modern heroines' (*Old Maid* 2, 22 November 1755). The insipid Julia has 'such inexpressible sweetness in her countenance, it has often occasioned a doubt of her understanding', together with a shyness which occasions her 'propensity to be silent in company' (*ibid*.). Like the protagonists of *The Excursion* (1777) and *Julia Mandeville*, she is at a crucial stage of her development, having 'just turned eighteen', and is, in addition, an orphan with a fortune of £15,000 (*Old Maid* 2). Julia's friend Rosara is equally a lady of sentiment, since 'from passing the greatest part of her time in the country' she is 'inclined to be romantic' (*Old Maid* 7, 27 December 1755). Rosara is secretly engaged to a rich lover, Wilmot, who plans to marry him on her father's death, whilst Julia, by a neat contrast, is in love with a poor soldier called Bellville. In her timidity and fragility, Julia anticipates the female figures in *Julia Mandeville*. The eponymous protagonist of that novel is 'delicate and feminine to the utmost degree' (Brooke 1763: 42), while her friend Emily Howard, 'delicate almost to fragility', inspires 'that instinctive fondness one feels for a beautiful child' (Brooke 1763: 109).

Brooke's novels usually pair a high-minded heroine, who is the focus of the plot, with a witty, irreverent commentator, in a structure which echoes the contrast between Clarissa Harlowe and the lively Anna Howe in Richardson's *Clarissa* (1747–8). In *Julia Mandeville*, the sensible widow Anne Wilmot provides a foil to the saccharine heroine; in *Emily Montague*, the self-confessed coquette Arabella Fermor is contrasted with the scrupulous Emily; whilst in *The Excursion* the picaresque heroine Maria is opposed to her pale, timid twin sister, Louisa. In the *Old Maid*, Mary Singleton is the Anna Howe figure: a detached and ironic narrator, involved in, yet not central to, the action, with less beauty and delicacy but greater strength of character than her niece. It is an unusual role for a confirmed spinster. While Anna Howe possesses an independent spirit, it is clear throughout *Clarissa* that she will eventually marry the long-suffering Hickman. Arabella Fermor and Maria are also destined for happy marriages.

Brooke borrows some of the devices of the novel in her periodical. When Mary Singleton relates her own story, she prints the correspondence between herself and her faithless lover, giving her tale greater immediacy and bringing the periodical closer to an epistolary novel. The periodical approaches even closer to this model when the editor introduces us to a new set of characters: Dr. Hartingley and his wife and their young protégé Sir Harry Hyacinth (*Old Maid* 29, 29 May 1756). Dr. Hartingley gives Julia's friend Rosara a poetry album which had belonged to his daughter. When she takes it home, an intimate letter drops out, in the best traditions of the novel, offering a glimpse of Sir Harry's personality. Sir Harry hints tantalizingly that he has already chosen his future bride. Dramatic future plot developments are suggested when he tells his correspondent that his future wife's character should be tested before he will marry her: 'I must see her in danger, and I must see her in sorrow' (*ibid.*).

When news arrives of Rosara's mother's illness, the periodical's style changes from journalistic ease to breathless, Richardsonian writing-to-the-moment:

> This moment whilst I am writing, a servant of *Mrs. Montague*'s, *Rosara*'s Mother, is arrived, with the unpleasing intelligence, that his Lady is ill of a fever, and desires to see her Daughter immediately: the poor tender Rosara is half distracted; Julia is in Tears; nor can I myself help sympathising in the distress of this amiable young woman . . . *Rosara* will set out to night; I hear her ordering a Post-Chaise, I tremble for them.
>
> (*Old Maid* 28, 22 May 1756)

The shift into the present tense, the short, disjointed clauses designed to express agitation and the abrupt ending on a cliff-hanger are all characteristic of the epistolary novel. In *Julia Mandeville*, Lady Anne Wilmot receives the news of Harry Mandeville's imminent death whilst writing to her lover:

> The surgeon is come; he is now with Mr. Mandeville; how I dread to hear his sentence! the door opens – he comes out with Lord Belmont: horror is in the face of the latter – oh! Bellville! my presaging heart – they advance towards me – I am unable to meet them – my limbs tremble – a cold dew –
> Bellville! his wounds are mortal – the pen drops from my hand.
>
> (Brooke 1763: 197–8)

Mary Singleton's use of this style transforms her from the journalist addressing her public to the writer of an emotional letter to an intimate friend or lover within the epistolary novel.

It is not only within the periodical's frame narrative that we find representations influenced by the novelistic tradition, but also in the *Old Maid*'s correspondence. The periodical's most explicitly feminist statement, on the disparity between the treatment of sons and daughters (*Old Maid* 11, 24 January 1756), also reveals the influence of the sentimental novel. The correspondent E.F. writes in emotive language of the misplaced affection of fathers for a 'blockheadly son', whilst neglecting 'the modest, agreeable, and beautiful daughter' (*ibid.*). He assures fathers, 'Women communicate joy and happiness, from the time they come into the world, to the time they leave it' (*ibid.*). E.F.'s emotive appeal to other men to appreciate the sheer natural virtue and loveliness of women anticipates the letters of Ed Rivers in *Emily Montague* and Harry Mandeville in *Julia Mandeville*, the sensitive men who are able to appreciate and cherish these female paragons. Such rapturous appreciation of female merit would not be possible in most essay-periodicals of the mid-eighteenth century, unless accompanied by a heavy dose of irony. By introducing the language and plots of the sentimental novel into her periodical, Brooke attempts to endow the single life with dignity. It is significant, though, that Brooke chose to do this in a periodical, not in a novel. Novels of this period generally centre on a courtship plot and end with the female protagonist's marriage: the periodical, by contrast, is both more miscellaneous and more open-ended.

Frances Brooke's interest in periodical writing spans her career. The *Old Maid* was her first full-length publication. The correspondence between Brooke and Frances Burney shows that in 1783, towards the end of Brooke's life, she was planning another periodical in collaboration with the younger novelist (McMullen 1983: 205). It is tempting to speculate on the style of publication which the two women novelists together might have produced. Whilst women writers dominated the contemporary market for novels, within the periodical tradition women editor-writers are something of an anomaly. Only five women – Delarivier Manley, Lady Mary Wortley Montagu, Eliza Haywood, Frances Brooke and Charlotte Lennox – are known to have edited periodicals between 1690 and 1770.[60] Three of these five women chose to write under female pseudonyms (Montagu poses as an anonymous male journalist in her publication the *Nonsense of Common Sense*, as does Delarivier Manley in the *Examiner*). One of the essay-periodical's most important features was its use of a quirky but charming editorial persona, a practice inaugurated by Richard Steele with his portrait of Isaac Bickerstaff in the *Tatler*. However, whilst the elderly bachelor eschewing domestic life in favour of journalism could be seen as a loveable eccentric, the old maid writer was more frequently portrayed as a monstrosity whose literary activities compromised her respectability and her femininity. By combining elements from the novel and the periodical, Brooke helped to link the female journalist with the more widely accepted female novelist and to infuse the more charitable attitudes of the sentimental novel into the essay-periodical, with its heavy reliance on the misogynistic stereotypes of satire. She feminizes the essay-periodical and, as she does so, champions both the old maids of her title and female journalists in general.

9 'Studies proper for women'

The *Lady's Museum* and the periodical as an educational tool

Before 1760, there were very few, if any, magazines specifically addressed to women readers, although Eliza Haywood's *Female Spectator* (1744–6) anticipates many of the features of the genre, including a pronounced interest in women's education. In the 1760s, at least four such publications appeared: the *Court Miscellany* (1765–71), the *Royal Female Magazine* (1760) and the *Lady's Magazine; or, Polite Companion for the Fair Sex* (1759–63), in addition to Charlotte Lennox's *Lady's Museum*. The *Lady's Museum* attempted to endow the magazine with moral and intellectual respectability by presenting itself as a pedagogical work for women. This chapter will examine the strengths and limitations of the mid-century magazine as an informative and instructive publication for women.

Women's need for greater access to education is a recurrent theme of periodical editors throughout the century. Those who claim to champion women's cause do so by demonstrating their educability and calling for a more ambitious programme of female study. The editor of the *Free-thinker* proposes to set women 'upon the Level with my own Sex, in our boasted Superiority of Reason', commenting wryly that 'every Kind of Knowledge, will be much better comprehended over a Pot of Tea, than ... a Bottle of Wine' (3, 31 March 1718). The *Visiter* would not wish its female readers to 'sit down with knowing how to make a Pudding ... as the only Knowledge necessary for them', adding provocatively that 'a University erected for their Use' would 'produce much fewer Female Blockheads, than *Oxford* or *Cambridge* does of the Masculine' (2, 25 June 1723). A correspondent of the *Ladies Magazine* complains that her education is shamefully neglected because she is a beauty: 'What Opportunities have we of improving, when Men talk nothing but Nonsense to us; or what Encouragement to cultivate our Minds, when we are assured that Nobody will ever concern themselves about them?' (III.6, 8 February 1762). Dunton's *Athenian Mercury*, a publication which contains many positive portrayals of women, claims that women have 'a finer Genius, and generally quicker Apprehensions' than men and encourages them to be 'as learned now, as . . . Madam *Philips*, Van *Schurman*, and others have formerly been' (I.18, 23 May 1691).[61] The *Ladies Journal* asserts that 'there is an absolute necessity, for the ladies being as learned as the *Gentlemen*' (no. 2) and cites a list of learned women for their emulation (no. 3). John Tipper's publications the *Ladies Diary* and *Delights for the Ingenious* encourage female interest in mathematics, telling readers that 'there is no Thoughtful and Contemplative Person, but wou'd find unspeakable Pleasure and Satisfaction in the Study of it' (*Delights for the Ingenious* January 1711). Priscilla Termagant of the *Spring-Garden Journal* argues that women 'have a more delicate and penetrating Understanding' than men, using her own authorship of the periodical as an ironic proof of female genius (3, 30 November 1752). She cites Classical precedents for female aptitude for learning: 'Was not *Aspasia* so excellent in Philosophy, that *Socrates* attended her Lectures . . . *Tullia* shone in Oratory; and *Cornelia* taught Eloquence to the *Gracchi* . . . *Sappho* excelled in Poetry and one of the *Corynnae* overcame *Pindar*' (*ibid.*).

The *Court Magazine* contains articles on the house of Mecklenburg (September 1761), the island of Hispaniola (April 1762) and on British geography (September 1762), which are of pedagogical interest, but other educational material is scanty within the publication. However, the *Court* comments indirectly on the extent of the vogue for female learning by including a letter from a servant who has become learned from reading Milton, Otway and Locke aloud to her mistress and debating philosophy with the chaplain (October 1761). The magazine also dramatizes the contemporary interest in female education with an article entitled 'The History of Amanda' (*Court Magazine* September 1761), which relates the story of a 17-year-old woman who loves reading (the *Spectator* is one of her favourite books). She frequents the company of educated men, partly out of a love of learning and partly from pride in her own erudition: 'Tho' this desire [of male company] might in some measure arise from a laudable intention of improving by the conversation of the ingenious, I will not positively affirm that it had not its share of vanity too' (*ibid.*). One of these scholarly men flatters Amanda's pride in her intellect and persuades her to have an affair with him. After he deserts her, she marries a virtuous man, who is convinced of her fundamental innocence, despite the affair: 'I do not see', he tells her, 'your conduct was the effect of levity; but an unguarded greatness of soul' (*ibid.*). The couple live happily ever after, thereby proving, perhaps, that a woman with an education is worthy of a good husband, even when she has lost her virginity to another man.

Christopher Smart's publication the *Midwife* treats the contemporary obsession with female education in a comic manner. The editor, Mother

Midnight, argues that 'the Mind of Woman is capable of the same Improvements as that of Man' and exclaims, 'How greatly it is to be lamented, that
the Female Sex should be in a Manner disinherited from their Right of
common in the Fields of Learning?' (*Midwife* II.5). Smart surrounds his
persona with an elaborate apparatus of pseudo-erudition. Mother Midnight
has published an edition of Ovid's *Metamorphoses* (*Midwife* II.6) and a
14-volume *Treatise on Perspective* (*Midwife* II.2). She corresponds regularly
with the College of Physicians, the Royal Society, to whom she sends a proposal for the invention of an organ driven by cats (*Midwife* I.3), as well as
with the Society of Antiquarians, to whom she donates an essay on a piece of
petrified excrement (*Midwife* I.4). The editor also receives letters from other
learned women. The correspondent Mrs Susannah Coxeter, for example, has
prepared her son for university and compensates for the deficiencies of his
schoolmasters with her own extensive learning: '[I] retaught him his *Latin*,
and *Greek*, and *English*, together with as much of *Logic*, *Rhetoric*, *Geography*,
Astronomy, *Mathematicks* and *Morality*, as learned Men generally know, and
more of *Divinity* than they practise' (*Midwife* II.5). Mary Midnight provides
the second volume of the periodical with garbled mottoes in Greek, Latin
and Hebrew and corrects the Classical scholarship of *'all the Universities in
Europe'* (*Midwife* I.2). Smart's primary purpose in the *Midwife* seems to be to
satirize the incompetence of the male intellectual establishment, rather than
to champion the cause of female education, however. His satire is also
directed in part at John Hill's pretensions to disseminate learning to both
male and female readers in his 'Inspector' papers in the *Daily Advertiser*.
Hill's journalistic alter ego is a keen amateur scientist and polymath. A
contemporary pamphlet satirizes Hill as 'a Chymist, Critick, Journalist,
Physician /. . . / A *Farinelli*, actor, and a poet' (*The Inspector's Rhapsody* 1752).
The Inspector regales his readers with such fare as an account of embalming
(no. 11), a critique of Gray's 'Elegy Written in a Country Churchyard' (no.
2), a description of the microscopic creatures found in pond water (no. 8)
and a proposal for mining (no. 7).

The concern with female education evinced by so many editors is closely
connected with contemporary anxieties about women's novel-reading habits.
Editors often attempt to find safe alternative reading material for women.
The *Lady's Museum* comments:

> There is scarcely a young girl who has not read with eagerness a great
> number of idle romances, and puerile tales sufficient to corrupt her
> imagination and cloud her understanding. If she had devoted the same
> time to the study of history, she would . . . have found . . . instruction
> which only truth can give.

> (1: I.13)

The editor of the *Oxford Magazine* tells his female readers, 'Your minds are as capable of more rational studies as ours, and could we but once fix your education upon a more rational plan, your sex would not be the only one that would receive the benefits from it' (no. 2, supplement to vol. for 1768). He exhorts women to turn from perusing novels to emulating scholars such as Elizabeth Carter and Catharine Macaulay, who are 'of late, the glories of your sex' (*ibid.*). Periodical editors often provide reading lists or recommendations for study, such as Steele's *Ladies Library* (1714), whose forthcoming publication is announced, somewhat prematurely, in *Tatler* 248. Eliza Haywood provides an impressive programme of reading in the *Female Spectator*. She recommends the study of botany, history – including the Old Testament, Cicero's correspondence, Velleius Paterculus, Sallust, Herodotus, Thucydides, Dion, Xenophon, Herodian, Suetonius, Plutarch, Josephus, Livy, Justinus, Publius Annius Florus and Tacitus (all in translation) – as well as poetry and travel writing – including Aubry de la Mottraye, Bernard de Montfaucon, William Dampier, Jean-Baptiste Du Halde, François Misson, Cornelis de Bruyn, Jean-Baptiste Tavernier and Jean Chardin (bk XV: 91–8). The editor, we are told, could have continued this list, but her friend the 'noble Widow' interrupts to warn her that 'the Crowd of Authors I have mentioned will be apt to fright some Ladies from taking up any one of them' (bk XV: 3.98). In a later issue, the Female Spectator goes on to recommend astronomy, suggesting the study of the works of Pierre Gassendi, Joseph Privat de Molières, Domenico Cassini, Euclid, Copernicus, Galileo, Newton, Descartes, Robert Hooke, John Flamsteed and Edmund Halley (bk XVII: 3.168–9). The editor also appears to recommend the study of medicine, citing the example of an aristocratic Lancashire lady who cures patients 'judged incurable by the Faculty' (bk XVII: 3.174).

While not explicitly an educational periodical, the *Female Spectator* has been aptly described by Kathryn King as 'something of an *omnium gatherum* for mid-century intellectual life' (Haywood 2001: 5). The periodical includes articles on politics (bk IX: 309–22, 329–33), literary criticism (bk XX: 3.257–62), astronomy (bk XVII: 3.167–75), zoology (bks XV: 82–90, XIX: 239–42) and theology (bk XXIII: 356–61), as well as suggestions for a new system for educating women. Throughout her publication, Haywood stresses the importance of female education. She proposes reading as a cure for female aversion to solitude (bk IV: 2.119–27). She attributes women's restlessness and melancholy to their lack of intellectual stimulation – 'those Vapours, those Disquiets we often feel . . . would be no more, when once the Mind was employ'd in the pleasing Enquiries of Philosophy' (bk X: 2.359) – and claims that the study of philosophy 'corrects all the vicious Humours of the Mind, and inspires the noblest Virtues' (bk X: 2.358). Her correspondent Cleora claims that education also improves women's morals: the errors they commit, she argues, are 'most commonly the Fault of a wrong Education' (bk x: 2.354). The editor diagnoses 'Want of something else wherewith to employ ourselves' as the source of women's propensity towards gossip, slander and jealousy (bk xiii: 3.5). More practically, Haywood also suggests that a good education will enable women to escape being married off against their will, since it will give them the ability to earn an independent living (bk xx: 3.275). The Female Spectator herself provides a role model for her readers: offering her own disquisition on the immortality of the soul (bk xi: 2.389–96, 399–404), observing the planets through a telescope (bk xvii: 3.168–73) and conducting zoological experiments (bk xvii: 3.161–5).

Haywood's recommendation of astronomy as a suitable subject for female study reflects contemporary interest in popularizing the work of natural scientists in books specifically aimed at a female audience. We have no record of the actual readership of these works, and they may have appealed at least equally to men wishing to broaden their knowledge, but they always represent their ideal reader as a young woman. The most well-known of these are translations of Bernard le Bovier de Fontenelle's *Entretiens sur la pluralité des mondes* (1686), first translated into English in 1687, and Francesco Algarotti's *Il Newtonianismo per le dame* (1737), translated into English by Elizabeth Carter as *Isaac Newton's Philosophy Explain'd for the Use of the Ladies* (1739). A 1737 edition of Fontenelle, entitled *A Week's Conversation on the Plurality of Worlds*, sports a frontispiece showing a young lady and gentleman conversing in a formal garden, the lady listening attentively, while the young man, gesticulating with both hands, explains an element of Fontenelle's thought. '*I have introduced a* LADY', the author tells us, '*to be instructed in Things of which she never heard; and I have made use of this Fiction, to render the Book the more acceptable, and to give Encouragement to Gentlewomen, by the Example of one of their own Sex*' (Fontenelle 1737: iv). Haywood satirizes the vogue for Fontenelle in her conduct book *The Wife* (1756), where she describes women 'with a kind of philosophic turn, who have their minds strangely busy about the planets' and 'would fain know whether those vast and luminous orbs . . . are habitable worlds or not' (2000c: 102). Algarotti cites Fontenelle as the inspiration behind his own approach in *Isaac Newton's Philosophy Explain'd*. In terms remarkably similar to Addison's in *Spectator* 10, in which he hopes that the periodical has brought philosophy 'out of Closets and Libraries, Schools and Colleges, to dwell in Clubs and Assemblies, at Tea-Tables, and in Coffee-Houses', Algarotti claims that Fontenelle 'first softened the savage Nature of Philosophy, and called it from the solitary Closets and Libraries of the Learned, to introduce it into the Circles and Toilets of Ladies' (Algarotti, trans. Carter 1739: ii). Like Fontenelle's work, Algarotti's takes the form of a dialogue: between the author and a marchioness, whom he entertains with disquisitions on Newtonian physics, interspersed with poetry, as they stroll through her beautiful and extensive grounds.

Fontenelle, Algarotti and the magazine editors who imitate them, all claim that women have a special aptitude for the natural sciences because they are based on observation and experiment, rather than on theoretical knowledge. Haywood's correspondent Philo-Naturae writes that biology requires no special study – 'we need but *look* to be *informed*' (*Female Spectator* bk xv: 3.89) – and makes the exciting suggestion that women might be able to make a significant contribution to human knowledge in that field: they 'would doubtless perceive Animals which are not to be found in the most accurate Volumes of Natural Philosophy; and the Royal Society might be indebted to every fair *Columbus* for a new World of Beings to employ their Speculations' (bk xv: 3.88). The Female Spectator demonstrates her own aptitude for scientific observation. She notices an alteration in the pigmentation of some caterpillars. A male friend, relying on his theoretical knowledge, suggests that the caterpillars change colour with changing weather conditions, but the editor ascribes the caterpillars' colour to their diet and plans an experiment to test her thesis (bk xvii: 162), pitting female empiricism against male learning. Benjamin Martin also claims that women may be as capable of understanding the natural sciences as men because of their empirical nature: 'The Senses are the general Inlets and Means of Knowledge, and are formed as accurately and just as perfect, in one Sex as the other, therefore these philosophical Subjects must be, in this Way, equally intelligible to both' (*General Magazine of Arts and Sciences*, Preface: vi).

Martin's *General Magazine of Arts and Sciences* (1755–66) adopts a similar format to the works of Fontenelle and Algarotti. Its title page promises 'a particular and accurate SURVEY of the WORKS of NATURE, by way of DIALOGUE', a 'NATURAL HISTORY of the WORLD', a 'compleat SYSTEM of all the PHILOLOGICAL SCIENCES' and 'A BODY of MATHEMATICAL INSTITUTES'. The frontispiece shows a young gentleman and lady sitting in a well-appointed library, by a globe of the skies and a telescope. She is holding a book and listening intently as the young man explains something, one hand poised on the globe and the other gesturing through the window at the starry night sky (Figure 9.1). We later learn that the couple are Cleonicus, newly returned from college, and his sister Euphrosine. Cleonicus gives his sister a copy of the *Philosophical Transactions of the Royal Society* to read and supplements her reading by conducting discussions with her on scientific subjects as they 'walk round the Park, or over the Fields and Meadows' on moonlit 'vernal Evenings' ('The Young Gentleman and Lady's Philosophy', dialogue I, *General Magazine of Arts and Sciences*: 4). Martin claims that the work is the first of its kind – 'a Body of *Arts and Sciences* has never yet been attempted in any monthly periodical Publication, under the Title of a MAGAZINE' (*General*

Figure 9.1 Frontispiece of Benjamin Martin's 'Young Gentleman and Lady's Philosophy' in the *General Magazine of Arts and Sciences* (1755–66).

Magazine of Arts and Sciences, Preface: iv). He claims that the periodical is a particularly convenient way of publishing educational material,

> not only as it suits with the Humour and Taste of the present Age, but also because it will be the easiest Way to communicate Subjects of this Sort, and attended with less Expence and Trouble as well to the Publisher as the Reader; not only so, but a whole Body of Arts and Sciences poured out on the Public at once, might not perhaps be quite so pleasing and acceptable as when retailed out in monthly Portions.[62]
>
> (*ibid.*)

The magazine is aimed at both men and women and defines its audience as those who do not have the time or money to obtain a more extensive education and who do not have the patience or aptitude to read large volumes of science. It is clearly of special relevance to female readers, however, since, as Martin points out, 'Gentlemen have generally an Opportunity of coming to the Knowledge of these Things, in a Way different from that of the Fair Sex' (*ibid.*). The periodical will form a means of self-education for those women who are not lucky enough to have a brother to expound science to them and who are not normally privy to conversations on scientific topics. As Martin points out, 'Such Subjects . . . come but too rarely on the Carpet in any Conversation, especially that of your Sex' ('The Young Gentleman and Lady's Philosophy', dialogue I: 1). Cleonicus reassures his sister that the study of science will not compromise her femininity: 'It is now growing into a Fashion for the Ladies to study Philosophy; and I am very glad to see a Sister of mine so well inclined to promote a Thing so very laudable and honourable to her Sex' (*ibid.* 1–2).

The *General Magazine*'s scientific syllabus is an impressive one. Cleonicus teaches his sister to calculate an eclipse (dialogue VI) and to use an ephemeris (dialogue XIII: 85–94), a stellated planetarium (dialogue XIV: 95–9), an Orrery (dialogues VII–XIII: 198–254) and a barometer (dialogue VIII, 327–37). The siblings cover an extensive range of subjects including astronomy, meteorology and fluid mechanics and conduct a number of experiments, for example with an air pump (dialogues XI–XIII: 357–407). Despite the poetry and digressions on Classical mythology interspersed throughout to provide light relief, this isn't easy science. The magazine is bristling with diagrams, calculations and mathematical formulae.

While few publications are as ambitious as Martin's, many lay claim to similar aims. The *Young Misses Magazine* (c.1760) and its sequel the *Young Ladies Magazine* (1760) 'by Mrs. Le Prince de Beaumont' also take the form of educational dialogues, this time between '*a Discreet Governess and Several Young Ladies of the First Rank Under her Education*', according to the subtitle of the *Young Ladies Magazine*.[63] As the *Critical Review* points out, the *Young Misses Magazine* aims to instruct governesses as much as their pupils: 'It will be equally useful to the pupil and the tutress. The ignorance of the latter is often very lamentable' (August 1757). The magazine offers a series of conversations between a small group of 12-year-old girls with allegorical names such as Lady Witty, Lady Trifle and Lady Sensible. The first half of the magazine contains a number of moral reflections on the correct form of female education and shows Lady Trifle being weaned off dolls onto books and Lady Witty learning the difference between 'two kinds of sense', the first of which will make women vain, proud and pedantic, while the second 'renders us mild, amiable and virtuous' (*Young Misses Magazine* I.7), underlining the fact that the *Magazine* is at least as concerned with teaching women how to behave as it is with academic knowledge. The lessons taught are largely ethical ones. The governess relates Oriental tales and fairy tales, carefully pointing out their morals. The stories are interspersed with very brief and elementary lessons in geography, such as recognizing geographical features such as islands and continents on a globe (I.131), identifying the main British rivers and cities (I.14) and learning the history of the Roman occupation of France (II.101–4). There is a very strong emphasis throughout on religious knowledge. The girls are taught their catechism (II.169–74) and told a number of Biblical stories, beginning with Adam and Eve (I.33–6) and ending with the worship of the golden calf (II.287–98). The first volume alone narrates the tales of Cain and Abel (I.40–2), Noah's ark (I.72–5), Ham, Shem and Japheth (I.97–9), the Tower of Babel (I.100–5), Sodom and Gomorrah (I.122–5), Abraham and Isaac (I.125–6, 143–9), Jacob and Esau (I.161–5), Joseph and Pharaoh (I.179–86, 197–202), Moses and the flight out of Egypt (I.220–7, 234–9, 247–55, 270–6, 287–94) and Balaam's ass (I.297–9).

The *Young Ladies Magazine* offers a similar, but more ambitious programme. Aimed at girls of 'about fourteen or fifteen' (*Young Ladies Magazine* xiii), it combines snippets of natural science and philosophy with 'the wholesome maxims of Jesus Christ' (p. xvi). The editor comments approvingly on the current vogue for female education and hopes to provide young women with a companion to their academic reading: 'Now-a-days ladies read all sorts of books, history, politicks, philosophy and even such as concern religion. They should therefore be in a condition to judge solidly of what they read and able to discern truth from falshood' (p. xxi–xxii). The lessons the governess offers her pupils include French language, French and English history, Biblical history, moral philosophy and geometry. The editor encourages independent thought among her charges – expressing approval when her pupil Mrs Rural disagrees with some of the ideas proposed by John Locke, for instance (p. 38) – and commends women who attend lectures on philosophy (*ibid.*). She particularly recommends geometry as a science which 'accustoms the mind to a regular process, to an exact calculation' (p. 46), qualities not usually associated with women at this period. She also teaches her pupils creative writing, in order to 'form a stile, and accustom you to write your thoughts in some order' (p. 140). However, the magazine's educational aims have serious limitations. For one thing, the women's use of their learning is to be confined to the home. They are being educated because they are to be married to 'gentlemen of great study' (p. 93) whom they must be able to entertain with intelligent conversation. The editor warns them against displaying their knowledge indiscriminately: 'We must conceal these little studies that are the subject of our meetings and behave with the ignorant, as if we were so' (p. 47). More importantly, while the publication repeatedly praises female education, the actual academic content of its pages is disappointing and largely restricted to pious maxims, Biblical tales, moral fables and analyses of the young ladies' characters.

The annual *Ladies Complete Pocket-Book* (1769–78) carries a series on female education, written by 'A MOTHER'. It is concerned, however, with the education of young children, rather than of the periodical's own female readership. The series comprises advice on breast feeding (1771), how to treat infants (1772), school education and, in particular, the importance of teaching grammar (1773), the dangers of boarding schools (1774, 1776) and of French governesses (1775) and ends with two poems (1777). The leader is very short (only two or three out of 45 pages) and is largely aimed at women as educators, rather than as recipients of education. It does, however, inculcate the importance of female education, though of a very limited kind. It advocates a knowledge of English grammar and encourages female reading, though not of 'novels and romances' or of 'French authors' whose lax principles might ruin a 'character for delicacy and virtue' (1775). In addition to discouraging a knowledge of French, the author of the series disapproves of boarding schools, since their curricula do not sufficiently inculcate female duty. Girls should be taught at home, she writes, since 'female education can have respect to little beyond the discharge of female duty, (the sphere of which is far from being extensive) all the knowledge necessary for the acquittal of such duty is contained in very narrow limits' (1776). In view of the strict boundaries which the periodical sets for female learning, its contentions that women are 'at least equally capacitated with men to excel in arts and sciences' (1773) and warnings against the dangers of female ignorance – 'an unedified, unprincipled woman being the most random, precarious being in the whole creation' (*ibid.*) – ring rather hollow.

The *Lady's Magazine; or, Polite Companion* (1759–63) also claims to be an educational work suitable for young women of quality. The paper's social and pedagogical pretensions are revealed in a letter dated from St. James's, in which the writer claims that the publication has been recommended to her by a duchess 'as a performance admirably calculated to form the minds of young ladies' (*Lady's Magazine* June 1761). A great deal of space in the *Magazine* is devoted to the subject of women's educability. The series 'Feyjoo's Defence of Women' (see Feyjóo y Montenegro 1760) lists a 'catalogue of learned women' and asserts that 'there is no inequality at all in the capacities of the one or the other sex' (January 1761). The editor argues that 'our sex are more pliant to instruction even than the other' (*ibid.*). The *Lady's Magazine* repeatedly celebrates female accomplishments, mainly through the gallant praises of male readers. One male reader reminds the editor, Mrs Stanhope, that 'it is incumbent on you, in a particular manner, to celebrate those, whose superior endowments are an ornament to their sex' (April 1761). He encloses a poem by a female friend, who is presumably too bashful to submit her own contribution. There are many thumbnail sketches of accomplished women within the magazine, usually submitted by men. The learned Hortensia is one such paragon, well read in the English and French historians and poets, but eminently modest: '[She] esteems it even a point of decency to throw a veil over the superior charms of her understanding' (*Lady's Magazine* June 1761). The *Lady's Magazine* is portrayed here as a forum in which Hortensia's accomplishments can be publicized, without violating her modesty. The magazine protects the individual woman's anonymity, while providing a framework within which to celebrate women's achievements as a group. Its tone is self-congratulatory, without being immodest or unfeminine.

While magazines do not always address the question of women's education directly, many provide numerous articles on a variety of scientific or literary subjects, which are often of academic interest. As Goldsmith sarcastically writes, 'History, politics, poetry, mathematics, metaphysics, and the philosophy of nature are all comprized in a manual not larger than that in which our children are taught the letters' (1966: 2.124). John Tipper's annual *Gentleman and Lady's Palladium*, an offshoot of his *Ladies Diary*, includes mathematical questions, articles on astronomy and explanations of elementary French grammar 'for the Pleasure and Service of *Both Sexes*, and proper for *Schools*' (1753, Preface). The editors of the *Oxford Magazine* claim to write out of 'a desire of dispersing, more effectually, the seeds of knowledge' and wish to provide 'complete systems of every branch of useful learning' (July 1768, Preface), while the *Scots Magazine* describes its aim as 'to suit the learning of the times to the purchase and opportunity of persons of every station' (vol. I, Preface). The editors of the *Imperial Magazine*, which has a strong focus on the natural sciences, promise to include '*whatever is either useful or entertaining in the circle of sciences*' (June 1762: 7). The magazine offers series of articles on geography and natural history, giving, for example, an account of terms such as *equator, horizon, ecliptic, meridian, continent, island* and *promontory* (*ibid.* 7–12). The ambitious *Royal Magazine* reprints the publications of foreign universities and learned societies, the Board of Longitude and the Society for the Encouragement of Arts, Manufactures and Commerce and includes mathematical theories, accounts of scientific and medical experiments, book reviews, poetry, foreign affairs and Parliamentary reporting (see October–December 1750). The editors claim that in their publication female readers 'will find an inexhaustible Fund of Knowledge … for the Improvement of their Mind', enabling them to participate in male conversation 'on most Subjects' (*ibid.* Preface). They warn that women whose education is neglected may meet the fate of Theodora, who 'fell a victim to the illiberal machinations of a villain', causing her mother and father to die of grief (*Royal Magazine* August 1765).

The attitudes of magazine editors towards women's education are often more ambivalent, however. In an article deceptively entitled 'The female genius equal to the male', a correspondent of the *Lady's Curiosity* claims that 'Learning is so far from improving a lady's understanding, that it is likely to banish the most useful science out of it, making her know nothing at all of what she is most concern'd to know' (no. 6). The knowledge which contemporary magazines provide is often of the pudding-making kind. The series 'The Compleat English Housewife' in the *Universal Magazine* is designed '*to assist our* Female *Readers with … Receipts in* Cookery *… and … other Branches of* good Housewifery' (June 1747). The annual *Ladies Complete Pocket-Book* offers such domestic advice as 'An easy BILL of FARE for Dinner and Supper every Month in the Year' (1769) and a '*Method of rearing* Turkies' (1769), as well as moral precepts such as verse hints 'for conjugal Happiness' (1769). The *Pocket-Book* does also contain an article which extols '*the Pleasure and Advantages of Reading*' (1770), but it does not recommend any specific reading material. Readers clearly regarded the publication as a collection of recipes and household hints; a contemporary has written a recipe for lavender water in the margin of the British Library copy of the 1771 volume. The *World* scornfully describes magazine editors as having 'ransacked the records of pastry-schools, and the manuscript cookery collections of good housewives' (147, 23 Oct. 1755).

When it is not purely domestic, educational material for women often takes the form of moral instructions and cautionary tales. The *Ladies Complete Pocket-Book* defines 'female Education' as 'some anecdote, fable, character, &c. tending to the edification … of the sex' (1771), whilst the *Monthly Review* praises the *Magazin de Londres* (1749) as an educational periodical because it contains 'reflexions and maxims of decency and good-breeding' (June 1749). The *Royal Female Magazine* does not harbour pretensions to pedagogy: the editor tells us that '*Entertainment* … alone is my humble design' (1, March 1760). Instead, he promises to focus on 'THE MORAL AND PRUDENTIAL DUTIES OF LIFE', specifically to provide 'a recreative unbending, to minds intent upon the more abstruse and weighty studies' (*ibid.*). The editors of the *Universal Museum* argue that a monthly magazine should aim to 'dissert, rather agreeably than deeply, upon the topic of the day', providing material which will appeal to 'those who desire to know the world, and mix with life', rather than those interested in 'deep research' (vol. I, 1765, Preface).

Many magazine editors present their periodicals as organs for the publication of the work of others, rather than vehicles for their own writing or collections of informative and educational articles. The editor of the *Ladies Complete Pocket-Book* is afflicted by poor health and old age and relies upon her correspondents to provide material: 'I most heartily subscribe to the superior geniuses of my livelier correspondents, whom I am extremely glad to patronize' (1778). The *Universal Museum* tells its readers that 'our Museum now almost entirely consists of voluntary contributions' (vol. I, 1765, Preface). The *Lady's Magazine* also presents its correspondence as its main selling point:

> The readers may be said in some measure to entertain each other, and write their endeavours in one single Magazine for their mutual instruction ... Here we ... read the world without the danger of its conversation.
>
> (January 1761)

The editor is one genteel amateur among others, without pretensions to high literary merit; she simply provides a safe public space for her readers to interact with each other, a written form of conversation, which lacks the sexual temptations and perils of society. The *Lady's Magazine*'s emphasis on the importance of correspondence undercuts its authority as an educational work. The editor does not claim any specialist knowledge or particular expertise and, instead, expects her readers 'to entertain each other' and to provide 'mutual instruction'. The slippage here from entertainment to instruction indicates that the editor has no clear educational programme: the 'instruction' will be fortuitous, rather than planned, and is more likely to consist of lessons of moral conduct – of how to behave in 'the world' – than it is of more scholarly material.

In the *Female Spectator*, correspondents frequently write in to provide articles of scholarly interest, such as Classical (or pseudo-Classical) texts, remarks on botany or astronomy or disquisitions on the immortality of the soul. Other mid-century editors also express the hope that their magazines will serve as vehicles for learned contributions. The *Gentleman's Magazine* prints letters on medicine, archaeology, astronomy, mathematics, optics, mechanics, veterinary medicine, electricity, biology and zoology. Pailler (1975) has shown that Cave's correspondents included at least two university professors and five Fellows of the Royal Society, as well as other eminent scholars.[64] As Pailler points out, the Secretary of the Royal Society also received a large volume of miscellaneous correspondence from amateur scientists hoping to see the results of their observations, theories or experiments published in the *Philosophical Transactions* (1975: 1.350). The editors of the *Imperial Magazine* 'invite the Learned and Ingenious to become Contributors to their Magazine' (January 1760, Introduction). Mark Akenside hopes that his *Museum* (1746–7) will attract similar correspondents, expressing the hope that '*the* MUSEUM *may become a general Vehicle by which the* Literati *of the whole Kingdom may converse with each other, and communicate their Knowledge to the World*' (vol. for 1746, Preface).

In many of the magazines of the 1750s and 60s, however, the correspondence is of a much more personal, less scholarly, nature. Editors frequently act as agony aunts. Both the *Court Miscellany* and the *Universal Museum* feature sections called 'The Oracle', which answer questions on love and marriage from readers, in a format modelled on Dunton's *Athenian Mercury*. Mrs Stanhope's readers in the *Lady's Magazine* confide their most intimate and inconsolable sorrows to her. A woman whose lover has been killed in action is certain that the editor 'will not disdain the correspondence of a person, who has no other qualifications to recommend her ... but nature and sincerity', since the only pleasure left to her is the 'small satisfaction of communicating my sorrows' (*Lady's Magazine* January 1760). A correspondent of Johnson's 'Idler' requests 'the common permission, to lay my case before you and your readers, by which I shall disburthen my heart, though I cannot hope to receive either assistance or consolation' (no. 95; 1969: 2.292). Even some primarily political publications are vehicles for similar declarations. A correspondent of Fielding's *Champion*, who has been jilted by his mistress, tells the editor that his motive for writing is that 'my Heart swells with Resentment, and I cannot be at Peace till I have discharg'd it' (325, 10 December 1741).

Mrs Stanhope of the *Lady's Magazine* clearly feels a moral obligation to print confessional letters of this kind and believes that their expressions of sincere feeling will appeal to her readership. She reprints the correspondence which passed between a soldier and his sweetheart, shortly before his death in battle, adding the editorial note, '*Mrs. Stanhope has not attempted to change a single word in the above letters, sensible that their natural simplicity must be more truly pleasing, than the most laboured accuracy*' (*Lady's Magazine* January 1761). The emphasis on 'laboured accuracy' may be a response to the popularity of Johnson's *Rambler*, which was by now a widely read work. Mrs Stanhope's comments valorize the communications of genuine readers above the artistry of professionals, the 'laboured performances, even of genius' (*Lady's Magazine* Jan. 1761). Her magazine is clearly 'calculated both for the head and the heart', as Goldsmith sarcastically expresses it in *Lloyd's Evening Post* (1 Feb. 1762; Goldsmith 1966: 3.188), rather than primarily for the former.

The high value which she places on authenticity, rather than wit and literary polish, is characteristic of editors of the mid-eighteenth century. The editor of the *Royal Female Magazine* is unusual in his frank assumption of 'the priviledge, which my periodical predecessors have always assumed, of writing to myself, particularly as the epistolary style is so much easier than the strict rule of a regular essay' (5, July 1760). The editor of the *World* reprints a letter on the dangers of ambition which 'has so genuine and natural an air' that he will print it without attempting to correct or refine it: 'without the alteration of a single word' (174, 29 April 1756). The *Imperial Magazine* prints a letter which 'may be depended on as genuine', adding that 'though the Stile is not elegant, the Sentiments are pathetic' (January 1760). Mary Midnight of the *Midwife* includes a letter reporting the sad story of a man imprisoned for debt, leaving his wife to die of grief and his children penniless. She comments, 'I have inserted this Letter . . . *verbatim*, without the least Alteration: Her Diction is the pure Language of Nature; and her Sentiments carry more Weight in her own Words, than they would do mangled by the most masterly Hand' (*Midwife* I.1). This focus on authenticity – on the emotive, rather than the learned, on readerly experience, rather than editorial instruction, on '*simplicity*' rather than '*accuracy*' – detracts considerably from any educational aims which these periodicals might have and seems to suggest that subjective, personal communications are more valued than objective, scientific or learned articles. If readers are to be educated, it will be a sentimental education, not a bookish one. In this context, Lennox's at times unrelentingly pedagogical focus in the *Lady's Museum* is even more striking.

The *Lady's Museum*, which combined the essay-serial 'The Trifler' with articles of educational interest and instalments of the novel 'The History of Harriot and Sophia', appeared monthly from March 1760 to January 1761 and was subsequently published in two bound volumes. The title page advertises the publication as 'By the Author of the Female Quixote'. Lennox appears to have written the periodical single-handedly and probably obtained a royal licence to protect the copyright of her serialized novel, which was republished as *Sophia* in 1762, since the publication's title page contains the royal arms of the lion and unicorn, with the motto *Dieu et mon droit*. *Sophia* is one of the first two novels to be initially published in instalments within a periodical. Tobias Smollett's *The Life and Adventures of Sir Launcelot Greaves* (1762) was also serialized in 1760–1, in his *British Magazine* (January 1760–December 1761).

The *Lady's Museum*'s preoccupation with women's education is immediately evident in the periodical's frontispiece.[65] A young and pretty woman is seated at a desk with her books before her, one open under her hand. Behind her are three semi-nude women in Classical garb – probably the Graces. Another female figure, dressed in a toga and wearing a crested helmet, probably Pallas Athena, stands protectively by her side, pointing towards a Classical temple, while at the same time a Cupid flies towards her, accompanied by a semi-naked youth, perhaps a suitor, who offers her a garland of roses. A woman is standing in front of the Cupid and appears to be disarming him of his bow and quiver. The image is a complex one, but seems to suggest a Choice of Hercules between love and learning. The presence of Pallas Athena, patron of scholars, and the disarming of the Cupid imply that the editor has chosen learning.

The opening issue of the *Lady's Museum* offers its readers three different portrayals of its editor: this frontispiece, an editorial preface and the introduction of the *eidolon* of an essay-series called 'The Trifler'. The editor distances herself from the essay-series, as if it were written by another hand, telling us that 'as I have but too much reason to distrust my own powers of pleasing, I shall usher in my pamphlet with the performance of a lady' whose 'sprightly paper' will, she hopes, meet with 'encouragement enough to dispel the diffidence natural to a young writer' (*Lady's Museum* 1: 1.1). Like the woman depicted in the frontispiece, Lennox's *eidolon* in 'The Trifler' is young, pretty and sexually available. She portrays reading as a virtuous occupation and associates writing with coquetry, describing it in sexual terms as a 'darling end' and a 'passion':

> *Cast your eyes upon paper, madam; there you may look innocently*, said a polite old gentleman of my acquaintance to me one day … It is indeed very clear … that my friend … recommended reading to eyes which he probably thought too intent upon pleasing; but I, with a small deviation from the sense, applied it, to what I freely own my predominant passion; and therefore resolved to write, still pursuing the darling end, though by different means.[66]
>
> (*Lady's Museum* 1: 1.2)

This portrayal of the female editor turning to journalism as an alternative means of 'pleasing' or as a kind of implicit flirtation with male readers was a common one. The Female Spectator, Mrs Crackenthorpe of the *Female Tatler* and Mary Singleton of the *Old Maid* all suggest that periodical writing can be an alternative to direct flirtation and a way of seeking admirers through print. Surprisingly, this sexualization of women's journalistic writing served to make female editorship of periodicals more, not less, respectable, since it implied that the journalism was not undertaken for money. The passage above clearly suggests that the *Lady's Museum* was launched to gratify a 'predominant passion', not from any financial motive. The portrait is far from being autobiographical: Charlotte Lennox seems to have struggled with poverty throughout her working life. In 1760, Andrew Millar, who had published Lennox's novels *The Life of Harriot Stuart Written by Herself* (1750) and *The Female Quixote* (1752), together with all her other works between 1750 and 1759, was declared bankrupt. John Newbery appears to have lent Lennox money at the outset of this crisis, which may have acted as an advance for her services as editor of the *Lady's Museum* (Small 1935: 29–30). Lennox is probably alluding to her *Museum* when she writes in October 1760 of her 'present slavery to the Booksellers, whom I have the more mortification to see adding to their heaps by my labours, which scarce produce me a scanty and precarious subsistence' (qtd. Small 1935: 27–8).

Lennox's visual and verbal portrayals of the editor of the *Lady's Museum* suggest more than simply a pose of gentility, however. While Brooke and Haywood present their *eidolons* as turning from attempts to attract men in their youth to attempts to please readers in their maturity, Lennox's editor-persona is notably young – she is 18 (*Lady's Museum* 1: 1.4) – and for her writing forms an alternative to love, rather than something to resort to in later life after admirers have become scarce. Brooke and Haywood contrast writing with coquetry and stress that writing is less dangerous and more useful to society. Brooke's Mary Singleton describes herself as 'very inoffensively blotting paper in the service . . . of my fellow citizens' (*Old Maid* 21, 10 April 1756); Haywood's Female Spectator has turned from 'Vanity and Folly' to a project which she describes as 'both useful and entertaining to the Publick' (*Female Spectator* bk I: 2.17–18). Lennox, however, depicts reading here as a respectable male-sanctioned activity, in explicit contrast to writing, which, she tells us, it is 'very clear' that the 'polite old gentleman' had no intention of encouraging. Periodical writing is depicted here as both more transgressive and more scholarly than it is in either Haywood or Brooke's publications. The editor dedicates herself to writing, rather than love, out of choice, not necessity. Although the Trifler describes herself as 'young, single, gay, and ambitious of pleasing', she makes it clear that her primary aim is not to gain the hearts of men. She is indeed ambitious – for her 'the desire of pleasing' is synonymous with the 'desire of fame'. The 'desire of pleasing', she writes, 'is the poet's inspiration, the patriot's zeal, the courtier's loyalty, and the orator's eloquence', as likely to result in 'the thunder of eloquence in the senate' as 'the glitter of dress in the drawing room' (*Lady's Museum* 1: 1.2–3). It is also women, rather than men, whose approbation the editor seeks: 'I shall be contented, if [the periodical] finds only a favourable acceptance with my own sex' (*Lady's Museum* 1: 1.4).

Unlike Haywood and Brooke, she also sees herself as part of a tradition of female editors, expressing the weary sense of the saturation of the periodical market shared by many editors of the 1750s and 60s: 'I should indeed have thought some apology necessary for an undertaking of this kind, had I not been persuaded, it was a mighty easy one, from its being so frequently attempted, and by persons too of my own sex' (*Lady's Museum* 1: 1.4).

The Trifler is the elder of two sisters and, despite her name, the less frivolous and more scholarly of the two. Her mother, who was forbidden reading as a girl because of a minor eye condition, has a

> high contempt for reading ... those of her female acquaintance who had made any proficiency that way were sure to be distinguished by her, with the opprobrious term of being *book-learned*, which my mother always pronounced with a look and accent of ineffable scorn.
>
> (*Lady's Museum* 1: 1.5)

The Trifler's mother neglects her in favour of her pretty, but shallow and uneducated, sister, but the author reads her way through her brother's library and is given 'a right education' by him when he returns from university (*Lady's Museum* 1: 1.8). On her mother's death, she goes to live with and keep house for him. The image of the editor as a young woman who turns to literary pursuits because of parental neglect and lack of beauty echoes Haywood's portrait of the editor Euphrosine in her *Young Lady*. Euphrosine's beauty is marred by an early bout of smallpox, and her mother's attentions are exclusively lavished on her frivolous, but pretty, sister. Euphrosine tells us that she 'betook myself to reading', which enables her to 'despise the ridiculous pursuits with which so many of my sex are infatuated'. The death of her parents leaves her free to 'pass the greatest part of my time among my books' (*Young Lady* 1, 6 January 1756), whilst a modest fortune in the stocks (see *Young Lady* 4, 27 January 1756) enables her to finance the publication of her periodical. The Trifler's scholarly bent is more pronounced than Euphrosine's, however: she has not had the smallpox and dedicates herself to writing because of a 'strong passion for intellectual pleasures' (*Lady's Museum* 1: 1.4).

The Trifler's name does not reflect her character, as her correspondents are quick to point out. A letter from Penelope Spindle urges her to follow Bickerstaff's example in the *Tatler* and provide a genealogy of her lineage as a trifler, but fears that 'you are claiming a character without right' (*Lady's Museum* 3: 1.162). She notes that, unlike most essayists, the Trifler has not even attempted to justify her choice of a sobriquet: 'None ever started from her own purpose so soon as the Trifler' (*Lady's Museum* 3: 1.163). In fact, the Trifler's name describes not her own personality, but that of the majority of her female contemporaries. As a letter from Anoeta, a genuine trifler, puts it, 'A greater consonancy between the title of this essay and the present complection of females, cannot well be imagined' (*Lady's Museum* 8: II.561). The Trifler's name also reflects the derision that she imagines her paper will meet with from her fellow-women. The correspondent Maria, another self-confessed trifler, tells her,

> In this polite age, love and courtship are meer trifles, marriage is a trifle; virtue is an egregious trifle; wisdom, morality, religion, all are trifles . . . when you talk of wit, learning, economy; when you recommend reservedness, and a contempt for fashionable amusements, there is not a fine lady in town who does not acknowledge the propriety of your title, and declare that you are an intolerable trifler.
>
> (*Lady's Museum* 4: I.242)

The pages of 'The Trifler' are filled with letters from frivolous, ignorant, superficial women, such as Parthenissa, who thinks 'a spelling dictionary, and Grey's Love Letters very ample furniture for a lady's library' (*Lady's Museum* 9: II.644),[67] and Grace Pythoness, who wishes to teach her grand-daughters to believe in 'spirits, hobgoblins, fairies, death-watches, and Will i'the wisp' (10: II.723). It is this 'numerous and powerful generation of *Triflers*' (*Lady's Museum* 3: I.161) – women who are 'too solicitous about their personal charms to attend to the improvement of their minds' (2: I.82) and have 'never been accustomed to bestow the least attention upon any thing but the adorning and exhibiting our dear persons' (9: II.643) – whom the magazine explicitly sets out to educate and reform. They are childlike in their ignorance and need to be coaxed into learning through the 'pretty stratagem' of capturing their wayward attention through what appears to be a witty Spectatorial essay-series, a method, as Parthenissa puts it, 'like teaching children their letters by gingerbread alphabets' (*Lady's Museum* 9: II.641).

The Trifler does not express the confidence of Bickerstaff and Mr Spectator that her educational programme will take effect. Her column is full of letters from women who defiantly declare themselves uneducable. The Trifler seems to be urging these women to leave something other than offspring for others to remember them by. It is not clear what form this contribution should take – perhaps a literary work, or a discovery in botany or zoology – but there are hints that women's education should lead to something more than simply self-improvement. Anoeta says of herself and her fellow-triflers that 'unless we should be encumbered by a few brats, can it be said of any of us, when we quit the scene, that we have left any monuments of our existence?' (*Lady's Museum* 8: II.564), while Penelope Spindle tells the editor that her 'grand-mother was a country gentlewoman, and has left little behind her except a scented paste' (3: 1.162). The Trifler is, perhaps, offering indirect encouragement to women to publish periodicals themselves.

The theme of female education is also central to Lennox's serialized novel 'The History of Harriot and Sophia'. Like the Trifler, Sophia, whose name, of course, appropriately means wisdom, is a scholarly young woman who lost her father at an early age and has been educated by a male mentor; the family friend Mr Herbert supplies her with books. She too is disliked by her mother, who prefers her ignorant and coquettish sister, Harriot. By the age of 13, Sophia is fluent in French and Italian, but also acting as a housekeeper for her lazy mother and sister, proving that 'the highest intellectual improvements were not incompatible with the humblest cares of domestic life' (*Lady's Museum* 1: 1.19).

The novel is a fable of an educated middle-class girl who marries an aristocratic reformed rake. Her learning is a crucial factor in securing and retaining his affections, something which Lennox is at pains to underline. In a plot which echoes Richardson's *Clarissa*, Sir Charles Stanley at first hopes to make Harriot his mistress, inflamed by her beauty, but on meeting Sophia he quickly transfers his attentions to her and woos her, fittingly, by buying her books. Lennox makes the implications of Sir Charles's preference crystal clear:

> No one could think it surprising that a man of sense should make the fortune of a woman who would do honour to his choice, and where there was such exalted merit as in Sophia, overlook the disparity of circumstances.
>
> But justly might it be called infatuation and folly, to raise to rank and influence a woman of Harriot's despicable turn; to make a companion for life of a handsome ideot.
>
> (*Lady's Museum* 1: 1.39)

When the couple finally marry, at the end of the novel, Sir Charles confesses to Mr Herbert that it is Sophia's 'charming mind' which keeps him faithful: 'Had my passion for Sophia been founded only upon the charms of her person, I might probably e'er now have become a mere fashionable husband; but her virtue and wit supply her with graces ever varied, and ever new' (*Lady's Museum* 11: 11.826). Like Lennox herself and the Trifler, Sophia is a writer, as well as a reader. On one occasion, Sir Charles visits her rooms in secret in her absence:

> Several compositions of her own now fell into his hands; he read them with eagerness, and, charmed with this discovery of those treasures of

wit, which she with modest diffidence so carefully concealed, he felt his admiration and tenderness for her encrease every moment.

(*Lady's Museum* 8: ii.581)

In 'The Trifler' and 'The History of Harriot and Sophia', the *Lady's Museum* offers its readers educated women as role models. The magazine also tackles the subject of women's education on a more theoretical level. A series of extracts from Fénelon's *Traité de l'éducation des filles* (1687), described as translated by '*a Friend of the Author of the Museum*' (*Lady's Museum* 4: i.294), in issues 4–11, offers advice on education. The series opens with the claim that 'nothing is more neglected than the education of daughters' (*ibid.*) and promises to redress this imbalance. The 'Treatise' addresses a perceived need to reform women's own practices as educators. In the *Lady's Museum*, it is mothers who neglect their daughters' education. The Trifler, disregarded by her mother, is educated by a man instead, as is Sophia. The Trifler's correspondent Perdita has a similar history. Her mother cuts short her education, removing her from boarding school at the age of 16 to give her 'a commerce with the fashionable world', but she learns far more from her father 'who was a man of sense and learning, and who took pleasure in cultivating my mind' (*Lady's Museum* 5: i.323). A letter from the correspondent Agnes Woodbine relates how a female cousin neglected her daughters' education: their only reading material was the newspapers 'when the upper servants had done with them', and they were never taught to write (*Lady's Museum* 4: i.291). She has recently learnt that the elder girl has run away with a soldier, and the younger has had a child by the butler, causing their mother to die of a broken heart (*Lady's Museum* 4: i.292).

However, the recommendations made in the 'Treatise' series bear little resemblance to the ambitious educational programmes outlined in the *Female Spectator*, the *General Magazine of Arts and Sciences*, the *Young Ladies Magazine* and other sections of the *Museum* itself. The 'Treatise' focuses primarily on very young children and seems to be addressed more to the magazine's readers as educators of their own children, than as people in need of education themselves. During most of the series, the author talks of children in general and uses *he* as the generic pronoun. When the 'Treatise' does discuss issues of specific relevance to women, its injunctions are mainly negative. The writer stresses the dangers of over-educating a woman: 'We ought to be very careful of making pedantick ladies', he tells us, and must avoid 'studies likely to disturb their heads' (*Lady's Museum* 4: i.295), such as those concerned with politics, military strategy or religious affairs. A young woman, we are told, should modestly conceal the extent of her knowledge: 'As to subjects out of the reach of women in general, she should not speak upon them at all, though well informed' (*Lady's Museum* 11: ii.846). We are told that 'the education of her children . . . the government of her domestics . . . the disbursements of house-keeping, the method of living with oeconomy . . . the letting of farms, and receiving rents' should form 'the bounds of female information', even though this focus on domestic affairs will lead women of lively intellectual curiosity to feel dissatisfied and 'put under great restraints' (*Lady's Museum* 11: II.847). Education is described not as a means to develop women's mental capacities, but to restrain and correct their bad tendencies. The writer views the most important objective of female education as correcting female narcissism: 'There is nothing we ought so much to guard against as vanity in young ladies' (*Lady's Museum* 11: II.840).

The emphasis is on curbing, not exciting, female imagination. Predictably, the writer proposes that 'the pleasures which the understanding affords, as conversation, news, histories, and divers games of application' (*Lady's Museum* 8: II.631) will prevent young women from becoming addicted to what he calls 'dangerous entertainments' exciting 'violent passions' (*ibid.*). The most perilous of these imaginative stimulants is, of course, fiction – 'all the books that can feed their vanity . . . romances . . . plays . . . stories . . . chimerical adventures' (*Lady's Museum* 5: I.370):

> A poor girl, full of the tender and the marvellous . . . is astonished not to find the world afford any real personages resembling her heroes. She fain would live like the imaginary princesses . . . alas! what mortification for her to descend from a state of heroism to the little cares of domestic life.
>
> (*Lady's Museum* 5: I.370–1)

Arabella, the protagonist of Lennox's *The Female Quixote*, is one such woman. Her reading has been entirely confined to her late mother's library of French romances and her inflated perception of her importance borders on psychosis. Education is portrayed both in Lennox's periodical and her *Female Quixote* as designed to humble women and deflate their exaggerated pretensions.

The presence of the 'Treatise' within the *Lady's Museum* reveals the ambivalence and confusion which often characterizes attitudes towards women's education in this period. On the one hand, it could be seen as justifying the periodical's pedagogical content, offered as an antidote to more frivolous and treacherous forms of female reading. On the other hand, the magazine features a novel within its own pages. The novel is not stuffed with 'the tender and the marvellous', nor does it feature 'princesses' or describe 'a state of heroism'. However, it does encourage women to think that education may enable them to better themselves socially and financially, an ambition which may prove just as chimerical as that of becoming a princess. The correspondent W.M. claims that a woman's chances of upward mobility through marriage are slender, the rich marrying each other 'it has been computed' 19 times out of 20 (*Lady's Museum* 3: 1.183). The magazine also contains several serialized biographies, which are sensational and lurid, full of aristocratic family feuds, sexual intrigues and sudden and violent deaths (see 'The history of the Dutchess of Beaufort' (*Lady's Museum* 1–2); letters from A.B. on the trial and execution of Lord Ferrers (no. 4); 'The history of the Count de Comminge' (nos. 2, 3, 4, 5, 6, 7, 8, 11); 'The history of Bianca Capello' (nos. 5, 6, 7); and a history of Castruccio Castracani, sent in by the correspondent E.F. (no. 7)). Each issue of these features ends on a cliff-hanger, a method suggested in the 'Treatise' as an effective way to teach history (*Lady's Museum* 10: II.776–7). The magazine's narrative content seems designed to pique female curiosity and encourage female ambition.

In addition, the *Museum*'s educational articles span a wide range of academic subjects, and there is no mention of the domestic topics which the 'Treatise' recommends as the most suitable subjects of female study. Instead, the *Lady's Museum* offers its readers such fare as a history of Great Britain from prehistoric to early medieval times (in nos. 3, 4, 6, 8 and 11), a description of the solar system (in no. 2), descriptions of the islands of Amboyna (in no. 2) and Sri Lanka (in nos. 9, 10 and 11), an account of animal metamorphoses (in no. 2) and of the behaviour of predatory insects (in no. 4) and a life of Van Dyke (in no. 10).

The importance of allowing women access to a wide range of academic disciplines is discussed in the periodical's opening issue in an article entitled 'Of the studies proper for women', ostensibly written by a male correspondent, perhaps to lend these thoughts more authority. While the editor herself offers us narratives of educated women – in 'The Trifler' and 'The History of Harriot and Sophia' – it is men who offer the more general, theoretical commentary on the issue. Like the editors of the *Lady's Magazine*, the writer of 'Of the studies proper for women' is keen to emphasize the female potential for intellectual development: 'When we consider the happy talents which women in general possess . . . we cannot without indignation observe the little esteem they have for the endowments of their minds' (*Lady's Museum* 1: 1.9). The correspondent recommends history and natural science as the female fields of study, assuring the *Museum*'s female readers that history is of direct relevance to their concerns: 'Women have at all times had so great a share in events . . . that they may with reason consider our archives as their own' (1: 1.13). He goes on to name women who have written histories themselves – Monpensier, Nemours, Motteville, Christine de Pisan and Anna Comnensus[68] – and suggests that such subjects might be discussed at salons modelled on those of the Sevignés, Lafayettes and Rochefoucaults, where 'ladies of the first rank' could mingle with 'men of sense and learning [who] would then frequent their assemblies' (*Lady's Museum* 1: 1.15). Like the *Female Spectator*, the *Lady's Museum* advocates mixed-sex social gatherings, in which scholarly subjects are discussed in a relaxed domestic setting, and learned men are encouraged to disseminate their wisdom. In addition, the *Lady's Museum* seems to wish to offer readers a salon within the periodical, where history and the natural sciences are to be given special prominence.

'Of the studies proper for women' does not express many overtly feminist views. Nothing is said about personal fulfilment or individual rights. Women are to be educated for social reasons. As in 'The History of Harriot and Sophia', education will enable women to attract men – 'something more than beauty is necessary to rivet the lover's chain' (*Lady's Museum* 1: 1.9–10) – and retain their affections – 'barrenness of ideas in women ... renders men unfaithful' (1: 1.10). As a poem sent in by a reader puts it, 'wit, and virtue' are more captivating than 'mere outward charms' (*Lady's Museum* 1: 1.48). The correspondent is keen to stress that he does not propose that women should write history themselves:

> If their sex has produced Daciers and Chatelets, these are examples rarely found, and fitter to be admired than imitated: for who would wish to see assemblies made up of doctors in petticoats, who will regale us with Greek and the systems of Leibnitz. The learning proper for women is such as best suits the soft elegance of their form, such as may add to their natural beauties, and qualify them for the several duties of life.
>
> (*Lady's Museum* 1: 1.11)

This passage seems at first to be warning against female pedantry and, in particular, female learning in the Classics and natural sciences. There is a cautionary portrait of a woman who has pretensions to Classical learning in 'The History of Harriot and Sophia'. In her affectation and ignorance, she 'murdered so many hard words, that her discourse was scarcely intelligible' (*Lady's Museum* 6: II.417), and her suggestion that a farmer '"ought to have taught his daughters a little Greek and Latin, to have distinguished them from meer country girls"' (6: II.424) is treated with derision. However, footnotes in the magazine carefully identify the allusions in the above passage to Anne Dacier (1651–1720), translator of and commentator on Terence and Homer, and Gabrielle Emilie le Tonnelier de Bréteuil du Châtelet (1706–49), exponent of Leibnitz and Newton. These scholarly women are not held up to ridicule. They may not be presented as models for imitation, but they are, explicitly, fit for admiration. It is in itself very unusual for a periodical to have footnotes, and their presence strengthens its claims to be an educational publication. The footnotes are used here to make women aware of a tradition of female learning. While the *Museum* stops short of suggesting that its readers become scholars, the 'Daciers and Chatelets' prove that the female sex is capable of understanding academic subjects.

The reader is offered a preview of the *Museum*'s educational programme in the opening issue of the series 'Philosophy for the Ladies', where we are told that the editor will always concentrate on matters of human interest: in history 'those movements of the human heart on which depend the happiness or ruin of individuals'; in geography 'human nature diversified by different laws, by different constitutions, and different ideas' (*Lady's Museum* 2: 1.131). The editor stresses that the publication will not be dry and pedantic. She wishes

> to obviate the horrid idea which the word philosophy might otherwise impress on the minds of our female readers, who might from that term expect to find a work . . . loaded with dry and abstruse investigations . . . which if they were attained would stand a chance of more than ten to one of exciting the outcry of the world against them.
>
> (*Lady's Museum* 2: 1.131–2)

The *Lady's Museum*, she reassures her readership, will render women 'conversable rather than scientific' (2: 1.130). Yet at the same time, very grand claims are made for the periodical's all-embracing subject matter:

> One Number of our work perhaps shall leave us admiring the stupendous fabric of the immense extended universe; the next shall find us aiding our limited sight by the help of glasses in observations on a world of unknown beings contained within a drop of fluid.
>
> (*Lady's Museum* 2: 1.133)

The periodical, rather than encouraging its readers to carry out experiments (as the *Female Spectator* does) is itself both telescope and microscope: it offers descriptions both of the entire universe 'as considered under a general view' (*Lady's Museum* 2: 1.134–44) and a tiny parasite which lives on caterpillars (6: II.471–3). The women's scientific studies are to be conducted at second hand, through the descriptions contained in each 'Number of our work', making them 'conversable, rather than scientific'. No single subject will be entered into in depth, we are told: 'The plan we have determined to proceed on, [is] of not dwelling too long on any one subject' (*Lady's Museum* 5: 1.388).

The monthly perusal of the magazine's educational articles is designed, we are told, to allay female sexual appetite and encourage devotion: 'to calm our ruffled passions, and, by a regular transition, convey our contemplations from the creature to its Creator' (*Lady's Museum* 2: 1.136). Female learning is frequently recast as piety by periodical editors, in an attempt to allay anxieties about the moral effects of female interest in the Classics or natural sciences. Nestor Druid, for example, recommends Homer to his women readers for '*his* piety . . . *and* strict morality' (*Lady's Curiosity* 9), and includes a description of Newtonian physics in the form of 'Sir *Isaac Newton*'s Creed' (*Lady's Curiosity* 11). One of the *Female Spectator*'s correspondents tells readers that 'the Study of *Nature* is the Study of *Divinity*' (bk xv: 3.89). The *Lady's Museum* tells us 'in defence of the study of philosophy' that 'the observations we cannot avoid making in the course of it, may be employed with great propriety towards humanizing the heart, and producing the most amiable effects in the general oeconomy of life and government' (3: 1.233). Studying the metamorphoses of insects, for example, 'might form to us, by analogy, the idea of a future and more exalted state' (*Lady's Museum* 3: 1.234).

The educational articles in the *Lady's Museum* do not simply serve a moral purpose, however. The editor is keen to emphasize the accuracy of her reports and the extent of her research. In her series on early British history, for example, she tells us that she has consulted 'biographical lexicons' (*Lady's Museum* 8: II.593) and offers readers two different accounts of the Picts, from the works of Bishop Stillingfleet and 'Tyrrhel', giving a page reference and also referring readers in a footnote to Innes's Essays (8: II.605).[69] She encourages further reading on the topic and offers tips to readers wishing to conduct independent research, telling us that 'dictionaries are always voluminous, but always useful; they are lesser libraries, and the compilers of them are entitled to the highest acknowledgements from all lovers of learning' (*Lady's Museum* 8: II.593).

In the periodical's most daring statement of female intellectual capacity, the editor suggests history and natural philosophy as areas in which women may equal and even excel men:

> Undisturbed by the more intricate affairs of business; unburthened with the load of political entanglements; with the anxiety of commercial negotiations; or the suspence and anguish which attend on the pursuit of fame or fortune, the memories of the fair are left vacant to receive and to retain the regular connection of a train of events, to register them in that order which fancy may point out as most pleasing, and to form deductions from them such as may render their lives more agreeable to themselves, and more serviceable to every one about them. Their more exalted faculties, not being tied down by wearisome attention to mathematical investigations, metaphysical chimeras, or abstruse scholastic

learning, are more at liberty to observe with care, see with perspicuity, and judge without prejudice, concerning the amazing world of wonders round them than those of men.

(*Lady's Museum* 2: I.129–30)

This passage bears the hallmarks of a separate spheres philosophy, in which women are regarded as having no part to play in the male worlds of business, politics and commerce and as excluded from the 'fame and fortune' that reward male successes. Drawing on a traditional view of scholarship as a way of life opposed to active involvement in state politics, a view in which learning is incompatible with political or financial ambition, Lennox portrays women as more natural scholars than men. Their minds are 'more exalted', 'more at liberty' – they have both the time and the mental disinterestedness required by serious study. Rather than describing women's studies as more limited than men's, Lennox makes male intellectual activity seem pointless, pedantic, obscure and esoteric: a 'wearisome' pursuit of 'abstruse' and 'scholastic' 'chimeras'. Like Eliza Haywood, Benjamin Martin and other writers, Lennox praises women's capacity for empirical science based on observation: they 'observe with care, see with perspicuity'. She goes further than Haywood and Martin, however, in her claims for the female intellect. While Haywood depicts women as acute observers, she regards women's minds as lively, rather than well-disciplined, with a 'Vivacity' and 'Quickness' which excel men's, but a tendency towards confusion. Women's thoughts, Haywood writes, can rush to an object 'like a Crowd of Mob round the Stage of a Mountebank, where all endeavouring to be foremost, obstruct the Passage of each other' (*Female Spectator* bk X: 2.360).[70] Lennox, by contrast, emphasizes not only women's quick apprehensions and powers of observation, but also their skills in logic: their understanding of 'a regular connection', ability to make 'deductions', to 'see with perspicuity' and 'judge without prejudice', in explicit contrast with men. Most strikingly, Lennox suggests that women's intellects, by contrast with men's, have a very wide field in which to range. Far from being confined to domestic concerns, women can mentally explore 'a world of wonders'. In the final issue of the *Lady's Museum*, she proposes an unbounded programme of natural science for women:

Could the prosecution of our plan have been pursued . . . even to the farthest stretch of time, our researches into the wonders of Nature's inexhaustible storehouse, would have been no other than the pursuance of an apparent horizon, the boundaries of which are ever flying before us.

(11: II.857)

Whatever the limitations of the magazine itself, the potential subjects for female study are 'inexhaustible'.

Lennox's statements of women's intellectual potential, together with her portrayals of educated women and her more theoretical articles on female education, are intended to flatter, coax and reassure her female readers into study. Above all, in all its rhetoric on education, the *Museum* is simply attempting to create a demand and then satisfy it. It tells women to educate themselves and then provides the necessary material within its pages. With their aspirations towards universality and comprehensiveness, mid-century magazines aimed to provide both a microcosm of society and a complete course of reading in themselves: grandiose aims which were seldom fulfilled. Often, magazines express grand ambitions for women's education, but fail to deliver on these promises. The *Lady's Museum* is typical in that in devotes as much space to discussing the need for female education as it does to educational material itself. Mid-eighteenth century journalism often contains lively debate about women's education and vociferous expressions of support for it, but the provision of a substantial academic programme of learning for women was a long way off. In the later years of the century, as women's need for education became a more pressing concern and magazines were increasingly segregated into publications aimed at a specific gender, most periodical publications also gradually abandoned their pedagogical focus and intellectual ambitions. The wishes of Lennox and some of her contemporaries to turn the magazine for women into a serious educational vehicle were to be disappointed. In the last decades of the eighteenth century, magazines specifically aimed at women were to specialize in fashion plates, recipes and household hints, a trend which continues to this day.

10 'Buried among the essays upon liberty, eastern tales, and cures for the bite of a mad dog'
Oliver Goldsmith and the essayist in the age of magazines

In his essay 'The state of literature', published in *Lloyd's Evening Post* (1 February 1762), Oliver Goldsmith vividly describes the state of the contemporary periodical press:

> Never was the publication of periodical works, calculated for both the head and the heart, so frequent before; more than ten agreeable Magazines in a month came flying abroad fraught with instruction and entertainment. The Gentleman's Magazine, remarkable for its gravity and age. The London Magazine, judiciously compiled from compilations; the Universal Magazine, fricasseed from Dictionaries; the Royal Magazine, written by a Society of Gentlemen; the Imperial Magazine . . . the sensible British Magazine, the orthodox Christian's Magazine; the Lady's Magazine . . . the Library Magazine . . . the Court Magazine . . . all serious, chaste, temperate compilations, calculated to instruct mankind in the changes of the weather and to amuse them with eastern tales, replete with grave essays upon wit and humour, and humorous essays upon the cultivation of madder and hemp.[71]
>
> (Goldsmith 1966: 3.188–9)

In the years between the launch of Edward Cave's *Gentleman's Magazine* in 1731 and Goldsmith's article a plethora of publications appeared, exploiting what seemed to be an insatiable demand for magazines. The editors of the *Literary Magazine* (1756–8) admit that 'there are already many such periodical compilations' and hope modestly only to engage those who are not already regular readers of a rival magazine (vol. I, Preface). Although some of these periodicals were short-lived, most ran for at least a year, and many were to continue in print for half a century or more. Cave's own publication, which appeared until 1907, J. Wilford's *London Magazine* (1732–97), the *Scots Magazine* (1739–1826) and the *Universal Magazine of Knowledge and Pleasure* (1747–1815) were to enjoy particular longevity. Bonnell Thornton comments 10 years before Goldsmith that 'the very name [*magazine*] will secure to you the custom of the country' (*Drury-Lane Journal* 3, 30 January 1752). By the 1760s, the term *magazine*, as Goldsmith's comments demonstrate, announced a well-defined formula. Travel accounts, Oriental tales and allegories, serialized novels, sentimental fragments, Biblical commentary and practical articles on such topics as gardening, furniture making and cures for common ailments take their place beside political essays and news items in these bulky publications. Their title pages usually voice grandiose claims to inclusiveness. Each issue of the quarterly *Royal Magazine* is 480 pages long, with its own index. The editors announce, '*No Performance can justly lay Claim to the Title of* MAGAZINE, *but that which gives a full and complete Collection* ... *of all the Pieces of Knowledge, Religion, Policy, Art, Wit, Humour, Love, Gallantry, Satire, &c. printed in the Period preceeding its Publication*' (I, October–December 1750, Preface). The *Universal Magazine of Knowledge and Pleasure* (1747–1815) aspires to the comprehensiveness of its title, promising readers '*News, Letters, Debates, Poetry, Musick, Biography, History, Geography, Voyages, Criticism, Translations, Philosophy, Mathematicks, Husbandry, Gardening, Cookery, Chemistry, Mechanicks, Trade, Navigation, Architecture, and Other Arts and Sciences*' (subtitle). Christopher Smart satirizes the extravagant claims of these bulky publications in his parody the *Midwife* (1750–3), whose grandiose subtitle announces:

> *Containing all the Wit, and all the Humour, and all the Learning, and all the Judgement, that has ever been or ever will be Inserted in all the other Magazines, or the Magazine of Magazines, or any other Book Whatsoever: so that those who Buy this Book will Need no Other.*

Priscilla Termagant makes a similarly sarcastic claim when she tells readers, 'This Journal should be an Epitome of Mankind' (*Spring-Garden Journal* 2, 23 November 1752). The magazines' grand pretensions often resulted in a jumble of material: 'incongruous Hashes of Gazette-Accounts, and News-paper Essays, Plagiarisms from Books, and a few flimsy, unimproving, and unmeaning Productions from Men of little Learning, and less Knowledge of the World', as the *Imperial Magazine* puts it (January 1760, Introduction).

The magazines' increasing success was at least partly due to the Stamp Tax on newspapers. In 1757 an act was passed which doubled the rates of the 1725 Stamp Tax. Although there was no clear legal definition of a newspaper, in practice the regulations were only applied to weekly or semi-weekly publications, making monthly magazines an even more attractive alternative to consumers and leading to a further expansion in their numbers and sales figures.

The essay-periodical is a genre overwhelmingly associated with the sophisticated world of London society. Whilst Cave adopted the pseudonym of Sylvanus Urban, emphasizing the breadth of his readership, editors like Mr Town of the *Connoisseur* (1754–6) and Adam Fitz-Adam of the *World* (1753–6) stressed their metropolitan affiliations. Magazines had always held a particular appeal for provincial readers. The *Royal Magazine* promises to keep 'Gentlemen who live in the Country' informed '*(tho' perhaps at a great Distance from the Metropolis) in all the Affairs of the* Beau Monde' (I, October–December 1750, Preface). The correspondent T.H. tells the editor of the *Court Magazine* that 'particular advantage arises to your country readers from this work . . . as the transactions of the Court must be a very agreeable part of an evening's conversation, and with which the generality of Magazine readers have been hitherto totally unacquainted' (September 1761: 18). Country-dwellers did not have the same easy access to a wide range of daily and weekly publications as the clientele of the London coffee-houses and were far more willing to wait until the end of the month to read summaries of the news, since they had always received news and current affairs publications far later than their metropolitan counterparts. Improved transport and communications enabled magazine editors to distribute their publications throughout the country. Magazines were often associated with a naïve and ill-informed rural audience. Thornton comments that 'a professing to *contain more in quantity than any other work of the same kind*, has doubtless had its weight with many a prudent country person, who thought he got a great bargain every month for his six-pence' (*Drury-Lane Journal* 3, 30 January 1752).

In view of an expanding national readership and a demand for greater variety, the essay-periodical, modelled on the works of Addison and Steele, had begun to appear outdated. As Robert D. Spector has shown, during the Seven Years War (1756–63) short essay-papers with a purely literary content became increasingly unpopular with a reading public hungry for foreign news (1966). Essayists failed to adapt to the changing political and literary climate and continued to take the *Tatler* and *Spectator* as their models, although both publications were nearly half a century old by 1760. Magazines were able to swallow essay-series whole, reprinting them in their pages as a regular feature. Addison and Steele's contemporaries read the *Spectator* in single sheets. Johnson's *Rambler*, in 1750–2, on the other hand, sold less than 500 copies in its original format, but was widely plagiarized by the London and provincial press. It reached a very large audience, but it was an audience of magazine readers.

For professional journalists who wished to make a living, contributing to the magazines was the only viable option. Despite his satirical comments, Goldsmith supplied essays to a wide variety of newspapers and magazines in the 1750s and 60s. Richard Taylor has traced Goldsmith's contributions to at least 15 publications of this period. These range from the daily newspaper the *Public Ledger* (1760–1837), to the pious and didactic *Christian Magazine* (1759–67) and include four of the periodicals – the *Royal*, *British*, *Christian* and *Lady's* magazines – lampooned in the article cited above.[72] As Taylor notes, as a poor, unknown Irish writer in London, the periodicals provided Goldsmith with an opportunity to earn money and attract the attention of the capital's publishers and booksellers, yet his journalistic work is marked by 'the unavoidable tension created by the author's expressed contempt for a profession in which he hoped to achieve fame' (1993: 76). Goldsmith's work for the *Critical Review* in 1757–8 marked the beginning of a lifelong association with the powerful bookseller John Newbery who introduced him to a circle of writers which included Johnson and Smollett (Taylor 1993: 89–103). Despite his own involvement with both major reviewing journals, the *Critical* and the rival *Monthly Review*, Goldsmith was to depict 'book-answerers' in his 'Chinese Letters' of 1760–1 as 'wretches . . . kept in pay by some mercenary bookseller . . . as all that is required is to be very abusive and very dull' (1966: 2.60). As Taylor has shown, this is a very distorted portrayal of Ralph Griffiths' and Tobias Smollett's professional staff, who enjoyed considerable independence and whose reviews were more often characterized by modest praise than by rancorous attacks (1993: 32–8, 100). Goldsmith's bitterness reveals his deeply ambivalent attitude towards his journalistic career. His essays contain both defiant vindications of the professional writer and attempts to distance himself from what he viewed as a degrading and servile occupation. This chapter will explore the tensions and contradictions of Goldsmith's depictions of himself as a periodical writer.

Goldsmith's complaints of his dependence on the booksellers reflect changing patterns of ownership and control of periodicals. Lady Mary Wortley Montagu complains in 1737 that printers and booksellers refuse to accept publications which threaten to be unprofitable and her own 'Ingenious Printer' has made unauthorized alterations to her copy, adding, as she exclaims indignantly, 'a little Bawdy at the end of a Paragraph, that no way led to any Idea of that sort' (*Nonsense of Common Sense* 2). These were only minor infringements, however: the concept and material were supplied by Montagu. Addison and Steele had been personally responsible for the contents of the *Spectator*, while magazine writers like Goldsmith and Lennox were in the hands of a publisher who dictated the shape of each issue. The editor of the *Court Magazine* tells his readers that it is 'the bookseller, who has very little literary vanity in his composition' who 'is generally the person who draws it up; he is a kind of godfather to the various writers concerned in the undertaking' (September 1761). Goldsmith's *Bee* was published by John Wilkie, one of a number of close business associates of John Newbery, who included the editor Griffith Jones and the printers Jonathan Richardson and William Faden, who printed the *Rambler*. Newbery's influence on the periodicals of the 1760s can hardly be overestimated. He seems to have had a financial stake not only in the *Bee*, but in most of the other periodicals with which Goldsmith was involved: the *British Magazine, Critical Review, Literary Magazine, Lloyd's Evening Post, London Chronicle, Public Ledger, Royal Magazine* and the *Universal Chronicle*, as well as the *Lady's Magazine; or, Polite Companion* and Lennox's *Lady's Museum* (see Taylor 1993: 87).

Although the *Nonsense of Common-Sense* is not strictly an essay-periodical, as it also contains a news section, it was primarily a vehicle for Montagu's writing. Goldsmith's 'Chinese Letters' were published in very different circumstances. They appeared irregularly at the average rate of 10 letters each month between 24 January 1760 and 14 August 1761 in the *Public Ledger*, published by Newbery and edited by Griffith Jones. The *Ledger* is a daily paper, dominated by military, shipping and domestic news, as well as featuring an index to the advertisements in other periodicals, which must have been of particular interest to a mercantile readership. Goldsmith's was only one of a number of leaders, some of which were literary, like the series 'The Visitor', published under the *nom de plume* of Philanthropy Candid. In other issues, foreign news or shipping lists replaced the essays on manners and morals. Goldsmith produced 119 letters in all, for which he was paid the not miserly stipend of £100 p.a. His reliance on Newbery was more than symbolic: during the publication of the 'Chinese Letters', Goldsmith, who was constitutionally financially inept, seems to have lived with Newbery and his relatives. The costs of room and board were subtracted from his salary (Kirk 1967: 33). When the 'Chinese Letters' ended on 14 August, Goldsmith immediately began the new 'Series of Literary Essays', the first of which appeared on 19 August.

Many of Newbery's ventures were highly successful. They anticipate the periodicals of the twenty-first century in many respects. Their length made it impractical for any single person to provide all the copy, whilst their longevity meant that successive generations of writers and publishers would become involved in the production of the same title. As with most modern-day periodicals, individual writers were expected to conform to a house style. For Goldsmith, these publications provided a vital livelihood and vehicle for his writings, yet on the other hand they were commercial enterprises that compromised his desire for literary respectability. Goldsmith did not want to be merely another hack. His journalism constantly responds to this perceived threat to his artistic integrity.

Goldsmith comments extensively on the new position of the Addisonian essayist in an age of magazines. He is very untypical in this respect. There were many essay-serials within newspapers and magazines, but most writers chose discreetly to ignore the context of their publication. The essay-series as a genre relies heavily on the persona of its narrator, usually portrayed as a gentleman (sometimes as a lady) and an eccentric who writes out of a mixture of pique, personal vanity and public spirit, with little or no profit motive. Female editors were frequently described as indulging their constitutional loquacity. The editor of the *Parrot*, a 'single Woman possess'd of a good Fortune' (3, 9 October 1728), confesses, 'I cannot hold my Tongue; for I must speak and write when the Humour takes me' (1, 25 September 1728). Similarly, the editor of Eliza Haywood's *Parrot* (1746) declares that he wishes 'to gratify my own insatiable Itch of talking' (no. 1). Nicholas Babble of the *Prater* has turned to writing a periodical because he 'was always of an inquisitive, communicative disposition' and has been persuaded that he would make a good journalist: 'My friends have at last flatter'd me into a belief that I have as much right to attract the attention of the Town as the daily, weekly, and monthly chatterers of the age' (1, 13 March 1756). Mr Babble is a denizen of fashionable society: 'Sometimes I have the honour to breakfast with a Lady of Quality before she is up, and to be taken notice of by a Great Man before he goes to Court' (*Prater* 3, 27 March 1756). He possesses 'a great deal of . . . public-spiritedness' and plans to 'scribble away . . . for the good of my Country' and give them the benefit of his lucubrations '*pro bono*' (*Prater* 1). His 16-year-old cousin Martha Chatter makes occasional contributions to the paper, motivated by the 'excessively delightful' opportunity of talking 'in Print', since all her personal acquaintances are weary of her incessant prattle (*Prater* 6, 17 April 1756).

Frontispiece illustrations, like that of the 1747 volume of the *Universal Magazine*, often depict editors seated pensively at desks in libraries, quill pen in hand (Figure 10.1). 'The Meddler', in the contemporary *Royal Female Magazine*, a widely travelled gentleman of leisure educated at Eton and Oxford, is a typical specimen of the financially disinterested editor. The 'title of this paper', he confesses, 'is the characteristic of my mind, the ruling passion of which, now that I have arrived at that stage of life, wherein ability for *active meddling* fails me, irresistibly impells me to this *speculative* indulgence of it' (1, March 1760). Adam Fitz-Adam, the editor of the *World*, is a gentleman who has access to polite society: both the metropolitan assemblies of people like the urbane Lady Townley, who prides herself on being a woman of fashion (151, 20 November 1755), and the estates of country squires like Sir John Jolly (153, 5 December 1755), whose aim is to make his country estate a copy of London society, with the addition of constant hunting parties.

This pretence of financial and intellectual independence is difficult to maintain if the writer admits that his essays were commissioned by a magazine editor. Steele comments playfully on every aspect of the *Tatler* from its poor quality paper to its advertisements and its publisher, Charles Lillie.[73] The contributors to the magazines are unable to maintain such a consistent

Figure 10.1 Frontispiece of the *Universal Magazine*, vol. for 1747.

character, and the Steelian persona frequently appears to be merely an outworn convention. The writer of 'The Meddler' tells his readers that 'the usual way, with my periodical predecessors, has been to give ... [a] history of themselves', but laments that 'many lamentable miscarriages ... have long since made that method ineffectual' (*Royal Female Magazine* 1, March 1760). However, he does adopt a persona: that of a melancholy traveller nursing a secret sorrow. Mark Akenside does not adopt an editorial persona of any kind in his *Museum*. In the *Town and Country Magazine*, correspondence is simply addressed 'To the Printer'. Mrs Stanhope of the *Lady's Magazine* remains a shadowy, undeveloped figure, and correspondents often unselfconsciously address her as 'Sir'. Likewise, the editor of the annual *Ladies Complete Pocket-Book* is simply and anonymously 'a LADY', while the editors of the *Court Magazine* and Matilda Wentworth of the *Court Miscellany* are never described to the reader. The editors of the *Universal Magazine* refrain from taking a stance on any issue, declaring, 'It is not our business to form any discussion ... our principal concern is to find matter of good entertainment for our Readers' (XXXVIII, 1766, Preface). We sense a weariness and impatience with the Spectatorial conventions in Goldsmith's *Bee*:

> There is not, perhaps, a more whimsically dismal figure in nature, than a man of real modesty who assumes an air of impudence; who, while his heart beats with anxiety, studies ease, and affects good humour. In this situation, however, a periodical writer often finds himself, upon his first attempt to address the public in form.[74]
>
> (1, 1 October 1759; Goldsmith 1966: 1.353)

Goldsmith's work for the magazines was anonymous and had no copyright. His work is often obscured by the sheer mass of other material contained in the magazines, coming forth, as he writes in *The Vicar of Wakefield*, 'in the mist of periodical publication, unnoticed and unknown' (Goldsmith 1966: 4.111). Essayists frequently describe the magazines as merely 'Monthly Heaps of second-hand, damag'd and stolen Goods' (*Daily Post* 23 February 1737), while readers like Tim Lovelady request 'more original pieces ... than I have yet met with' (*Lady's Curiosity* 6). Goldsmith complains that his essays have been so extensively plagiarized that they have become hackneyed and outdated even before publication in volume form:

> Most of these essays have been regularly reprinted twice or thrice a year, and conveyed to the public through the kennel of some engaging compilation ... I have seen some of my labours sixteen times reprinted, and claimed by different parents as their own.
>
> (Goldsmith 1966: 3.1)

Goldsmith's own journalism is highly plagiaristic (see Taylor 1993: 81), yet he is concerned to protect his intellectual property and even envisages a critical edition of his journalism. He writes in a letter of 1758, 'There will come a day . . . when the Scaligers and Daciers will . . . give learned editions of my labours, and bless the times with copious comments on the text' (Goldsmith 1928: 38–9). This semi-serious joke is repeated in the fourth issue of the *Bee* (27 October 1759) where the author imagines 'Scaligers, Daciers, and Warburtons of future times commenting with admiration upon every line I now write', adding the wry comment that 'the world may forsake an author, but vanity will never forsake him' (Goldsmith 1966: 1.416). These grand visions of posterity poring over an established Goldsmith canon contrast with the fragmented and depersonalized world of magazine publication, where writings are continually borrowed, adapted and distorted.

Goldsmith describes the production of a magazine as a highly mechanized process. Lady Mary Wortley Montagu also complains in 1737 that 'the Art of Poetry is now grown so thoroughly Mechanical, that, if my Conscience would suffer me, I would bind my youngest Son 'Prentice to an eminent Poet' (*Nonsense of Common Sense* 9). Whilst for Montagu, however, it is the financial motive which demeans poetry, for Goldsmith, it is the extreme division of literary labour. In the *Bee* (1, 6 October 1759), a bookseller explains:

> One writer excels at a plan, or a title-page, another works away the body of a book, and a third is a dab at an index. Thus a Magazine is not the result of any single man's industry; but goes through as many hands as a new pin, before it is fit for the public.
>
> (Goldsmith 1966: 1.354)

Goldsmith's views are confirmed by the *Court Magazine*, which describes how 'a few authors' specialize in 'Introduction writing' and 'receive half a crown . . . for three or four preparatory pages at the head of a performance' (September 1761). The mechanized nature of magazine publication is further emphasized when T.D. offers his services as a journalist on the strength of having 'wrought for several magazine-shops' (*Court Magazine* October 1761). The editor tells his readers 'we consider the republic of letters as a commercial state and look upon the different professors as a kind of mechanics' (*Court Magazine* November 1761).

For Goldsmith, the magazine is a huge, bland, anonymous, money-making venture. The individual writer's personality is swamped by the sheer mass of other material. Writers of essay-periodicals might have had to try to attract a readership in an overcrowded market, but for the modern magazine writer, the competition is from other articles within the magazine itself.

Each reader turns to his or her own favourite section and ignores the rest. The essayist's work is packaged for an audience of magazine-readers, that is, for a readership below his or her dignity and unappreciative of his or her merits. Later in the same issue, Goldsmith warns that 'should the labours of a writer who designs his performances for readers of a more refined appetite fall into the hands of a devourer of compilations, what can he expect but contempt and confusion' (1996: 1.356). Writing for the magazines is regarded as in itself demeaning. In his essay-series 'The Indigent Philosopher', Goldsmith laments:

> Alas! how ill do I support the dignity of a Scholar or a Gentleman, by thus consigning my little acquirements to the same vehicle that must too often necessarily convey insipidity and ignorance! How cold a reception must every effort receive that comes thus endeavouring to regulate the passions, in a place where almost every paragraph tends to excite them; where readers of taste seldom seek for gratification; and where readers of politicks and news seldom require more than the objects of their peculiar curiosity.
>
> (*Lloyd's Evening Post* 22 January 1762; Goldsmith 1966: 3.182)

The audience of *Lloyd's Evening Post*, the essayist argues, have bought the publication primarily for its focus on current affairs and trading reports. Preoccupied by 'politicks and news', they lack the detachment and disinterestedness requisite for the appreciation of philosophy. Political polemic and controversy, together with reports which stimulate mercantile hopes and fears, 'excite' the passions, and moral essays are disregarded as irrelevant. Readers of sufficient taste and discernment to appreciate Goldsmith's work would never, he claims, stoop to buying such a publication. In the *Bee* (1, 6 October 1759), he writes that 'if . . . like labourers in the Magazine trade, I humbly presume to promise an epitome of all the good things that were ever said or written, those readers I most desire to please may forsake me' (Goldsmith 1966: 1.353–4). Goldsmith sometimes seems to suggest that even an essay-periodical is a demeaning medium for his writing. His own persona Lien Chi Altangi of the 'Chinese Letters' declares that 'essays upon divers subjects can't allure me' (Goldsmith 1966: 2.388). Goldsmith's fears that the medium in which his essays appeared would affect their reception appear to have been justified. A contemporary reviewer of the collected version of the 'Chinese Letters', published in book form as *The Citizen of the World* in 1762, comments:

> Were we to examine these reflections of our *Citizen of the World* by the standard of originality, our pleasure would be greatly diminished . . .

these letters, if we mistake not, made their first appearance in a daily news-paper, and were necessarily calculated to the meridian of the multitude.

(Critical Review May 1762)

Goldsmith's attempts to distance himself from these mechanical 'labourers', denied originality and forced to 'eccho the million' (Chinese Letter LI; Goldsmith 1966: 2.214), can be most clearly seen in his periodical the *Bee* (1759). The weekly publication is a hybrid of the essay-periodical and the magazine, a kind of miniature magazine without the news section. Its political essays, allegories, Oriental tales, biographies and poems are typical magazine fare, and many of them were recycled by Goldsmith during his probable editorship of the *Lady's Magazine*, as well as plagiarized by other contemporary magazines. Only about half of the material is original, the rest compiled by Goldsmith, or translated from French sources (see Taylor 1993: 81). Yet the *Bee* is full of hostile comment on magazines and constantly claims not to be one itself. It is portrayed as far more exclusive and indeed unpopular than the magazines:

> Should I estimate my fame by its extent, every News-Paper and every Magazine would leave me far behind. Their fame is diffused in a very wide circle, that of some as far as Islington ... while mine ... has hardly travelled beyond the sound of Bow-bell.
>
> *(Bee* 4, 27 October 1759; Goldsmith 1966: 1.414)

The writer is depicted as a disinterested essayist in the Addisonian mould who has fallen upon evil times, in a degenerate age in which the essay-periodical is no longer appreciated. He complains:

> The Spectator, and many succeeding essayists, frequently inform us of the numerous compliments paid them in the course of their lucubrations ... I have received *my letters* as well as they; but alas! not congratulatory ones ... One gentleman assures me, he intends to throw away no more three-pences in purchasing the BEE ... Were my soul set upon three-pences, what anxiety might not such a denunciation produce! But such does not happen to be the present motive of publication! I write partly to show my good-nature, and partly to shew my vanity.
>
> *(ibid.*; Goldsmith 1966: 1.419)

The essayist is presented here as a disinterested, genteel amateur, writing for his own personal satisfaction. Goldsmith claims that the very form of his publication proves it was not written for money, since no publication modelled on the *Spectator* could be expected to make a profit in the 1760s. If he had wished to accumulate three-pences, the editor writes, 'I should have written down to the taste and apprehension of the many', or, in other words, produced a magazine:

> I had thought of changing the title into that of the ROYAL BEE, the ANTI-GALLICAN BEE, or the BEE'S MAGAZINE.[75] I had laid in a proper stock of popular topics, such as encomiums on the king of Prussia ... the history of an old woman whose teeth grew three inches long ... a rebus, an acrostic ... and a journal of the weather.
>
> (*ibid.*; Goldsmith 1966: 1.418)

Goldsmith's flippant summary implies that magazines are both easy to produce and all alike. His list of topics echoes the heterogeneous contents pages of many contemporary publications. A letter from a repentant former prostitute follows an account of a scientific experiment in the *Imperial Magazine*, for example (January 1760).

Although, in the *Bee*, Goldsmith distances himself from the mercenary hack, he often defends the professional writer. He introduces his 'Series of Literary Essays', a sequence of brief book reviews and extracts printed in the *Public Ledger*, in a defiant manner:

> In the execution of a task of this nature neither great abilities nor profound learning will be exerted by the writer, and no great discernment or sagacity will be required on the part of the reader. I could wish that we both brought only our common-sense to the business.
>
> (*Public Ledger* 19 August 1761; Goldsmith 1966: 3.159)

The preface to his *Essays* defends them against the charge of being 'trifling and superficial' with the admission that 'in some measure ... the charge is true ... but I would ask whether in a short essay it is not necessary to be superficial?' (Goldsmith 1966: 3.2). Goldsmith implies that journalism must be judged by its own set of standards. He reminds his readers that even such a humble profession requires care and skill. However low its status, journalism is a competitive field: 'It is not every scholar who pretends to despise this prostitution of talents, whose works have sufficient beauty to allure our employer to propose terms of similar prostitution' (*Lloyd's Evening Post* 22 January 1762; Goldsmith 1966: 3.182). The bitterness of Goldsmith's sarcasm reveals the tensions between his desire to elicit sympathy for journalists and his shame at his own involvement in the profession.

Claims of editorial gentility are ubiquitous in mid-eighteenth century journalism. The editors of the *Court Magazine* complain of 'the insolent claim, every little pretender to genius, shall make to the character of a gentleman. From the writer of an humble Acrostic in the Daily Gazetteer, to the sensible compiler of an Evening's Essay in the St. James's Chronicle' (November 1761). The *Court*'s editors are themselves described as 'a Society of Gentlemen ... Who have generously united their Abilities for ... the Benefit of Mankind' (I [for 1761], 1763, Preface). Magazine editor Nestor Druid is proud to be '*of no Profession*' (*Lady's Curiosity* 1, Introduction), while Jeffrey Broadbottom of the political journal *Old England* tells his printer '*your profession is getting Money, and mine getting Fame*' (20, 18 June 1743). Jeoffry Wagstaffe of the *Batchelor* claims to have 'an easy competency, so as to make me independent' and to write 'meerly to gratify my humour, or for amusement' (1, 29 March 1766). In his *Covent-Garden Journal*, Fielding, writing as Sir Alexander Drawcansir, sarcastically claims that matters of profit are 'infinitely below my Consideration', since he wished 'to distribute these Papers *gratis*', but was dissuaded by his profit-hungry bookseller (1, 4 January 1752).[76] The editors of the *Scots Magazine* feel obliged 'to offer our *motives*, as to our *performance*, to the judgment of our readers' (vol. I, Preface). They admit that they do not 'pretend to be free from all desire of gain', but promise that any profit will be 'carefully applied toward making *this Magazine* more acceptable' (*ibid.*).

The *Universal Visiter* claims to have been written by 'a society of gentlemen' (subtitle). The frontispiece to vol. 1 for 1756 shows a man sitting contemplatively at a desk in a library. The room is decorated with the busts of Chaucer, Spenser, Shakespeare, Waller and Dryden, and the shelves above contain volumes of English authors from Gower to Tillotson. The picture suggests that the periodical is the work of a single, leisured gentleman, an amateur who writes from the well-appointed library in his own spacious home. The reality behind the image was very different: Christopher Smart and Richard Rolt signed a notorious contract which bound them to provide one third of the magazine's copy and to write for no other publication for a term of 99 years (see Gedalof 1983: 349–54) (Figure 10.2).

In Goldsmith's writing, the figure of the poor author starving in his garret is not always satirized. He makes an implicit distinction between writing for profit and writing for subsistence. Goldsmith mocks the genteel pretensions of magazine editors in 'The Indigent Philosopher' with an advertisement for an imaginary *Infernal Magazine* written by 'a Society of Gentlemen of distinction', who 'disdain to eat or write like Hirelings ... and ... are resolved to sell our Magazine for sixpence merely for our own amusement' (Goldsmith 1966: 3.192). By contrast, Goldsmith's indigent philosopher makes a bargain with his readers which seems frank and fair: 'Let the reader then only permit me to eat, and I will endeavour to encrease his pleasures' (*Lloyd's Evening Post* 22 January 1760; Goldsmith 1966: 3.183).

Figure 10.2 Frontispiece of the *Universal Visiter*, vol. I, 1756.

Goldsmith's 'Indigent Philosopher' is a latter-day Diogenes, recalling Classical Athens, rather than Grub Street. Like the narrator of the 'Chinese Letters', he is an impoverished, but wise and disinterested, philosopher. He is fiercely independent and proud, despite his poverty, a neglected genius publishing his moral wisdom for the benefit of a sadly unappreciative world. He makes a passionate appeal to our sense of justice, exclaiming, 'And shall I be ashamed of being paid a trifle for doing this, when Bishops are paid for scarce preaching on Sundays! . . . *By Heavens I . . . glory in it*' (*Lloyd's Evening Post* 22 January 1762; Goldsmith 1966: 3.183). In his 'Chinese Letters', he voices the view that professional writers have far greater artistic freedom than their predecessors who were forced to become the sycophants of aristocratic patrons: 'At present the . . . poets of England no longer depend on the Great for subsistence, they have now no other patrons but the public, and the public, collectively considered, is a good and generous master' (Goldsmith 1966: 2.344). In the 'Chinese Letters', Goldsmith describes 'a polite age', in which 'almost every person becomes a reader' (1966: 2.311), and every 'polite member of the community by buying what he [the professional author] writes, contributes to reward him' (1966: 2.344). The necessity of earning money, rather than restricting a writer, acts as a spur to creativity. He assures readers that professional writers are far from being a manifestation of modern depravity: 'Homer is the first poet and beggar of note . . . Terence was a slave, and Boethius died in a jail' (Goldsmith 1966: 2.342). Goldsmith's Chinese philosopher asserts proudly that 'almost all the excellent productions in wit . . . were purely the offspring of necessity; their Drydens, Butlers, Otways and Farquhars, were all writers for bread' (Goldsmith 1966: 2.376).

Goldsmith's ambivalence towards his occupation as a professional journalist is symptomatic of a larger problem confronting the periodicalists of the mid-eighteenth century. In the late 1750s and early 1760s, periodical essayists and editors were forced to redefine themselves and adopt new literary strategies. In a market dominated by newspapers and magazines, the essay-periodical seemed threatened with extinction. Essayists continued to invoke the sacred names of Addison and Steele in defence of their undertaking, but these had lost a lot of their talismanic power. The essay-serial seemed like a quaint period-piece from Queen Anne's reign, within the more modern idiom of the magazine or newspaper. The changes which had taken place were to have lasting consequences. Like the magazines of the 1760s, most modern periodicals are published by a complex hierarchy of publishers, editors, sub-editors and staff writers. The material submitted by individual contributors is carefully edited and is usually expected to conform to a house style. Editorials and regular columns have come to replace the Spectatorial essay, occupying only a small proportion of space in most publications. Whilst some columnists express outspoken or maverick views, very few adopt a fictional persona. Less precedence is given to readers' letters, yet they remain a persistent feature of journals, and women's magazines, in particular, place a high premium on authenticity. Publications like *Cosmopolitan* and *Marie Claire* feature confessional first person accounts of traumatic events in their readers' lives, surveys and problem pages, as well as letters to the editor. Readers are encouraged to identify with their staff writers, who present themselves not as professional journalists, but as ordinary people sharing the troubles and pleasures of their audience. It is often difficult to tell whether their correspondence is genuine or fictional. Whilst a number of men's magazines were launched in the 1980s and 90s, magazines are still associated primarily with women readers and have been unable to lose their frivolous and trivial image. Newspapers have diversified to include articles on travel, the arts and entertainment, particularly in their Sunday supplements, which carry a slim glossy magazine folded in their pages. Whilst eighteenth-century newspapers and magazines have evolved into current-day forms, the essay-periodical, with its colourful fictitious editor, was already moribund in 1760 and was never to recover its original vitality.

In the *Bee* (5, 3 November 1759), Goldsmith describes a vision of the future, which he calls a 'Resverie [*sic*]', an allegorical fantasy. The essayist has been considering the growing commercialization of literature, reflecting that although 'every writer who now draws the quill seems to aim at profit, as well as applause, many among them are probably laying in stores for immortality' (Goldsmith 1966: 1.444). He allows his mind to wander and daydreams of a coachyard full of vehicles, each symbolizing a different motivation for writing. Passing by the *'pleasure stage-coach'*, the *'waggon of industry'*, the *'vanity whim'* and the *'landau of riches'*, the writer eagerly approaches a coach with the inscription the *'fame machine'*. The coachman has just carried a generation of writers – Addison, Swift, Pope, Steele, Congreve and Colley Cibber – to the Temple of Fame and has returned to collect their successors. The editor offers a copy of the *Bee* as his credentials, but the driver 'assured me he had never heard of it before'. Samuel Johnson soon approaches, weighed down by the bulky volumes of his *Dictionary*, but the coachman refuses to take him on board until he spots a 'little book ... peeping from one of his pockets'. On asking to see it, he is told it is a 'mere trifle ... it is called the Rambler'. On hearing this, the driver exclaims in rapture:

> The Rambler! ... I beg, sir, you'll take your place; I have heard our ladies in the court of Apollo frequently mention it with rapture; and Clio, who happens to be a little grave, has been heard to prefer it to the

Spectator, though others have observed, that the reflections, by being refined, sometimes become minute.

(Goldsmith 1966: 1.447–8)

Ironically, it is a periodical, that most ephemeral and fragile of publications, written hurriedly and for money, that provides a passport to posterity where lengthy volumes fail. Even the *Rambler*, the most earnest and didactic of periodical papers, is considered by its own author as a 'trifle' and is depicted as a work of entertainment for a female audience: it is the *ladies* of the court of Apollo who are keen *Rambler* readers. Johnson's periodical provides, for Goldsmith, decisive proof of the literary worth of journalism: 'Their Johnson's and Smollet's are truly poets; though for aught I know they never made a single verse in their whole lives' (Chinese Letter XL; Goldsmith 1966: 2.171). While Goldsmith's evaluation of the *Rambler* has been vindicated by posterity, few other eighteenth-century periodical writers have retained their seats in the fame machine, not, in any case, for their journalistic work. This study has attempted to show that it is time to revise that judgement, to return to a unique moment in literary history and reappraise the work of eighteenth-century periodical editors.

Notes

1 The *New Royal and Universal Magazine; or, the Gentleman and Lady's Companion* (1751–9), *Universal Museum; or, Gentleman and Lady's Polite Magazine of History, Politics and Literature* (1762–72), *Curiosity; or, Gentleman and Lady's Repository* (1740) and *Gentleman and Lady's Palladium* (1750–79).

2 For more detailed information on reviewing periodicals, see Donoghue 1996 and Roper 1978.

3 There were at least two periodicals of this name: the *Court Miscellany in Prose and Verse* (1719) and *Court Miscellany; or, Ladies New Magazine* (1765–71), continued as *Court; or, Gentleman and Lady's New Magazine*.

4 One important exception is Laurence Sterne, whose writing was heavily influenced by Addison and Steele in particular (see Golden 1987).

5 Hugh Kelly's 'Babbler' essays appeared in *Owen's Weekly Chronicle* (1758–70) between 1761 and 1767 and were reprinted as a collection in 1767.

6 See the bibliography of periodicals for publications of these names, with eponymous editor-figures.

7 The character 'Euphrosine' first appears in Haywood's *Female Spectator* (1744–6), where, however, she is rather different from her incarnation in the *Young Lady*.

8 See the advertisement for Smart's show in the *Public Advertiser* (13 March 1753), as well as 'The prologue to Mary Midnight's Oratory' in the *Ladies Magazine* (III.6, 8 February 1752).

9 The *OED* does not cite any examples of the word *museum* used to signify a type of periodical.

10 For further details about Steele's life, see Winton 1964 and 1970.

11 The sexual mores of the Restoration theatre, with its ubiquitous rakes and cuckolds, are also challenged in plays like Steele's *The Tender Husband* (1705) and *The Conscious Lovers* (1722). In *The Tender Husband*, the young aristocrat Clerimont marries the city girl Biddy Tipkins, rather than attempting to seduce her. Her uncle-guardian, a rich banker, is happily married to a faithful wife. The aristocratic Bevil jr. of *The Conscious Lovers* is a morally exemplary young man, who wishes to marry Indiana, even though he believes that she is penniless and of low birth.

12 For Addison's papers on wit, see *Spectators* 58–65.

13 For places where Bickerstaff *does* categorize women, see *Tatlers* 4, 17 and 67.

14 Steele does occasionally satirize individual women in the *Tatler*. *Tatler* 63 contains a veiled attack on Mary Astell, Elizabeth Elstob and Delarivier Manley.

15 Deborah Payne has questioned the assumption that Restoration and early eighteenth-century actresses were regarded primarily as sex objects. However, she still sees them as, at best, a 'social group on . . . precarious social footing' (Payne 1995: 20).

16 One issue is unaccounted for here: I have been unable to locate a copy of *Female Tatler* 63.

17 Manley's novel *The New Atalantis* (1709) attacks Steele as Monsieur L'Ingrate (see Manley 1992: 101–5). She claims that he was the father of her illegitimate child. Steele retaliates in *Tatlers* 63, 167 and 229.

18 Mrs Crackenthorpe alludes to the Society for the Reformation of Manners, which printed inspirational tracts and a broadside *Black List*, containing the names of people allegedly punished by the Society for such misdemeanours as drunkenness, swearing and violating the Sabbath. In 1709, the *Black List* was replaced by *Accounts*, which recorded 10,000 names in 1708–9 (R.P. Bond 1971: 72).

19 The *British Apollo* retaliates with satirical verse (nos. 45, 47, 49, 50 and 51).

20 Lucinda alludes to Bickerstaff's description of himself as a mastiff in *Tatler* 115.

21 Isaac Bickerstaff is also a member of a club: he attends a nightly meeting of elderly men at the Trumpet tavern, where the monotony of the club's proceedings acts as a natural soporific, enabling Bickerstaff to drop off to sleep easily afterwards. This club, however, features in only one issue (*Tatler* 132) and is pointedly *not* a source of writerly inspiration or lively discussion.

22 For a clear and succinct account of the *Spectator*'s politics and contemporary reactions to them, see Smithers 1968: 213–6 and Winton 1964: 138–50.

23 Quotations from the *Englishman* are taken from Steele 1955.

24 Quotations from the *Lover* are taken from Steele 1725.

25 Bond has calculated that Addison's papers contain 202 independent essays and 49 made up wholly or in part by contributed material or letters; Steele's 89 and 162 respectively (D.F. Bond 1965: lix).

26 Quotations from 'The Idler' are taken from Johnson 1969.

27 For papers on prostitution in the first series, see, for example, *Spectators* 182, 205, 266, 274, 276, 286 and 410. For those on other forms of sexual immorality, see *Spectators* 151, 154, 156, 190, 203, 260 and 298.

28 *Examiners* 46 (14 June 1711) to 52 (27 July 1711) have been attributed to Delarivier Manley (Burke 1983: 113–19).

29 For an excellent biographical account of the relationship between the *Nonsense of Common Sense* and Montagu's life and political convictions at this period, see Grundy 1999: 371–8.

30 For a further account of the journalism of this period, see Goldgar 1976: 134–62; Harris 1987: 21–7 and Hanson 1936: 114–17.

31 This is an issue also broached by Steele in the *Spinster* (1719).

32 See *Spectators* 67, 334 and 376.

33 See *Tatlers* 19, 41 and 195.

34 From 1732 onwards, the title was the *Gentleman's Magazine; or, Monthly Chronicle*. In 1738, this was changed to the *Gentleman's Magazine and Historical Register*.

35 This rubric was omitted after 1731.

36 For contemporary evidence of this, see *Grub-Street Journal* 353 (12 October

1736), which records the complaints of former staff-writer Joseph Ilive, and Boswell 1964–71: 3.332.

37 'Ad Urbanum' first appeared in the *Gentleman's Magazine* VIII, March 1738, in Latin. I am citing an anonymous translation.

38 The judge ruled against allowing the booksellers to publish the translation, however, as the work, Thomas Burnet's *Archaeologica Philosophica* (1685), contained 'reflections against religion', unfit for the perusal of the uneducated who could not read the Latin original.

39 The division of the book review into headings began in April 1732.

40 For an interesting discussion of the implications of the Stamp Tax for the establishment of a distinction between journalism and history, see Davis 1983: 95–100.

41 This preface was written after Cave's death: he died in January 1754.

42 Issues of the *Female Spectator* were neither numbered nor dated, but published in 'Books'. References to the *Female Spectator* are to the book nos. of the original 1744–6 collected edition of the periodical, followed by volume and page no. in Haywood 2001.

43 The editorship of the *Lady's Magazine; or, Polite Companion for the Fair Sex* (1759–63) has been tentatively attributed to Goldsmith, writing under the alias of 'the Hon. Mrs Caroline Stanhope' (see Taylor 1993: 87).

44 While it is never explicitly stated, I assume that the Female Spectator is a spinster, since she conforms closely to the stereotype of the coquette-turned-old maid (see Chapter 8).

45 See bk xx: 3.253; bk xxiii: 3.361; bk ix: 2.302; bk v: 2.156; bk viii: 2.288; bk xvi: 3.111; bk xx: 3.276; bk xii: 2.422; and bk viii: 2.294.

46 I am indebted to Boulard for pointing out the spurious nature of these letters (2000: 187*n*33).

47 The *Bee; or, Universal Weekly Pamphlet* (1733–5), the *Bee Reviv'd; or, the Prisoner's Magazine* (1750), the *Royal Magazine; or, Quarterly Bee* (1750–1) and the *Bee* (1759).

48 Republished in 1756 under the more familiar title *The Pleasures of the Imagination*.

49 *Ramblers* 30, by Catherine Talbot; 44 and 100, by Elizabeth Carter; and 97, by Samuel Richardson.

50 *Ramblers* 10, with contributions by Hester Mulso, later Chapone; 15, with a letter attributed to David Garrick; and 107, with a letter from 'Amicus', attributed to Joseph Simpson (see Bate and Strauss 1969: xxi*n*1).

51 James Woodruff has shown that a number of the *Rambler* papers do refer implicitly to contemporary events. These allusions remain veiled, however: the *Rambler* does not invite its readers to make connections between the editor's subject matter and topical concerns (see Woodruff 1982: 27–64).

52 See *Gentleman's Magazine* March 1750 (*Rambler* 11); January 1751 (*Rambler* 83); February 1751 (*Rambler* 91); March 1751 (*Rambler* 107); June 1751 (*Ramblers* 130 and 133); October 1751 (*Rambler* 161); December 1751 (*Ramblers* 186 and 187); January 1752 (*Rambler* 191) and March 1752 (*Rambler* 208).

53 See *Ramblers* 11, 50, 74, 79, 160, 162 and 196, respectively.

54 'The Life of Dr. Herman Boerhaave, Late Professor of Physic in the University of Leyden in Holland' first appeared in *Gentleman's Magazine* 9 (January–April 1739). See Murphy (ed.) 1825: 6.238–55.

55 This section of my chapter is indebted to Grundy's remarks on the importance of competition in Johnson's thought.

56 The *Dictionary of National Biography* (1997) entry on Frances Brooke dates her marriage as 'around 1756'. However, as Lorraine McMullen has noted, since Brooke signs her contributions 'B', she was probably married before she began the paper in November 1755 and certainly before it ended in July. Letters of this period, signed with her married name, confirm this (McMullen 1983: 30).

57 Mary Singleton claims to remember Marlborough's campaigns in the War of the Spanish Succession (1701–14) (*Old Maid* 35, 10 July 1756).

58 The issues of the *Student* are neither numbered nor dated, but organized in volumes. Each issue of each volume is named after one of the Muses.

59 The *Old Maid* was published at a time of heightened political interest, on the eve of the Seven Years War. Wild points out that Brooke's confident appropriation of political discourse is unusual for a woman writer of this period. I would argue that it is even more surprising in a writer who has adopted the persona of an old maid. A discussion of Mary Singleton's politics is beyond the scope of this chapter. See Wild 1998: 421–36.

60 Delarivier Manley briefly assumed the editorship of the *Examiner* (1710–16) in 1711. See also Lady Mary Wortley Montagu's *Nonsense of Common Sense* (1737–8), Eliza Haywood's *Female Spectator* (1744–6), *Parrot, With a Compendium of the Times* (1746) and *Young Lady* (1756) and Charlotte Lennox's *Lady's Museum* (1760–1). In addition, some critics have attributed the *Female Tatler* (1710–11) to Delarivier Manley. See Anderson 1931: 354–60 and Morgan 1992: vii–viii.

61 The writer is probably referring to the poet Katherine Philips, often known as 'Orinda' (1632–64), and the Dutch painter and Classical scholar Anna Maria van Schurman (1607–78).

62 Quotations from the *General Magazine of Arts and Sciences* are taken from the 1755 bound edition of the first part of the periodical, 'The Young Gentleman and Lady's Philosophy'.

63 References to the *Young Ladies Magazine* are taken from the 1760 collected edition of the periodical, which is not divided into separate numbers. Quotations from the *Young Misses Magazine* are taken from the two-volume second edition of 1767. I have not been able to locate an earlier edition.

64 According to Pailler, these correspondents were Charles Alston, Regius Professor of Botany (1683–1760); Benjamin Kennicott, Fellow of Exeter College, Oxford (1718–83); an unnamed 'Professor of Poetry at Oxford'; N. Duillier Facio F.R.S.; Stephen Hales (1677–1761) F.R.S., foreign associate of the Royal Academy of Paris; Alexander Monro, F.R.S.; J.H. Winkler F.R.S., 'Professor at Leipzic'; and Samuel Sharpe, F.R.S., surgeon at Guy's Hospital. See Pailler 1975: 2.660.

65 This frontispiece was unavailable for inclusion in this book. It can be viewed in the British Library copy of the *Lady's Museum* (classmark C.175.n.15).

66 References to the *Lady's Museum* are by issue number, followed by volume and page number in the two-volume collected edition of 1761. The page numbering is continuous through both volumes.

67 Parthenissa is probably referring to Aphra Behn's *Love-Letters Between a Nobleman and his Sister* (1684–7), which purported to be an edition of the real letters of Ford Grey, Earl of Tankerville, and his sister-in-law Lady Henrietta Berkeley.

68 The writer is referring to Anne-Louise d'Orléans, duchesse de Monpensier

(1627–93), author of *Mémoires* (1637–43); Marie d'Orléans-Longueville, duchesse de Nemours (1635–1707), author of *Mémoires* (1718); Françoise Bertaut de Motteville (c.1621–89), author of *Mémoires pour servir à l'histoire d'Anne d'Autriche* (1723); Christine de Pisan (c.1364–c.1430); and Anna Comnena (1083–c.1153), Byzantine historian and author of the *Alexiad* (c.1148).

69 Lennox is probably referring to Edward Stillingfleet's *Origines Britannicæ* (1685), reprinted in his *Works* (London, 1710); James Tyrrell's *General History of England, both Ecclesiastical and Civil* (London, 1696–1704); and Thomas Innes's *A Critical Essay on the Original Inhabitants of the Northern Parts of Britain or Scotland* (London, 1729).

70 For a fuller discussion of Haywood's interesting theories of the female mind, see *Female Spectator* bk x: 2.358–64 and Mullan 1993.

71 Goldsmith refers to the *Gentleman's Magazine; or, Trader's Monthly Intelligencer* (1731–1907), *London Magazine; or, Gentleman's Monthly Intelligencer* (1732–97), *Universal Magazine of Knowledge and Pleasure* (1747–1815), *Royal Magazine; or, Gentleman's Monthly Companion* (1759–71), *Imperial Magazine* (1760–2), Tobias Smollett's *British Magazine; or, Monthly Repository for Ladies and Gentlemen* (1759–67), the *Christian Magazine; or, a Treasury of Divine Knowledge* (1759–67), *Lady's Magazine; or, Polite Companion to the Fair Sex* (1759–63), *Library; or, Moral and Critical Magazine* (1761–2) and *Court Magazine; or, Royal Chronicle* (1761–5).

72 Publications to which Goldsmith contributed include the *Bee* (1759), *British Magazine*, *Busy Body* (1759), *Critical Review* (1756–1817), *Christian Magazine*, *Christian's Magazine; or, the Sunday Entertainment* (n.d.), *Grand Magazine of Universal Intelligence* (1758–60), *Lady's Magazine; or, Polite Companion*, *Lloyd's Evening Post* (1757–1808), *Monthly Review* (1749–1844), *Public Ledger; or, Daily Register of Commerce and Intelligence* (1760–96), *Royal Magazine; or, Gentleman's Monthly Companion*, *Royal Magazine; or, Quarterly Bee* (1750–1) and the *Weekly Magazine; or, Gentleman and Lady's Polite Companion* (1759–60).

73 On the quality of the paper see *Tatlers* 101 and 160; on advertisements see *Tatler* 224 and for Charles Lillie see *Tatlers* 92, 94, 96, 101, 103, 110, 129, 138, 140, 142, 166, 200, 213, 250, 252, 257, 259, 264 and 265.

74 I am quoting from the original *Bee*. The passage printed in Friedman (1966) is slightly different, but he includes this version in 1.353*n*.

75 Contemporary publications with similar names include the *Bee Reviv'd; or*, the *Prisoner's Magazine* (1750), *New Royal and Universal Magazine; or, the Gentleman and Lady's Companion* (1751–9), *Royal Magazine; or, Gentleman's Monthly Companion*, Hugh Kelly's *Court Magazine; or, Royal Chronicle* (1761–5) and the *Royal Westminster Journal* (1741–1825). The ambivalence of Goldsmith's attitude towards the magazines is vividly illustrated by the fact that he himself contributed to several similar works, including the *Royal Magazine; or, Quarterly Bee* and the *Royal Female Magazine* (1760).

76 At $3\frac{1}{2}$ pence per issue, the *Covent-Garden Journal* was, in fact, particularly expensive. Most weekly journals cost 2 pence.

Bibliography

Periodicals

Adventurer (1752–4).

Alchymist; or, The Spirit of Fog Reviv'd, or an Atonement for the Loss of that Late Hero (1736).

Applebee's Original Weekly Journal (1713–37).

Athenian Gazette, Resolving Weekly All the Most Nice and Curious Questions Propos'd by the Ingenious, later the *Athenian Mercury* (1691–7).

Athenian News; or, Dunton's Oracle (1710).

Auditor (1733–4).

Batchelor (1769–73) Dublin.

Beauties of All the Magazines Selected (1762–4).

Bee (1759).

Bee; or, Universal Weekly Pamphlet (1733–5).

Bee Reviv'd; or, the Prisoners Magazine (1750).

British Apollo; or, Curious Amusements for the Ingenious (1708–11).

British Magazine; or, Monthly Repository for Gentlemen and Ladies (1760–7).

Busy Body (1759).

Censor (1715–17).

Champion; or, British Mercury (1739–43).

Christian Magazine; or, a Treasury of Divine Knowledge (1759–67).

Christian's Magazine; or, the Sunday's Entertainment (n.d.).

Common Sense; or, the Englishman's Journal (1737–43).

Compleat Library; or, News for the Ingenious (1692–4).

Conjuror (1736), Edinburgh.

Connoisseur (1754–6).

Country Magazine; or, the Gentleman and Lady's Pocket Companion (1736–7).

Court and City Magazine; or, a Fund of Entertainment for the Man of Quality (1770–1).

Court Magazine; or, Royal Chronicle (1761–5).

Court Miscellany in Prose and Verse (1719).

Court Miscellany; or, Ladies New Magazine (1765–71). Continued as *Court; or, Gentleman and Lady's New Magazine*.

Covent-Garden Journal (1752).

Craftsman, Being a Critique on the Times (1726–50).

Critical Review; or, Annals of Literature (1756–1817).

Curiosity; or, Gentleman and Lady's Repository (1740).

Daily Courant (1702–35).

Daily Gazetteer; or, London Advertiser (1735–96).

Daily Post (1719–46).

Delights for the Ingenious; or, a Monthly Entertainment for the Curious of Both Sexes (1711).

Devil (1755).

Dreamer (1754).

Drury-Lane Journal (1752).

Edinburgh Review (1755–6).

Englishman (1713–15).

Evening Post (1709–33).

Examiner; or, Remarks upon Papers and Occurences (1710–16).

Female Spectator (1744–6).

Female Tatler (1709–10).

Flowers of Parnassus; or, Lady's Miscellany (1734–6).

Flying-Post from Paris and Amsterdam (1695–1753).

Freeholder (1715–16).

Free-thinker; or, Essays on Ignorance (1718–21).

Friendly Writer and Register of Truth (1732–3).

General Magazine of Arts and Sciences, Philosophical, Philological, Mathematical, and Mechanical (1755–66).

General Postscript (1709).

Gentleman and Lady's Palladium (1750–79).

Gentleman's and London Magazine (1741).

Gentleman's Journal; or, the Monthly Miscellany (1692–4).

Gentleman's Magazine; or, Trader's Monthly Intelligencer (1731–1907).

Grand Magazine of Magazines (1758–9).

Grand Magazine of Universal Intelligence (1758–60).

Gray's-Inn Journal (1753–4).

Grouler; or, Diogenes Robb'd of His Tub (1711).

Grub-Street Journal (1730–8).

Grumbler. By Squire Gizzard (1715).

Guardian (1713).

Heraclitus Ridens (1703–4 and 1718).

Hermit (1711–12).

High-German Doctor (1714–15).

History of the Works of the Learned; or, an Impartial Account of Books Lately Printed in All Parts of Europe (1699–1712).

Humours of a Coffee-House (1707–8).

Hyp Doctor (1730–41).

Imperial Magazine; or, Complete Monthly Intelligencer (1760–2).

Jacobite's Journal (1747–8).

Jesuite (1719).

Knight-Errant (1729).

Ladies Complete Pocket-Book (1769–78).

Ladies Diary; or, the Women's Almanack (1704–1871).

Ladies Journal (1727) Dublin.

Ladies Magazine (1749–53).

Ladies Mercury (1693).

Lady's Curiosity; or, Weekly Apollo (1752).

Lady's Magazine; or, Entertaining Companion for the Fair Sex (1770–1832).

Lady's Magazine; or, Polite Companion for the Fair Sex (1759–63).

Lady's Museum (1760–1).

Lady's Weekly Magazine (1747).

Lay-Monk (1713–14).

Library; or, Moral and Critical Magazine (1761–2).

Literary Magazine; or, Universal Review (1756–8).

Little Review; or, an Inquisition of Scandal (1705).

Lloyd's Evening Post and British Chronicle (1757–1808).

London Chronicle; or, Universal Evening Post (1757–1823).

London Daily Advertiser (1751–3).

London Gazette, also *Oxford Gazette* (1665–present day).

London Magazine; or, Gentleman's Monthly Intelligencer (1732–97).

Lover (1714).

Magazin de Londres (1749).

Magazine of Magazines (1750–1).

Medley (1710–12).

Memoirs for the Ingenious (1693–4).

Memoirs of the Royal Society (1665–1735).

Midwife; or, the Old Woman's Magazine (1750–3).

Miscellaneous Correspondence (1742–8).

Miscellaneous Observations upon Authors, Ancient and Modern (1731–2).

Miscellany [also *Weekly Miscellany*] (1732–41).

Mist's Weekly Journal (1716–28).

Momus Ridens; or, Comical Remarks on the Public Reports (1690–1).

Monthly Chronicle (1728–31).

Monthly Entertainments (1713).

Monthly Review (1749–1844).

Mountebank (1732).

Museum; or, the Literary and Historical Register (1746–7).

New Miscellany (1734–9).

New Royal and Universal Magazine; or, the Gentleman and Lady's Companion (1751–9).

News from the Dead (1715–16).

Nonsense of Common-Sense (1737–8).

Norwich Post (1708), Norwich.

Observator; or, a Dialogue Between a Countryman &c. (1705–6).

Old England; or, the Constitutional Journal (1743–53).

Old Maid (1755–6).
Old Whig (1719).
Old Whig; or, the Consistent Protestant (1735–8).
Orphan Reviv'd; or, Powell's Weekly Journal (1718–20).
Owen's Weekly Chronicle; or, Universal Journal (1758–70).
Oxford Magazine; or, University Museum (1768–76), Oxford.
Parrot (1728).
Parrot, With a Compendium of the Times (1746).
Patrician (1719).
Philosophical Transactions of the Royal Society (1665–present day).
Phoenix Britannicus (1731).
Pilgrim (1711).
Plain Dealer (1724–5).
Plebeian (1719).
Post-Angel; or, Universal Entertainment (1701–2).
Post Boy Foreign and Domestick (1695–1735).
Prater (1756).
Prattler (1747).
Projector (1721).
Prompter (1734–6).
Public Advertiser (1752–94).
Public Ledger (1760–1837).
Rambler (1750–2).
Reader (1714).
Records of Love; or, Weekly Amusements for the Fair (1710).
Remembrancer; or, National Advocate (1747–51).
Review (1704–13)
Rhapsodist (1757).
Royal Female Magazine (1760).
Royal Magazine; or, Gentleman's Monthly Companion (1759–71).
Royal Magazine; or, Quarterly Bee (1750–1).
Royal Westminster Journal and London Political Miscellany (1741–1825).
Scots Magazine; or, General Repository of Literature, History and Politics (1739–1826).
Spectator (1711–12, 1714).
Spinster (1719).
Spring-Garden Journal (1752).
St. James's Magazine (1762–4).
Student; or, the Oxford (and Cambridge) Monthly Miscellany (1750–1) Oxford.
Supplementary Journal of Advice to the Scandalous Club (1704–5).
Tatler (1709–11).
Tatling Harlot (1709).
Theatre (1720).
Town and Country Magazine; or, Universal Repository of Knowledge, Instruction and Entertainment (1769–95).
True Patriot and the History of Our Own Times (1745–6).

Universal Chronicle; or, Weekly Gazette. Continued as *Payne's Universal Chronicle* (1758–60).

Universal Magazine of Knowledge and Pleasure (1747–1815).

Universal Museum; or, Gentleman and Lady's Polite Magazine of History, Politics and Literature (1762–72).

Universal Spectator and Weekly Journal (1728–46).

Universal Visiter and Monthly Memorialist (1756–8).

Visiter (1723–4).

Weekly Amusement; or, the Universal Magazine (1734–6).

Weekly Comedy (1699).

Weekly Magazine; or, Gentleman and Lady's Polite Companion (1759–60).

Weekly Miscellany – see *Miscellany*.

Weekly Oracle; or, Universal Library (1734–7).

Weekly Pacquet (1678).

World (1753–6).

Young Ladies Magazine; or, Dialogues between a Discreet Governess and Several Young Ladies of the First Rank under her Education (1760).

Young Lady (1756).

Young Misses Magazine (c.1760).

Other primary sources

Algarotti, Francesco (1737) *Il Newtonianismo per le Dame;* trans. Elizabeth Carter (1739) *Sir Isaac Newton's Philosophy Explain'd for the Use of the Ladies,* London.

Austen, Jane (1988) *Northanger Abbey* (1818), in R. W. Chapman (ed.) *The Novels of Jane Austen,* Oxford University Press.

Boswell, James (1964–71) *Boswell's Life of Johnson, Together With Boswell's Journal of A Tour to the Hebrides and Johnson's Diary of a Journey into North Wales,* G.B. Hill and L.F. Powell (eds), Oxford: Clarendon.

Brooke, Frances (1763) *The History of Lady Julia Mandeville,* London.

—— (1769) *The History of Emily Montague,* London.

—— (1777) *The Excursion,* London.

Buckingham, George Villiers, Duke of (1976) *The Rehearsal* (1671), D.E.L. Crane (ed.), University of Durham Press.

Burnet, Thomas (1685) *Studio et Opera,* Edinburgh.

Centlivre, Susannah (1709a) *The Busie Body,* London.

—— (1709b) *The Man's Bewitch'd; or, The Devil to Do About Her,* London.

—— (1722) *The Artifice,* London.

Chambers, Ephraim (2nd edn 1738) *Cyclopædia; or, An Universal Dictionary of Arts and Sciences,* London.

Coleridge, Samuel Taylor (1983) *Biographia Literaria* (1817), James Engell and W. Jackson Bate (eds) Princeton, NJ: Princeton University Press.

Considerations for Establishing a College for Old Maids in Ireland (1790) Dublin.

Dunton, John (1705) *The Life and Errors of John Dunton,* London.

Fénelon, François de Salignac de la Motte (1687) *Traité de l'éducation des filles,* Paris.

Feyjóo y Montenegro, Benito Gerónimo (c.1760) *An Essay on Woman; or, Physiological and Historical Defence of the Fair Sex*; trans. Anon, London.

Fielding, Henry (1974) *The Jacobite's Journal and Related Writings*, W.B. Coley (ed.) Oxford University Press.

—— (1988) *The Covent-Garden Journal and A Plan of the Universal Register-Office*, Bertrand A. Goldgar (ed.) Oxford: Clarendon.

—— (2001) *Joseph Andrews* (1742) Ontario: Broadview.

Fontenelle, Bernard le Bovier de (1686) *Entretiens sur la pluralité des mondes*, Amsterdam.

—— (1737) *A Week's Conversation on the Plurality of Worlds*; trans. William Gardner London.

Gay, John (1711) *The Present State of Wit*, London.

Gildon, Charles (c.1693) *The History of the Athenian Society*, London.

—— (1710) *The Life of Mr. Thomas Betterton, the Late Eminent Tragedian*, London.

Goldsmith, Oliver (1762) *The Citizen of the World*, London.

—— (1928) *The Collected Letters of Oliver Goldsmith*, Katherine C. Balderston (ed.) Cambridge University Press.

—— (1966) *The Collected Works of Oliver Goldsmith*, Arthur Friedman (ed.) Oxford: Clarendon.

Hawkins, Sir John (1787) *The Life of Samuel Johnson, LL.D.*, London.

Haywood, Eliza (1720) *Love in Excess; or, the Fatal Enquiry*, London.

—— (1725) *Memoirs of a Certain Island Adjacent to the Kingdom of Utopia*, London.

—— (2000a) *Epistles for the Ladies* (1749–50), in Kathryn R. King and Alexander Pettit (eds) *Selected Works of Eliza Haywood*, series I, vol. 1, London: Pickering and Chatto.

—— (2000b) *The Tea-Table: Or, A Conversation between Some Polite Persons of Both Sexes, at a Lady's Visiting Day* (1725), in Kathryn R. King and Alexander Pettit (eds) *Selected Works of Eliza Haywood*, series I, vol. 1, London: Pickering and Chatto.

—— (2000c) *The Wife* (1756), in Margo Collins and Alexander Pettit (eds) *Selected Works of Eliza Haywood*, series I, vol. 3, London: Pickering and Chatto.

—— (2000d) *The Young Lady* (1756), in Kathryn R. King and Alexander Pettit (eds) *Selected Works of Eliza Haywood*, series I, vol. 2, London: Pickering and Chatto.

—— (2001) *The Female Spectator* (1744–6), in Kathryn R. King and Alexander Pettit (eds) *Selected Works of Eliza Haywood*, series II, vols 2 and 3, London: Pickering and Chatto.

Hill, Aaron (1746) *The Art of Acting*, London.

Hogarth, William (1732) *A Harlot's Progress*, British Museum: London.

The Inspector's Rhapsody; or, Soliloquy on the Loss of his Wigg (1752) London.

Johnson, Samuel (1755) *A Dictionary of the English Language*, London.

—— (1905) *Lives of the English Poets*, George Birkbeck Hill (ed.) Oxford: Clarendon.

—— (1969) *The Yale Edition of the Works of Samuel Johnson*, W.J. Bate and Albrecht B. Strauss (eds) New Haven and London: Yale University Press.

—— (1992) *The Letters of Samuel Johnson*, Bruce Redford (ed.) Oxford: Clarendon.

Kippis, Andrew (1778) *Biographia Britannica; or, the Lives of the Most Eminent Persons Who Have Flourished in Great Britain and Ireland, from the Earliest Ages, to the Present Times*, London.

Lennox, Charlotte (1750) *The Life of Harriot Stuart Written by Herself*, London.

—— (1752) *The Female Quixote; or, the Adventures of Arabella*, London.

—— (1762) *Sophia*, London.

Lillie, Charles (1725) *Original and Genuine Letters to the Tatler and Spectator, During the Time Those Works were Publishing*, London.

Locke, John (1975) *An Essay Concerning Human Understanding*, Peter H. Nidditch (ed.) Oxford: Clarendon Press.

Manley, Delarivier (1992) *Secret Memoirs and Manners of Several Persons of Quality of Both Sexes, From the New Atalantis*, Ros Ballaster (ed.) London: Penguin.

Memoirs of the Society of Grub Street (1737) London.

Montagu, Lady Mary Wortley (1947) *The Nonsense of Common Sense*, Robert Halsband (ed.) Seattle: Northwestern University Press.

—— (1967) *Complete Letters of Lady Mary Wortley Montagu*, Robert Halsband (ed.) Oxford: Clarendon.

—— (1993) *Essays and Poems and Simplicity, A Comedy*, Robert Halsband and Isobel Grundy (eds) Oxford: Clarendon Press.

Murphy, Arthur (ed.) (1825) *The Works of Samuel Johnson, L.L.D.*, Philadelphia.

The Mysteries of Virginity; or, a Full Discovery of the Difference Between Young Maids and Old Ones (1714) London.

Newbery, John (1994) *Trade and Plumb-Cake for Ever, Huzza!: The Life and Work of John Newbery, 1713–1767*, John Rowe Townsend (ed.) Cambridge: Colt Books.

A Philosophical, Historical, and Moral Essay on Old Maids (2nd edn 1786) London.

Pope, Alexander (1951) *The Twickenham Edition of the Poems of Alexander Pope*, John Butt (ed.) London: Methuen.

A Practical Essay on Old Maids (n.d.) London.

A Satyr Upon Old Maids (1713) London.

Sheridan, Richard Brinsley (1975) *Plays*, Cecil Price (ed.) Oxford University Press.

Steele, Richard (1705) *The Tender Husband; or, the Accomplish'd Fools*, London.

—— (1714) *The Ladies Library*, London.

—— (1722) *The Conscious Lovers*, London.

—— (1725) *The Lover; to which is added, the Reader*, London.

—— (1955) *The Englishman: a political journal by Richard Steele*, Rae Blanchard (ed.) Oxford: Clarendon.

—— (1968) *The Correspondence of Richard Steele*, Rae Blanchard (ed.) Oxford University Press.

Swift, Jonathan (1974) *Journal to Stella*, Harold Williams (ed.) Oxford: Blackwell.

Willson, Joseph ([1795]) *'Tis Pity to Die an Old Maid*, London.

Secondary sources

Adburgham, Alison (1972) *Women In Print: writing women and women's magazines from the Restoration to the accession of Queen Victoria*, London: George Allen and Unwin.

Anderson, Paul Bunyan (1931) 'The history and authorship of Mrs. Crackenthorpe's *Female Tatler*', *Modern Philology*, 28: 354–60.

—— (1936) 'Splendor out of scandal: the Lucinda–Artesia Papers in *The Female Tatler*', *Philological Quarterly*, 15: 286–300.

—— (1937) 'Innocence and artifice: or, Mrs. Centlivre and *The Female Tatler*', *Philological Quarterly*, 16.4: 358–75.

Ballaster, R. *et al.* (1991) *Women's Worlds: ideology, femininity and the woman's magazine*, London: Macmillan.

Bate, Walter Jackson (1984) *Samuel Johnson*, London: Hogarth Press.

Bate, Walter Jackson and Strauss, Albrecht B. (1969) Introduction, *The Yale Edition of the Works of Samuel Johnson*, New Haven and London: Yale University Press.

Berry, Helen (2003) *Gender, Society and Print Culture in Late-Stuart England: the cultural world of the Athenian Mercury*, Aldershot: Ashgate.

Bhowmik, Urmi (2003) 'Facts and norms in the marketplace of print: John Dunton's *Athenian Mercury*', *Eighteenth-Century Studies*, 36.3: 345–65.

Black, Jeremy (1991) *The English Press in the Eighteenth Century*, Aldershot: Gregg Revivals.

Black, Scott (1999) 'Social and literary form in the *Spectator*', *Eighteenth-Century Studies*, 33.1: 21–42.

Bloom, Edward A. (1957) *Samuel Johnson in Grub Street*, Providence, RI: Brown University Press.

Bloom, Edward A. and Bloom, Lillian D. (1980) *Addison and Steele: the critical heritage*, London: Routledge and Kegan Paul.

Blouch, Christine (2000a) Introduction, in Kathryn R. King and Alexander Pettit (eds) *Selected Works of Eliza Haywood*, series I, vol. 1, London: Pickering and Chatto.

—— (2000b) 'What Ann Lang read: Eliza Haywood and her readers', in Kirsten T. Saxton and Rebecca P. Bocchicchio (eds) *The Passionate Fictions of Eliza Haywood: essays on her life and work*, Lexington KY: University of Kentucky Press.

Bond, Donald F. (1965) Introduction, *The Spectator*, Oxford: Clarendon.

—— (1987) Introduction, *The Tatler*, Oxford: Clarendon.

Bond, Donovan H. and McLeod, W. Reynolds (1977) *Newsletters to Newspapers: eighteenth-century journalism*, Morgantown: School of Journalism, West Virginia University.

Bond, Richmond P. (1959) *New Letters to the Tatler and Spectator*, Austin: University of Texas Press.

—— (1969) *Growth and Change in the English Periodical Press*, Lawrence, Kansas: University of Kansas Libraries.

—— (1971) *The Tatler: the making of a literary journal*, Oxford University Press.

Boulard, Claire (2000) *Presse et socialisation féminine en Angleterre de 1690 à 1750, conversations à l'heure du thé: étude du Gentleman's Journal, du Spectator et du Female Spectator*, Paris: L'Harmattan.

Brewer, John (1997) *The Pleasures of the Imagination: English culture in the eighteenth century*, London: Harper Collins.

Browne, Alice (1987) *The Eighteenth-Century Feminist Mind*, Brighton: Harvester.

Burke, Edward J. (1983) '*The Examiner*', in Alvin Sullivan (ed.) *British Literary Magazines: the Augustan age and the age of Johnson, 1698–1788*, vol. 1, Westport, CT: Greenwood Press.

Clery, E.J. (1991) 'Women, publicity and the coffee-house myth', *Women: A Cultural Review*, 2.2: 168–77.

Clifford, James L. (1980) *Dictionary Johnson: Samuel Johnson's middle years*, London: Heinemann.

Crane, R.S. and Kaye, F.B. (1927) *A Census of British Newspapers and Periodicals 1660–1800*, Chapel Hill, NC: University of North Carolina Press.

Davis, Lennard (1983) *Factual Fictions: the origins of the English novel*, New York: Columbia University Press.

DeMaria, Robert (1993) *The Life of Samuel Johnson: a critical biography*, Oxford: Blackwell.

Dictionary of National Biography (1997) Oxford University Press.

Donogue, Dennis (1996) *The Fame Machine: book reviewing and eighteenth-century literary careers*, Cambridge University Press.

Firmager, Gabrielle M. (ed.) (1993) *The Female Spectator*, Bristol: Bristol Classical Press.

Gedalof, Alan J. (1983) '*The Universal Visiter and Memorialist*', in Alvin Sullivan (ed.) *British Literary Magazines: the Augustan age and the age of Johnson, 1698–1788*, vol. 1, Westport, CT: Greenwood Press.

Golden, Morris (1987) 'Periodical context in the imagined world of *Tristram Shandy*', *The Age of Johnson: a scholarly annual*, 1: 237–60.

Goldgar, Bertrand A. (1976) *Walpole and the Wits: the relation of politics to literature, 1722–42*, Lincoln, NE: University of Nebraska Press.

Graham, Walter (1926) *The Beginnings of English Literary Periodicals: a study of periodical literature 1665–1715*, New York: Oxford University Press.

—— (1930) *English Literary Periodicals*, London.

Grundy, Isobel (1986) *Samuel Johnson and the Scale of Greatness*, Leicester University Press.

—— (1999) *Lady Mary Wortley Montagu*, Oxford University Press.

Habermas, Jürgen (1989) *The Structural Transformation of the Public Sphere: an inquiry into a category of bourgeois society*; trans. Thomas Burger, London: Polity Press.

Halsband, Robert (1956) *The Life of Lady Mary Wortley Montagu*, Oxford: Clarendon.

Hanson, Laurence (1936) *Government and the Press, 1695–1793*, Oxford University Press.

Harris, Michael (1978) 'The structure, ownership and control of the press', in George Boyce, James Curran and Pauline Wingate (eds) *Newspaper History from the Seventeenth Century to the Present Day*, London: Constable.

—— (1987) *London Newspapers in the Age of Walpole: a study of the origins of the modern English press*, London: Associated University Presses.

Hill, Bridget (2001) *Women Alone: spinsters in England 1660–1850*, London: Yale University Press.

Hunter, Jean E. (1976) 'The eighteenth-century Englishwoman: according to the

Gentleman's Magazine', in George Boyce, James Curran and Pauline Wingate (eds) *Woman in the Eighteenth Century and Other Essays*, Toronto: Stevens Hakkert.

—— (1977) 'The *Lady's Magazine* and the study of Englishwomen in the eighteenth century', in Donovan H. Bond and W. Reynolds McLeod (eds) *Newsletters to Newspapers: eighteenth-century journalism*, Morgantown: School of Journalism, West Virginia University.

Hunter, J. Paul (1977) 'The loneliness of the long-distance reader', *Genre*, 10: 455–84.

—— (1990) *Before Novels: the cultural contexts of eighteenth-century English fiction*, London: Norton.

Ketcham, Michael (1985) *Transparent Designs: reading, performance and form in the Spectator papers*, Athens: University of Georgia Press.

Kirk, Clara M. (1967) *Oliver Goldsmith*, New York: Twayne.

Korshin, Paul J. (1989) 'Johnson's *Rambler* and its audiences', in Alexander J. Butrym (ed.) *Essays on the Essay: redefining the genre*, London: University of Georgia Press.

Laurence, Anne (1999) *Women in England 1500–1760: a social history*, London: Phoenix Giant.

Luttrel, Narcissus (1857) *A Brief Historical Relation of State Affairs*, Oxford.

McEwen, Gilbert (1972) *The Oracle of the Coffee-House: John Dunton's Athenian Mercury*, San Marino, CA.: The Huntingdon Library.

McKeen Wiles, Roy (1968) 'The contemporary distribution of Johnson's *Rambler*', *Eighteenth-Century Studies*, 2.2: 155–72.

—— (1976) 'The relish for reading in provincial England two centuries ago', in Paul Korshin (ed.) *The Widening Circle: essays on the circulation of literature in eighteenth-century Europe*, Philadelphia: University of Pennsylvania Press.

—— (1979) 'Middle-class literacy in eighteenth-century England: fresh evidence', in R.F. Brissenden (ed.) *Studies in the Eighteenth Century 4: papers presented at the fourth David Nichol Smith memorial seminar*, Canberra: Australian National University Press.

McMullen, Lorraine (1983) *An Odd Attempt in a Woman: the literary life of Frances Brooke*, Vancouver: University of British Columbia Press.

Maurer, S.L. (1998) *Proposing Men: dialectics of gender and class in the eighteenth-century English periodical*, Stanford, CA: Stanford University Press.

Mayo, Robert D. (1962) *The English Novel in the Magazines 1740–1815*, Evanston, IL: Northwestern University Press.

Morgan, Fidelis (1986) *A Woman of No Character: an autobiography of Mrs. Manley*, London: Faber and Faber.

—— (1992) Introduction, *The Female Tatler*, London: Everyman.

Mullan, John (1993) 'The gender of knowledge: women and Newtonianism, 1690–1760', in Marina Benjamin (ed.) *Women, Science, and Literature*, New Brunswick, NJ: Rutgers University Press.

Nicoll, Allardyce (1980) *The Garrick Stage: theatres and audiences in the eighteenth century*, Manchester University Press.

Pailler, Albert (1975) *Edward Cave et le Gentleman's Magazine (1731–1754)*, Lille University Press.

Paulson, Ronald (1967) *The Fictions of Satire*, Baltimore, MD: The Johns Hopkins University Press.

Payne, Deborah C. (1995) 'Reified object or emergent professional: retheorizing the Restoration actress', in J. Douglas Canfield and Deborah C. Payne (eds) *Cultural Readings of Restoration and Eighteenth-Century English theatre*, London: University of Georgia Press.

Plumb, J.H. (1983) 'Commercialization and society', in Neil McKendrick, John Brewer and J.H. Plumb, *The Birth of a Consumer Society: the commercialization of leisure in eighteenth-century England*, London: Hutchinson.

Prescott, Sarah and Spencer, Jane (2000) 'Prattling, tattling, and knowing everything: public authority and the female editorial persona', *British Journal for Eighteenth-Century Studies*, 23.1: 43–57.

Rizzo, Betsy (1989) 'Johnson's efforts on behalf of authorship in *The Rambler*', in *Transactions of the Seventh International Congress on the Enlightenment*, Oxford: The Voltaire Foundation at the Taylor Institute.

Rogers, K.M. (1982) *Feminism in Eighteenth-Century Literature*, Brighton: Harvester.

Roper, Derek (1978) *Reviewing Before the 'Edinburgh' 1788–1802*, London: Methuen.

Rose, Mark (1993) *Authors and Owners: the invention of copyright*, London: Harvard University Press.

Sands, Mollie (1987) *The Eighteenth-Century Pleasure Gardens of Marylebone, 1737–1777*, London: Society for Theatre Research.

Sherbo, Arthur (1967) *Christopher Smart: scholar of the university*, East Lansing, MI: Michigan State University Press.

Shevelow, Kathryn (1989) *Women and Print Culture: the construction of femininity in the early periodical*, London: Routledge.

Shields, David (1997) *Civil Tongues and Polite Letters in British America*, Chapel Hill, NC: University of North Carolina Press.

Sitter, John (1982) *Literary Loneliness in Mid-Eighteenth Century England*, Ithaca, NY: Cornell University Press.

Small, Miriam Rossiter (1935) *Charlotte Ramsay Lennox: an eighteenth-century lady of letters*, New Haven: Yale University Press.

Smith, John Harrington (1952) 'Thomas Baker and *The Female Tatler*', *Modern Philology*, 49.3: 286–300.

Smithers, Peter (2nd ed 1968) *The Life of Joseph Addison*, Oxford: Clarendon Press.

Solomon, Harry M. (1996) *The Rise of Robert Dodsley: creating the new age of print*, Carbondale, IL: Southern Illinois University Press.

Spacks, Patricia Meyer (1999), Introduction, *Selections from the Female Spectator*, Oxford University Press.

Spector, Robert D. (1966) *English Literary Periodicals and the Climate of Opinion during the Seven Years War*, The Hague: Mouton.

Stewart, James D., Hammond, Muriel E. and Saenger, Erwin (eds) (1995) *British Union-Catalogue of Periodicals: a record of the periodicals of the world, from the seventeenth century to the present day, in British libraries*, London: Butterworths.

Sullivan, Alvin (1983) '*The London Magazine*', in Alvin Sullivan (ed.) *British Literary*

Magazines: the Augustan age and the age of Johnson, 1698–1788, Westport, CT: Greenwood Press.

Taylor, Richard C. (1993) *Goldsmith as Journalist*, London and Toronto: Associated University Presses.

Teiman, Gillian (1993) Review of Fidelis Morgan (ed.) *Female Tatler*, in *The Scriblerian and the Kit-Cats*, 15.2: 233.

Todd, William B. (1965) 'A bibliographical account of the *Gentleman's Magazine, 1731–1754*', *Studies in Bibliography: papers of the bibliographical society of the University of Virginia*, 18: 81–109.

Trayer, Howard William (1946) *Ned Ward of Grub-Street: a study of sub-literary London in the eighteenth century*, Cambridge, MA: Harvard University Press.

Van Tassel, Mary M. (1988) 'Johnson's elephant: the reader of the *Rambler*', *SEL: studies in English literature 1500–1900*, 28.3: 461–71.

Welsh, Charles (1885) *A Bookseller of the Last Century: being some account of the life of John Newbery and of the books he published*, London.

Whicher, George Frisbie (1915) *The Life and Romances of Mrs. Eliza Haywood*, New York: Columbia University Press.

White, C.L. (1970) *Women's Magazines, 1693–1968*, London: Michael Joseph.

White, R.B. (1974) 'The rivalry of the *Female Tatlers*: periodical piracy in the early eighteenth century', in Larry S. Champion (ed.) *Quick Springs of Sense: studies in the eighteenth century*, Athens, GA: University of Georgia Press.

Wild, Min (1998) '"Prodigious Wisdom": civic humanism in Frances Brooke's *Old Maid*', *Women's Writing*, 5.3: 421–36.

Winton, Calhoun (1964) *Captain Steele: the early career of Richard Steele*, Baltimore, MD: The Johns Hopkins Press.

—— (1970) *Sir Richard Steele, M.P.: the later years*, Baltimore, MD: The Johns Hopkins Press.

Woodruff, James F. (1982) 'Johnson's *Rambler* and its contemporary context', *Bulletin of Research in the Humanities*, 85.1: 27–64.

Woolf, Virginia (1979) 'A scribbling dame', in Michèle Barret (ed.) *Women and Writing*, London: The Women's Press.

Wroth, Warwick and Wroth, Arthur Edgar (1979) *The London Pleasure Gardens of the Eighteenth Century* (1896), reprinted London: Macmillan.

Zionkowski, Linda (1992) 'Aesthetics, copyright, and "the Goods of the Mind"', *British Journal for Eighteenth-Century Studies*, 15: 163–74.

Index